BRITISH FOOTBALL AND SOCIAL EXCLUSION

Editor

STEPHEN WAGG
Roehampton University

Routledge
Taylor & Francis Group

LONDON AND NEW YORK

First published 2004
by Routledge
2 Park Square, Milton Park, Abingdon, Oxon OX14 4RN

Simultaneously published in the USA and Canada
by Routledge
270 Madison Ave, New York, NY 10016

Routledge is an imprint of the Taylor & Francis Group

Typeset in Times New Roman by
Taylor & Francis Books Ltd

Printed and bound in Great Britain by
TJ International, Padstow, Cornwall

British Library Cataloguing in Publication Data
A catalogue record for this book is available from the British Library

Library of Congress Cataloging-in-Publication Data
A catalog record for this title has been requested

ISBN 0–7146–5217–2 (hbk)
ISBN 0–7146–8204–7 (pbk)

Sport in the Global Society

General Editor: J.A. Mangan

SPORT IN THE GLOBAL SOCIETY

General Editor: J.A. Mangan

The interest in sports studies around the world is growing and will continue to do so. This unique series combines aspects of the expanding study of *Sport in the Global Society*, providing comprehensiveness and comparison under one editorial umbrella. It is particularly timely, with studies in the political, cultural, anthropological, ethnographic, social, economic, geographical and aesthetic elements of sport proliferating in institutions of higher education.

Eric Hobsbawm once called sport one of the most significant practices of the late nineteenth century. Its significance was even more marked in the late twentieth century and will continue to grow in importance into the new millennium as the world develops into a 'global village' sharing the English language, technology and sport.

Other Titles in the Series

Football, Europe and the Press
Liz Crolley and David Hand

The Future of Football
Challenges for the Twenty-First Century
Edited by Jon Garland, Dominic Malcolm and
Michael Rowe

Football Culture
Local Contests, Global Visions
Edited by Gerry P.T. Finn and Richard
Giulianotti

France and the 1998 World Cup
The National Impact of a World Sporting Event
Edited by Hugh Dauncey and Geoff Hare

The First Black Footballer
Arthur Wharton 1865–1930: An Absence of
Memory
Phil Vasili

Scoring for Britain
International Football and International Politics,
1900–1939
Peter J. Beck

Women, Sport and Society in Modern China
Holding Up *More* than Half the Sky
Dong Jinxia

Sport in Latin American Society
Past and Present
Edited by J.A. Mangan and Lamartine P.
DaCosta

Sport in Australasian Society
Past and Present
Edited by J.A. Mangan and John Nauright

Sporting Nationalisms
Identity, Ethnicity, Immigration and
Assimilation
Edited by Mike Cronin and David Mayall

The Commercialisation of Sport
Edited by Trevor Slack

Shaping the Superman
Fascist Body as Political Icon: Aryan Fascism
Edited by J.A. Mangan

Superman Supreme
Fascist Body as Political Icon: Global Fascism
Edited by J.A. Mangan

Making the Rugby World
Race, Gender, Commerce
Edited by Timothy J.L Chandler and John
Nauright

Rugby's Great Split
Class, Culture and the Origins of Rugby League
Football
Tony Collins

The Race Game
Sport and Politics in South Africa
Douglas Booth

Cricket and England
A Cultural and Social History of the Inter-war
Years
Jack Williams

The Games Ethic and Imperialism
Aspects of the Diffusion of an Ideal
J.A. Mangan

Contents

Dedication   vii

Acknowledgements   viii

Series editor's foreword   ix

Introduction   xi

Notes on contributors   xvi

1. Fat city? British football and the politics of social exclusion
   at the turn of the twenty-first century   1
   Stephen Wagg

2. 'You're not welcome anymore': the football crowd, class
   and social exclusion   26
   Tim Crabbe and Adam Brown

3. 'Giving something back': can football clubs and their
   communities co-exist?   47
   Neil Taylor

4. A day out with the 'old boys'   67
   Pat Slaughter

5. 'With his money, *I* could afford to be depressed':
   markets, masculinity and mental distress in the
   English football press   90
   Stephen Wagg

6. Still a man's game? Women footballers, personal experience
   and tabloid myth   110
   John Harris

7. Out on the field: women's experiences of gender and sexuality
   in football   127
   Jayne Caudwell

8. Talking to me? Televised football and masculine style   147
   Eileen Kennedy

9. 'Play the white man': identifying institutional racism in
   professional football   167
   Colin King

10. Football and social responsibility in the 'new' Scotland:
    the case of Celtic FC   186
    Raymond Boyle

11. Football for children or children for football?
    A contemporary boys' league and the politics of childhood   205
    Paul Daniel

12. Pick the best, forget the rest? Training field dilemmas and
    children's football at the turn of the century   224
    Simon Thorpe

    Select bibliography   242
    Index   259

For my brother Jeremy

and for the memory of Loughborough Corinthians Football Club
(Midland League 1925-1933), of whose home crowd Annie Hardy,
born in 1918 and later our mother, was a devoted member.

Acknowledgements

This book emerged from a telephone conversation with Tim Crabbe, who subsequently helped me to put it together. My chief debt in compiling this book is to him. Thanks also to colleagues in the School of Life and Sport Sciences at Roehampton University, for the study leave during which the book was completed. Among these colleagues Paul Norcross was always especially willing to help me to refine my arguments. My friend Roy Williams helped me, as so often, to find information when I needed it.

Details about Loughborough Corinthians FC, who have been talked of in my family for as long as I can remember and to whose memory this book is partly dedicated, came from the Football Club History Database.

Stephen Wagg
March 2004

Series editor's foreword

Let's be blunt! Domestic professional football is in a sorry state. The golden veneer of newly obtained premier league wealth is a thin honeyed glaze on a badly scratched surface. A glum editorial in *The Sun* recently lamented a game at the nadir of its 'moral degeneration'[1] : 'Paying fortunes to young men was always going to end in tears. Football has a last chance to clean up its act.' Perhaps.

The slow rolling cadences of muffled drums still seem a long way off. The fact that professional football has shed pragmatic principles like 'fair play' as easily as a spring ermine sheds its winter coat, has not stopped premier league attendance growing. The scrupulist, never mind the scrupulant, seems in too short supply.

Whatever the future, *British Football and Social Exclusion* offers reasons for soccer's degeneration over and above spoilt players, menial officials and vicious fans. The purpose of the collection is 'to relate recent and current developments especially in the English football world, to *the emergent politics of social exclusion*'.[2] The collection faces two immediate problems and confronts them both with candour: firstly, the elusiveness of the term 'social exclusion'. As frankly noted in the collection, the specific meaning of the term cannot be easily found[3] and, moreover, refers too often too vaguely only to life chances, and not to 'material circumstances';[4] and secondly, over and beyond 'a certain point, football cannot meaningfully address "social exclusion"… its real problems lie in lengthy hospital waiting lists, schools' inadequate resources, poor pensions, "sink" estates, decaying public transport infrastructures and so on'.[5] In a sentence, 'football cannot compensate for society'.[6]

In the absence of an adequate definition of 'social exclusion', an accepted definition of exclusion is at least a starting point: 'The action or an act of excluding; … shutting out from a place, debarring from an office or society, rejecting from consideration etc.'[7] It is not too difficult to relate this definition specifically to society. The collection relates exclusion specifically to soccer, covers inequalities of class, gender, racism and ageism and considers *inter alia* commodification, community schemes, youth strategies, media insensitivities and gender prejudices.

Obtudant gender prejudices are especially well handled from three perspectives: women and self-image, mythology and objectification. Sad and true observations are made regarding media conservation, lesbian mythologising and sexual stereotyping. However, happily, the final ensured conclusion in *British Football and Social Exclusion* which mirrors, incidentally, the conclusion in the recently published *Soccer, Women, Sexual Liberation* is that women are slowly but steadily winning access to football fields, unsensational appreciation for game skills, and unremarkable acceptance 'on the park'.[8]

British Football and Social Exclusion includes the assertion that FIFA has 'the power to define, influence and shape the future for women who play football'.[9] It is worth repeating, therefore, the observation in *Soccer, Women, Sexual Liberation* that 'FIFA could do no finer thing than set as its *top* priority women's classless access to soccer all over the world'.[10]

Soccer has torn a large hole in the aortic valve of its public's passionate heart. *British Football and Social Exclusion* makes it clear that before that heart can be mended, soul-searching is required by those at every level of the game who wish it well.

J. A. Mangan
International Research Centre for Sport, Socialization, Society
De Montfort University (Bedford)
November, 2003.

Notes

1   Quoted in *The Daily Telegraph*, Friday, November 28, 2003, Sports, 55.
2   Stephen Wagg (ed.), *British Football and Social Exclusion*, (London: Routledge, 2004), p. 1.
3   Ibid., p. 14.
4   Ibid., p. 16.
5   Ibid., p. 24.
6   Ibid., p. 24.
7   *The New Shorter Oxford Dictionary*, (Oxford: Clarendon Press, 1993), p. 875.
8   Fan Hong and J. A. Mangan (eds.), *Soccer, Women, Sexual Liberation: Kicking Off New Era*, (London: Frank Cass, 2003), see Prologue, Epilogue and passim.
9   Stephen Wagg (ed.), *British Football and Social Exlcusion*, p. xiii.
10 Fan and Mangan (eds.), *Soccer, Women, Sexual Liberation*, see the Series Editor's Foreword, p. xi.

Introduction

STEPHEN WAGG

This book has a simple purpose: to explore the various dimensions of social inequality that currently afflict the game of football in Britain. The contributors have written variously against a background of euphoric public discourse about football, with waning concern about football hooliganism, a string of new stadiums, the incessant tinkling of cash registers at the top clubs and relentless media invocations of 'the beautiful game'. This framing of the contemporary game has not, of course, gone unchallenged, and a paradigm of critical writing about British football and social division has been sustained. This paradigm, organised around the angry rhetorical question 'Whose game is it, anyway?', goes back at least to the early 1970s, and has always been centrally about social class and community.

I look at the progress of this paradigm in the first chapter of this book and relate it to the contemporary (some would say 'postmodern') politics of 'social exclusion' in Britain. This chapter is intended to provide an analytical overview of the British football world in the past two decades. It also provides a lead into, and a context for, the remaining chapters in the book.

In Chapter 2 Tim Crabbe and Adam Brown develop further the themes set out in the first chapter. They draw on their 25 years' experience as supporters, researchers and activists in discussing the shifting nature of identities in the football crowd, in relation to broader notions of social change. Specifically, they look at the commodification, or 'McDonaldisation', of football and the changing nature of the match day experience, with regard to social class, loyalty, authenticity and identity amongst fans. They also analyse political interventions, such as the football 'Task Force', and suggest that contemporary concerns with social exclusion are marginal in relation to a consumption-driven football industry and its associated supporter cultures.

Neil Taylor's chapter, which follows, is a thoroughgoing account of the world of the 'Football in the Community' scheme. The politics of social exclusion in the 1990s produced a new nexus of clubs, administrators, government, funding bodies and community workers, who have combined to sanction and carry out programmes for the 'socially excluded' in the name of 'giving something back' to 'the community'. Neil, who has run one such programme for a number of years, analyses the working of this nexus.

The football world threw up postwar Britain's most enduring folk devils: football hooligans. The subject of innumerable books, public debates and student dissertations, football hooligans seemed to disappear in the early 1990s. Their banishment has been proclaimed as part of the success story that is the new, commodified, consumer-friendly football world: but what happened to the 'hooligans'? Chapter 4, by Pat Slaughter, is an observer's account of a day out with a group of Leeds United fans who all, to a greater or lesser extent, embraced the soccer 'casual' or 'hooligan' culture of the mid-1980s. Each in his own way recognises that his present fan identity has been moulded by this earlier experience – hence the term 'old boys', which the group employs to distinguish itself from other fans. How, for these old boys, does a day out in today's football world compare to a similar day out back in the 1980s? In the 1980s the members of this group wore designer clothes; disdained the wearing of club colours and the chanting of club anthems; possessed a clandestine knowledge of the workings and personnel of other fighting crews; and sat or stood in a part of the ground that they identified as 'theirs'. These were exclusionary practices, which served to insulate the group from the 'squares' of majority fandom and to preserve the violent, 'cool' identity of the group. To what extent have these traditions survived? This chapter shows how the members of this group have negotiated life in the new football world and what is, for them, a clearly hostile environment with no obvious place for old, working-class macho forms of support.

My argument in Chapter 5 is also concerned with class and, more specifically, with media discourse on the modern football world. In the populist rhetoric of the contemporary football press the greater rewards that accrue to modern players disqualify those players from claiming mental distress. This, I contend, is part of life in an increasingly marketised society. People act and 'make choices'. They are efficient at what they do, or they are not. In failure they cannot cite mitigating circumstance – least of all mental distress, which is widely regarded as a self-indulgence of the rich and famous.

The next three chapters are variously about the ways in which the contemporary football world addresses women. It may appear that women's current involvement in football is unproblematic: a potential success story on the cusp of reality. In many ways the Women's World Cup in the United States in 1999, the final game of which attracted more than 90,000 spectators, can be used as an indicator of women's current opportunities to succeed in football. However, in Britain women have struggled to play for more than 100 years, facing exclusion and inequality throughout. The 'takeover' of the Women's Football Association (WFA) by the Football Association (FA) in 1993 represents an ironic twist in women's footballing history, as does the proposition by Joao Havelange of the Fédération Internationale de Football Association (FIFA) that the 'future of football is feminine'. In their separate ways these three chapters make it clear that Havelange's assertion raises problems.

Chapter 6, by John Harris, is based on his doctoral research and it explores two dimensions of the relationship between women and football. Firstly, Harris draws on an extensive ethnographic study to present an analytical and descriptive account of the life of a collegiate women's football team in the South of England. Highlighting a number of issues of equity and equality, he identifies the struggles faced by women in their quest to be taken seriously as football players. One important theme that emerges is the perceived association between women's football and lesbianism. Secondly, Harris looks at the relationship between women and football as it is portrayed in the popular press. Here his finding is that football remains depicted solely as a male activity, and that women remain subordinate and sexually objectified in the majority of sports coverage. Harris thus demonstrates that there is a degree of social exclusion of women from football. Nevertheless, the women's game emerges as a dynamic social space, in which dominant ideologies are not only perpetuated but also challenged and contested.

In Chapter 7 Jayne Caudwell pursues questions of gender, identity and sexuality in the football world. The efforts by predominantly patriarchal institutions to include women – and we can read this as 'feminine women' – in football can be seen to reflect a move towards equality. Both the FA and FIFA have the political and economic power to define, influence and shape the future for women who play football. Arguably, they have the power to define, influence and shape the concept of the 'female footballer' as it relates to the feminine. Caudwell explores the existing conceptions of the female footballer. Through a discussion of both quantitative and qualitative research material she shows how the terms 'butch' and 'tomboy' have real currency for women playing within the cultural arena of football. She offers an analysis of female masculinity as it functions in sport, specifically football, and highlights the conflation of gender 'deviance' with aberrant sexuality: that is, the annexing of female masculinity to lesbianism. She acknowledges the presence of lesbians within football and assesses the treatment of lesbian players. She highlights the tensions that exist here and argues that lesbianism, in particular the 'butch' lesbian, is and will continue to be positioned as an anathema.

Media theorists have suggested that television genres address specific audiences. Soap opera, for example, has been considered to address 'feminine-identified' viewers and may therefore be seen as, arguably, a gendered genre. However, the gendering of the type of television programmes that are popular with males has rarely been analysed to the same extent. In Britain, despite reports of its gentrification and feminisation, football has traditionally been associated with a male working-class audience: it therefore presents an interesting opportunity to analyse a 'masculine' television genre. In Chapter 8 Eileen Kennedy offers a reading of televised football in Britain, identifying a series of important 'masculine' textual markers. Kennedy goes on to discuss how far other issues – such as class, nationhood and 'race' – might inform this process and takes up other questions, such as the growing deployment of women in television football coverage. Finally, she assesses the extent to which the discourse of televised football could be called socially exclusive.

In Chapter 9 Colin King explores the experience of black footballers in English football. Taking his lead from the Macpherson report on the death of Stephen Lawrence, with its emphasis on the 'unwitting and unconscious', King seeks an understanding of the ways in which the institutional structures of English professional football might normalise the notions of 'whiteness' in the game. Adapting Macpherson's stress on the importance of 'canteen culture' and drawing on his experiences on an FA coaching course, he suggests that precisely the same sort of frameworks noted by Macpherson in the Metropolitan Police Service also prevail in the institutions of football – the boardroom, the dressing rooms and the training field.

In Chapter 10 Raymond Boyle examines the extent to which football clubs in Scotland are attempting to intervene in the wider policy field that relates to community and social identity. While work in England has concentrated on the issue of football and ethnic minorities, in Scotland discussion has been dominated by sectarian identities, actual and perceived. Focusing on Celtic Football Club, Boyle traces the evolving engagement of the club in addressing wider social concerns. Some of these concerns are broadly related to racialisation. They focused initially on sectarianism, but have recently been extended to include Asian and other ethnic minorities, and the wider political issue of social exclusion. Like Taylor, Boyle assesses the degree to which this shift by the club is driven by commercial and corporate imperatives, as the transformation of the club into a global business accelerates. He goes on to ask whether there is a role for football clubs in a new Scottish political environment where a greater intervention in social and cultural matters is possible.

While other growing social divisions within the game have received a lot of attention, this cannot be said of the increased tension in youth football. The two closing chapters seek to remedy this.

In Chapter 11 Paul Daniel examines the impact of the recently created academies and centres of excellence upon the culture of boys' football. Organised by parents and other enthusiastic amateurs, youth football has traditionally been based on an ethos of social inclusion and broad participation, at least for boys. The academies appear to have a different agenda, however. For the FA they are a means of raising the level of skill in the English game, to enable English teams to compete more successfully on the international stage, while for the clubs that run the academies they are a source of future marketable assets. We can expect that the academies will be closely monitored on these two counts, but that little, if any, attention will be paid by the football authorities to the impact that these new centres have on football-playing children and on the existing culture of youth football. Daniel examines this important issue by drawing upon primary research conducted within one of the largest youth football leagues in the country. He discusses the views and experiences of parents, of league officials, and, in particular, of the boys themselves.

The new guidelines laid down by the FA for the coaching of children have created a number of problems for coaches, who now have to grapple with a number of important moral problems. In particular, many of them wonder whether current specifications actually commit children to a regime of football drudgery and repetition? Are children's bodies being overdisciplined? When selecting teams, should they pick the players whom they perceive as the best or ensure that everyone gets a go? Are girls, despite the rhetoric of the football authorities, once again being marginalised? These issues are analysed by Simon Thorpe in Chapter 12, which is based on extensive participant observation of the coaching of a children's football team.

Contributors

Raymond Boyle is a Senior Lecturer and Vice Dean of the Faculty of Arts at the University of Stirling.

Adam Brown is a Senior Research Fellow in the Manchester Institute for Popular Culture, Manchester Metropolitan University.

Jayne Caudwell is a Senior Lecturer in the Sociology of Sport, Chelsea School, University of Brighton.

Tim Crabbe is Reader in Social and Cultural Studies in Sport at Sheffield Hallam University.

Paul Daniel lectures in Social Policy at Roehampton University in London.

John Harris is a Senior Lecturer at the University of Wales in Cardiff.

Eileen Kennedy is a Senior Lecturer in the School of Life and Sport Sciences, Roehampton University.

Colin King runs the Martin Shaw King Trust, which, among other things, helps to fight racism in football.

Pat Slaughter is a Lecturer in Criminology at Middlesex University.

Neil Taylor is in charge of the Leyton Orient Community Sport Programme in East London.

Simon Thorpe teaches at Southwark College in South London.

Stephen Wagg is Senior Lecturer in the School of Life and Sport Sciences at Roehampton University.

Fat city? British football and the politics of social exclusion at the turn of the twenty-first century[1]

STEPHEN WAGG[2]

> It may be good enough for the homeless, but not for an international striker.
> (Pierre van Hooijdonk, turning down a pay rise of £7,000 per week at Celtic Football Club, 1996[3])

> But the teams that pass through those doors won't be Grimsby, Rotherham and Crewe. It'll be Arsenal, Manchester United ...
> (reporter standing in the visitors' dressing room at Birmingham City, BBC TV *Ten O'Clock News*, 16 August 2002)

This essay attempts to take stock of English football culture in the early years of the new (twenty-first) century. Its primary purpose is to probe the political meanings of this culture: that is, to try to understand what contemporary football discourses might tell us, politically speaking, about English society during this apparently tumultuous period. In doing this I hope not to rehearse unduly the already well advanced debates over the commodification of football in Britain and the consequent sense on the part of many that the game has lost its soul to an alliance of merchandisers and 'inauthentic', Johnny/Jackie-come-lately supporters. I'm well aware that, to borrow Hamil *et al.*'s phrase, 'the tensions between the new commercialism and football's social purpose have become intense' (Hamil *et al.*, 1999: 13). Indeed, this essay, like all the others in this book, has been purposely conceived as a contribution to this now well entrenched 'Whose-game-is-it-anyway?' paradigm of writing about football and society. More specifically, the essay will try to relate recent and current developments, especially in the English football world, to the emergent politics of 'social exclusion'. In this context, it will discuss the relationship between football and the academy; the political implications of the Premiership; the ongoing campaigns to preserve the smaller football clubs; and the new nexus of football clubs, funding bodies (some governmental, some not) and community work.

The essay, from time to time, draws on my own experiences. Most of the contributors to this book have, after all, written as much out of a personal, as a political or intellectual, engagement and I have been involved, albeit in a very minor way, in some of the developments I'm describing.

I should also stress that the focus of this essay is primarily upon *social class* and on the economic dimensions of contemporary inequality. Other writers in the book are, quite properly, concerned with the other social fractures of gender, sexuality, racialisation and age.

Eat football, breathe football ...

Association football today seems to be everywhere. Shunned by polite society for much of the twentieth century, it is now apparently embraced by all sections of the British, and much of the world's, population. Most people now affect to know something about football and to follow the fortunes of a particular club. Young men with loud, patrician voices proclaim their affiliations on London subway trains. A conversation I witnessed travelling the Northern Line in the late 1990s recalled BBC TV's *The Fast Show*, in which two upper-class characters proclaim their love of 'soccer', a game they have clearly only recently discovered.

'You support *who*!' bellowed one young man-with-a-briefcase to another. '*Tottenham*? They're *rubbish*!'.

'No, they're not'.

'Yes they are. They're ... they're ... worse than ... er ... *Ipswich*!'.

'Ipswich are in a different division'.

'Well, they're worse than ... *Everton* then'.

To those witnessing it this conversation carried the sense that it was intended – rather as if it had been conducted via mobile phones – for public consumption. It seemed important to these 'something in the City' young males that they be seen to be 'into football', although their knowledge of it appeared minimal. By now this kind of public invocation of the people's game extended all the way to 10 Downing Street. John Major had made much of his admiration for Chelsea FC during his premiership (1990–7). His successor Tony Blair had in 1997 recalled to an interviewer on a local radio station that he had sat behind the goal at Newcastle United's ground as a lad and watched the club's great centre-forward Jackie Milburn. It was soon realised, however, that seats had only been installed in that part of the ground in the 1990s. Moreover, at the time of Milburn's retirement, in 1957, Blair had been only four years old (Assinder, 1999).

These vignettes evoke, I think, two important and connected factors in football's contemporary cultural presence. One is the ubiquitous, almost paradigmatic nature of the game now: it has become a sea of public discourse in which we all might care to swim. I compare this to the place of football in the post-war suburban home in which I grew up. Both my parents loved football and despite our comparatively comfortable circumstances there was never a hankering in our house for the greater social status that seemed to attach to rugby. My father liked to take me to matches when he could but he insisted that it was always better to play the game than to watch it and became impatient when football and the affairs of the local club became, as they so often did, my sole topic of conversation. If I couldn't shut up about them, he said to me in some exasperation when I was around fourteen, then why didn't I go and live with them. These values, in which doing was placed above consuming and people were enjoined to sample a diversity of cultural influences, were widely held in British suburbia in the middle of the twentieth century and were embodied in the BBC of Lord Reith (Wagg, 1992). A little bit of what you fancied did you good, but no appetite – be it for sport, music, plays, science, the discussion of current affairs – should be fed continuously or on demand. There should, for my father and many of his generation, be moderation in all things. We have, of course, seen a steady abandonment of these values over the last forty years. In the postmodern, consumer-led, pick-and-mix cultural supermarket of the twenty-first century, constraints upon consumption tend to be practical (time, money ...) rather than philosophical. With regard to football, following the Broadcasting Act of 1989, viewers in the United Kingdom with the appropriate reception equipment can have virtually as much of the game as they can digest. Through the spread of satellite TV in the 1990s watching football came to rival drinking as a motive for people to enter pubs. Football has thus become, in a sense, a *given* – part of the popular cultural air that the people of many societies breathe. And it is given, on the whole, as a social good, the publicist's favoured description of it as 'the beautiful game' having become all-pervasive. For example, when in August of 2002, Colonel Muammar Gadafy, political leader of Libya since 1969 and depicted for much of that time as an international pariah by the British and American governments, sought global rehabilitation, he is said to have considered football as a means to achieve this. The Western press reported his love of the game and his recent investment in Italian and Greek clubs (Morris *et al.*, 2002). Less than a year later, with British and American troops massed in the Persian Gulf for an expected war on Iraq, a team from the UK's *Channel 4 News* visited Baghdad and mingled with a football crowd. What did they think of US President Bush? 'Fuck Bush' they responded. They preferred to talk about Sir Alex Ferguson, wanting in particular to know when he was going to 'sort out the back four at Manchester United' (*Channel 4 News*, 31 January 2003). Meanwhile the England footballer David Beckham has become what the writer Dick Hebdige once called a 'living news item' (Hebdige, 1974: 5) – indeed, in February 2003 SFX, the player's agents, were reported to have signed a deal to provide 'a set number of Beckham stories each year' to the *Sun* newspaper (Chaudhary, 2003). With Beckham now a global popular cultural icon to rival Elvis Presley or James Dean, cultural analysis began in earnest: coverage of one study suggested that Beckham was now 'the most influential man in Britain' (Campbell, 2003).[4]

The other factor is the widespread sense that, in England, Association football has been appropriated and that it now belongs to interlopers – people who care little for its heritage or for its previously acknowledged social meaning. This, of course, goes well beyond the resentment of Johnny-come-lately football supporters jumping, without complete conviction, onto a popular cultural bandwagon. It expresses the often complex and contradictory politics that have resulted from the commodification of the game, and it has given rise to a body of academic and related writing on English football that we might call the 'Whose-game-is-it-anyway?' paradigm.

Whose game is it now?

The principal contradiction here, then, is that, on the one hand, football seems to belong to everyone and, on the other, the game – rather like the land in the enclosure movements of the seventeenth and eighteenth centuries – has been taken from the people and used for profit. In this latter formulation, then, the notion of British football's social and political history, from the Second World War to the turn of the twenty-first century, is founded on ideas of social exclusion.

One of the earliest and most important contributions to the fashioning of what became the 'Whose-game-is-it-anyway?' paradigm in public and academic writing on football was made by the sociologist Ian Taylor in 1971. Taylor addressed the emergent phenomenon of what was then called 'soccer hooliganism' – the clearly vexatious, and allegedly new, practice of young men fighting at football matches. Taylor saw this violence as an expression of cultural anguish on the part of a rising generation of English working-class males at the commercialisation of a game they believed was rightfully theirs. Football, he pointed out, was a popular obsession and the violence now being discussed was 'an index of that commitment' (Taylor, 1971: 134). Perhaps wrongly, Taylor asserted that football clubs had been 'participatory democracies' (p. 140); he was on much firmer ground in asserting that Football League clubs had not previously been 'organized bureaucratically in the pursuit of profit' (p. 144).

Subsequent academic writing on the English football culture of the time worked, as I've observed elsewhere (Wagg, 1998: 43), with these assumptions: Chas Critcher, for example, wrote what amounted to an endorsement and an elaboration of Taylor's argument. Critcher, like my own subsequent book (Wagg, 1984), noted the impact on football of professionalisation and the mass media. It met, he argued, with resistance from young working-class men anxious to assert their 'adolescent male working class identity' against the new mores of the 'selective consumer' and the 'armchair viewer': 'The football ground is the established venue for the exploration and expression of this identity. In the absence of alternatives, it is likely to remain so' (Critcher, 1979: 172–3).

Two decades later this was open to doubt. In 1997, with the top clubs now having formed a Premier League, with the connivance of the Football Association and floated by sponsorship and satellite television revenue (see for example Conn, 1997; Fynn and Guest, 1994: 45–59; Horrie, 1997; Kelly, 1999; King, 1998), BBC Radio 5 Live gave leading football researcher Rogan Taylor four programmes in which to explore 'The Death of Football'. 'Football', began Taylor, 'is engaged in a gigantic act of betrayal'. Working-class communities were experiencing a ripping of the umbilical cords that tied them to football clubs. 'There's very little walk-up trade now', John Williams of the Sir Norman Chester Centre for Football Research at Leicester University explained. There were now two types of discrimination – one by price and one by mode of application: now you 'have to have a bank balance. Have to have a credit card'. While no clear ground for the increase in admission charges could be identified, football now excluded the 'older, poorer fans' (BBC Radio 5 Live, 17 April 1997). 'It's not just a matter of nostalgia', continued Taylor. 'The very fabric of the crowd that wraps around a football match is changing, through a process of exclusion'. An anonymous voice observed: 'There is this gentrification ... with so much money around and everything we seem to have attracted this secondhand car dealer mentality ... [People who are] dodgy and strange [and accompanied by] brassy women ... '. 'I think we're looking at a regulated, a controlled, a managed, a pacified space', concludes Williams, '[occupied by] more of an audience than a crowd' (BBC Radio 5 Live, 1 May 1997). In the final programme, football manager Lawrie McMenemy offers a perfect evocation of Ian Taylor's original argument: 'The trouble is that the man in the street used to be able to touch the player. He admired him and he was envious and he would love to do what he did. But not now. He canna get near ... ' (BBC Radio 5 Live, 8 May 1997). This final programme is able to offer something of a scoop. The Labour Party has won the recent general election with a huge majority (179 seats) and Tony Banks, the newly designated Minister for Sport, has agreed to answer questions. After the congratulations, Rogan Taylor presses Banks: is there anything that this new government can offer us? Banks' replies seem wordy and evasive – he's 'a conservative in football terms', we should remember football clubs aren't run by the state, there must be 'long term planning' which can encompass all the problems raised in these programmes, but 'we don't want to frighten the clubs off'. To those listeners with sufficient political acuity and knowledge of the 'New Labour' tendency now dominating the party the message is clear enough: the incoming Labour government will not countenance significant interventions in the football market.

The vocabulary of social exclusion, then, is long established in discourses on English football. But it has begun, at the turn of the twenty-first century, to be re-inflected and challenged, both in academic and popular commentary.

Some resistance to the commercialisation of English football has been institutionalised in the form of the fanzine (Giulianotti, 1999: 61–3; Redhead, 1993). Much fanzine commentary is localised: most professional football clubs in the British Isles have at least one critical and irreverent publication attached to them. There is also the national fanzine *When Saturday Comes*, which was founded in 1986 and has a current circulation of 23,000 (http://www.wsc.co.uk/, accessed 2 March 2004). *WSC*, intelligent, ironic and populist, has always tried to express the elusive 'fan's point of view'. In practice it has remained broadly sympathetic to the aims of the Football Supporters' Association, formed in the aftermath of the Heysel Stadium tragedy of 1985 (and has run a dual membership scheme with the FSA). The FSA, now subsumed within the Football Supporters Federation, has always sought to mitigate the effects of market forces on football, and regularly, for example, campaigns to lower ticket prices.

In 1999 John Williams, by now the English game's leading academic observer, produced a booklet whose title asked *Is It All Over? Can Football Survive the Premier League?*. Williams' reply to his own question is tentative and less nostalgic than previous analyses: 'Football is hot and it is rich', albeit with the proviso that 'not everybody in football is either hot or rich' (Williams, 1999: 65).

Other writers now questioned the validity of the categories which had framed the debate about clubs and their supporters since the 1970s. Anthony King, for instance, having spent time studying the culture of Manchester United supporters, challenged the contention of 'the lads' who felt themselves to represent traditional and authentic support for the club, 'that new consumer fans (who do not sing) are not real supporters'. '[M]y interviews', argued King, ' … demonstrated that they experienced just as visceral an attachment to the club as any of the lads' (King, 1998: 197).

Finally, in his doctoral work completed in 2002, the sociologist and fanzine editor Carlton Brick calls into question the whole notion that football supporters can be meaningfully said to be either 'real' or 'inauthentic' in their relationship either to the game or to their preferred clubs (Brick, 2002).

All this betokens an English football world in which problems of exclusion have become, in effect, problems of corporate public relations. I'd like briefly to discuss two of these: the issues of growing inequalities in English football and the recurrent public reference to 'hooliganism'. These two issues are, ultimately, linked.

Rich man, poor man

Kelly Jones plays guitar for the Welsh rock band The Stereophonics. Early in 2002 he told *Observer Sport Monthly*, for their regular feature 'My team', that he was a longstanding supporter of Leeds United Football Club. 'Despite growing up in south Wales', he explained, 'I've never been interested in Cardiff or Swansea. My memories from growing up is [*sic*] that they were both always crap' (*Observer Sport Monthly*, no. 21, February 2002, 60). A public proclamation of this kind would have been unthinkable in the English football world of forty years ago. Its jaunty dismissal of the poorer relations in the national football family, especially those from the speaker's own locality, would have been thought to be in poor taste. Importantly, it uses language which endorses, indeed revels in, social exclusion of a certain kind. As another celebrity, comedian Frank Skinner, told the same magazine:

> I was born in West Bromwich so I was never going to support anyone else ... Nowadays *Sky* has given us a big Premier League supermarket where kids can choose anything they like. For them it's 'Why don't I just watch someone who's good?' rather than their nearest team.
> (*Observer Sport Monthly*, no. 18, October 2001)

There is a strong sense, then, in contemporary football culture that one should choose the best and forget the rest (a theme explored by Simon Thorpe elsewhere in this book in relation to children's football). This, as I argue in my other contribution to this book, is accompanied by an impatience with the idea of extenuating circumstance. Fewer people now care *why* some clubs are less successful than others; they just are – they're 'crap'.

Indeed, by the beginning of the twenty-first century, the hegemony of top-class football was starting to swamp not only the claims to legitimacy of the smaller clubs but wider notions of the game of football itself. I sensed this early in February 2003, when I went into the West End of London to buy a football shirt. I wanted plain red, red being the generic colour stipulated by my Sunday morning football team, which doesn't, currently, have an official set of shirts. But, although central London has, as one would expect, a large number of chain stores selling sports goods, few of them sell plain football shirts, of any colour. They only stock replica shirts of famous teams that play in red – Manchester United, Arsenal, England when wearing their change strip, and so on. My request registered only confusion and apology on the faces of the young shop assistants. But if the shirts weren't plain, the implications of this experience were. In the marketing strategies of the big stores, football is equated with the game that well known clubs and their celebrity employees play on television. Therefore to want to wear a red football shirt, whether to play football in it or not, is, in this framing, to seek some kind of communion with a global football brand of that hue. Of course, as I hack a ball through the municipal mud I shall feel no homage to these brands, nor shall I imagine myself to be Paul Scholes or Denis Bergkamp. But players like myself who wish to make their own clumsy football history in plain shirts of their own choosing are now a comparatively small blip on the radar of contemporary sport consumption.

The Premiership, moreover, has ushered in a new age of personal enrichment for professional footballers playing in England. Ian Taylor's seminal essay was in part inspired by the abolition of the English footballer's maximum wage restriction ten years earlier (in 1961). This meant that many English players were soon earning considerably more than skilled working-class males. Now, however, a Premiership player is likely to be paid more in a few days than a working-class male could get in a year. Top salaries in the Premiership are publicly estimated at between £50,000 and £100,000 per week. 'What we earn is not just a whacking amount by Dutch standards', Manchester United and Netherlands player Ruud Van Nistelrooy told *Voetball International* magazine in January 2003, 'it's obscene when you compare it to what is earned in the rest of Europe' (*Guardian*, 15 January 2003). Indeed, Van Nistelrooy's vocabulary may have failed him if he had looked further afield for his comparisons. After all it's now axiomatic that the Premiership, via satellite TV, is a global phenomenon. At the time of his remark, the estimate by the United Nations Development Programme of the number of people in the world who didn't have enough food stood at 800 million; the UNDP additionally advised that 500 million of them were malnourished (http://www.undp.org/teams/english/facts.htm, accessed 25 February 2003). Similarly, the campaigning organisation *Global Issues* stated that nearly three billion people in the world (that is, virtually half of its population) were living on less than two US dollars a day (http://www.globalissues.org/TradeRelated/Facts.asp, accessed 26 February 2003). In this context the top Premiership clubs walk a fine line. On the one hand, following a series of reforms in the 1980s and 1990s through which market forces became effectively unrestricted in the English football world, the clubs have, consciously or not, become a flagship for the neo-liberal policies and practices being urged on institutions throughout the world. Here they carry prior public sympathy since supporters throughout the world will want 'their' club to have the best players and to pay accordingly, and very likely rebuke them for 'lacking ambition' if they don't. As the writer Laura Thompson remarked recently: 'Everyone knows players' wages would be regarded as a scandal were they paid to company bosses ... In that sense football's hegemony is almost terrifying' (Thompson, 2002: 15).

But, on the other hand, top Premiership clubs now perceive a problem of public relations, especially given the readiness (discussed at greater length in my other chapter for this book) of the sports media to run stories of excessive behaviour among the highly remunerated practitioners of the 'people's' game. For example, when in December 2001 the Leeds United and England player Jonathan Woodgate was convicted of causing an affray in Leeds city centre, it was disclosed that he had been known, during a night's drinking, to take £20 notes from his wallet and set fire to them. Woodgate's weekly wage packet at the time was said to be nudging £15,000 (Bradshaw, 2001), meaning that he would have netted in roughly ten days the median annual income for a British household. Less than a year later Chelsea first teamers Jody Morris and John Terry stood trial of assaulting door staff at a London nightclub. Although they were acquitted, the court heard that Terry had called the doorman 'a wanker' and that Morris had shouted 'Do you know how much I earn? I earn more in a day than you earn in a week. Do you know who we are? We could get you sacked' (Kelso, 2002). Behaviour more calculated to emphasise the division between the socially included and the socially excluded is difficult to imagine. It unsettles investors and consumer/supporters, and the Premiership clubs are naturally anxious to deter it. In 2002 it was announced that youth academies at all the clubs would receive tuition on 'how to cope with relationships and the public spotlight, how to handle the media and money management skills' (Chaudhary, 2002c). The clubs are likely, moreover, to want to encourage the view that, for footballers, wealth carries responsibilities and that they, along with their employers, are 'putting something back' into society.

There are, of course, other important dimensions to the inequality in the British football world following the founding of the Premier League. One was represented by the huge disparities of the football labour market, themselves heightened in 2002 by the apparent saturation of the market for televised football. As the pay-TV company ITV Digital proposed to default on their deal, worth £315 million, to show Nationwide League football over a three year period, a number of clubs faced severe financial difficulty. For many players this meant redundancy, and the press were not slow to adapt this to the rich-man-poor-man framework: 'As Beckham gets set for £92,000 a week, 600 fellow footballers prepare for the dole' read a *Guardian* headline, not on the sports pages but in the news section (Fifield, 2002).

Meanwhile, many clubs, which were previous and longstanding members of the original ninety-two clubs of the Football League, now struggled to stay in business. Throughout the 1990s smaller clubs grappled with heavy debts. Several went into administration and a number spent the period 1992–2002 under virtually permanent threat of closure – York City, at the time of writing, being the latest example. In the time of the Premiership, Barnet, Barnsley, Bradford City, Bournemouth, Brighton and Hove Albion, Chester City, Chesterfield, Crystal Palace, Derby County, Hull City, Leicester City, Lincoln City, Mansfield Town, Nottingham Forest, Notts County, Oxford United, Portsmouth, Southend United, Swansea City and Swindon Town football clubs had all either entered administration or faced potentially terminal financial difficulty. As stated on all the websites which furnish this sort of information, this list is not exhaustive. And, significantly, around half those clubs named have aspired to, and for a time occupied, a place in the Premiership. The cost of competing with the big clubs, or 'brands' as they are now frequently termed, has been punitive and was reflected in the announcement in the early autumn of 2002 that twenty-one of the current twenty-four clubs in Nationwide Division One could not guarantee to fulfil their fixtures. Following the collapse of ITV Digital, at least ten of them were seeking talks with the Professional Footballers' Association over possible wage deferment (Cox, 2002). In February 2003, David Sheepshanks, chairman of Ipswich Town, relegated from the Premiership the previous season and the latest club to go into administration, said: 'I don't want this to sound like sour grapes but I shall be continuing my action to tackle the huge monetary gap between the Premiership and the First Division, which is increasing' (Collins, 2003). Meanwhile, the bigger fish of the Premiership were licking their corporate lips at the thought of still-untapped global markets. Fifteen months earlier, then Manchester United chief executive Peter Kenyon had spoken of competing, not with rival football clubs, but with 'global brands' such as Coca-Cola, Pepsi and Mercedes-Benz. This would involve turning the club's 'global army of fans – 10m in the UK,

20m in Asia and 20m elsewhere – into customers'. In August 2002 Nike were due to take over the club's merchandising in a deal worth £303 million (Campbell, 2002).

These inequalities are reflected on the field of play. 'Results', wrote John Williams recently, 'are becoming more predictable ... founded as they increasingly are on the wage bills of top clubs. Finishing positions in the Premier League now largely reflect who is paying what and to whom. High payers finish first' (Williams, 1999: 66). The League is invariably won either by Arsenal or by Manchester United. Only Blackburn Rovers, in 1994–5 and subsidised by the massive personal fortune of their benefactor Jack Walker, has ever breached this duopoly.

Hooliganism: the spectre at the feast

Football research and academic commentary on the game are now firmly established in universities across the world, and the principal catalyst for this has been the social and political concern, particularly in Britain, with 'football hooliganism'. As we've seen, the debate about 'hooliganism' was, at its inception, also a debate about social exclusion since, as Ian Taylor argued, it was feelings of social exclusion from the game as they had understood it that moved these young men to behave as they did. By the 1980s the argument initiated by Taylor was in full swing and the leading critics of his argument were based at Leicester University, where the Sir Norman Chester Centre for Football Research was founded in 1984. The work of the 'Leicester School' (see in particular Williams *et al.*, 1984; Dunning *et al.*, 1988; Murphy *et al.*, 1990) in turn provoked further academic dispute, increasingly global in its compass. This dispute, which was often as much about the Leicester writers' intellectual heritage in the work of the German social theorist Norbert Elias as it was about 'hooliganism', has been ably summarised elsewhere (Williams, 1991; Giulianotti, 1994; 1999: 39–65; Social Issues Research Centre; see also Armstrong, 1998, for a robust engagement with the literature).

The researchers of the Chester Centre led the debate in the 1980s and early 1990s and, from time to time, had the ear both of the government and of the football authorities. They dismissed Ian Taylor's notion that 'hooliganism' was a response to commercialisation and other changes to football in the 1960s. On the contrary it 'stretches back to before the First World War, though in its present form it dates from the 1950s and 60s'. Only since that time had it been defined as a social problem, largely because of changing public sensitivities toward this type of behaviour. The seed bed of hooliganism was a 'pattern of "aggressive masculinity" [which] ... if our evidence and analysis are right ... is characteristic, not solely but mainly, of the "rougher" sections of the working class' (Murphy *et al.*, 1990: 93). The testimony of many young males of Social Class V interviewed by the Leicester researchers suggested that they enjoyed fighting and this seemed to be confirmed by the purported memoirs of football hooligans themselves, which began to proliferate in the late 1980s. Colin Ward's *Steaming In* (Ward, 1989) comes to mind here, as do the copious, and apparently interchangeable, works of Doug and/or Eddie Brimson (see for instance Brimson, 1996).[5] Seen from this perspective, the problem lay predominantly with the 'hooligans' and no logical link between them and some cultural appropriation of the 'people's game' could be made. If the sons of the 'rougher' working class still wanted to watch top-class English football, they had better confront their 'aggressive masculinity' and maybe, given the decline in 'walk up trade', open a bank account.

It's fair to say that the heat has gone out of the hooligan controversy, both as a social and as an academic problem, but it remains as a spectre which the sports and other media may occasionally care to raise. Every now and again an incident, or apparent spate of incidents, of disturbance at a football match will cause some news organisation to pose the question: 'Are we seeing a return to the bad old days of *football hooliganism*?'. One such was in early 2002. Exuberant Cardiff City supporters ran onto the pitch to celebrate their team's FA Cup victory over Leeds on 6 January. Three days later a bottle was thrown at Stamford Bridge as Chelsea played Tottenham. Both these games, significantly, were televised. The following day an article in the *London Evening Standard* announced that football had been 'thrown into chaos' (Curtis and Stammers, 2002). The same day I was invited to assess this view. My article in the next evening's *Standard* was an attempt to be more polemic and nuanced about the whole matter of football violence, arguing in particular that class hypocrisy was at work. 'Football hooligans' were shunted off the premises and told to take their 'aggressive masculinity' elsewhere; Premiership footballers convicted of affray or assault went straight back into the first team squad. 'It's easier to indulge in hooliganism', I wrote, 'if you're a particularly expensive piece of human machinery' (Wagg, 2002). Invitations to appear on the BBC's *Breakfast* and on *Channel 4 News* now found their way onto my answerphone. That night, in a studio at ITN, Channel 4's sport correspondent sat down opposite me and asked sternly 'Well, Stephen Wagg, *are* we seeing a return to the 1970s?'.

This is a deceptively political discourse. A decade is used to symbolise a past now defined as misguided, dangerous or disruptive, and it is set against a present that is modern and no-nonsense. For example, in the 1980s right-wing social commentary often constructed 'the sixties' as a period of 'permissiveness' and ill discipline. Similarly, in the 1990s, as the writer-comedian Mark Steel recently pointed out, the 1970s became the time of trade union militancy, strikes and 'The Winter of Discontent' (Steel, 2001: 49). Similarly, the 'football hooliganism of the 1970s' has become a media motif. It stands for pre-modernity in football – for a time when clubs had no business plan. When the media raise the spectre of 'the bad old days of football hooliganism', it is a signal for a flurry of press conferences at which club communications directors, administrators and police intelligence personnel avow that appropriate steps are being taken and there will be no return to this dread decade. Sponsors thus receive an implicit assurance that, at the next televised game, there will be no 'noises off' and no unpleasantness, therefore, to be associated with their products.

On 27 January 2002, in another televised game, this time between Arsenal and Liverpool, the Liverpool defender Jamie Carragher was hit by a coin thrown from the crowd. He threw it back and was dismissed by the referee. 'Now, surely', wrote the respected sports journalist Richard Williams, 'something has to be done' (*Guardian*, 28 January 2002). Instead, the spectre of 'football hooliganism' for the most part dropped out of sight, its mileage as a current news 'story' having been extracted. And academic discussion of this matter, at its height following the deaths at Heysel stadium in May 1985 and consequent expulsion of English clubs from European competition, has also dwindled.

Meanwhile, football researchers, like all researchers, must seek their salvation in the marketplace, and for leading centres such as the Sir Norman Chester, this has meant putting its investigative facilities at the disposal of the Premiership. In September 2002, reflecting on the Centre's trajectory, its director John Williams showed a cool appreciation of this relationship and its implications for British football and social exclusion:

SW: Let me run some (clearly overlapping) questions together. Over the last decade or so roughly how much of your work has come from the Premier League? What, principally, has the Premier League wanted to find out? You mention a lot of recent work on profiling. To what extent, in your view, have the sponsors of this research been hoping to counter the popular view that football's now only for the well off? And, broadly speaking, does your research bear out this view or not?

JW: A lot of the recent funded research has come from the FA Premier League and more recently from the Football League. I think, initially at least, that this funding was reasonably 'open' in the sense that, under [Rick] Parry [Chief Executive of the FA Premier League 1992–6], there was a genuine interest in finding out who fans were and what fans thought about the game and the direction it was taking. There was also interest here, of course, in collecting information about the differences between fan groups and about their characteristics. On the issue of using the demographic data I think the P[remier]L[eague] has had much more complex aims.

On the one hand it was happy, in the right context, to have the data pointing to a more affluent crowd – for marketing and sponsorship purposes – and on the other it also liked to try to promote the continuing involvement of w/c [i.e. working-class] people in the sport as a means of showing it is not 'excluding' those who are less affluent. We also did some detailed research for the Football Task Force in 1999, which showed pretty clearly that exclusion was going on.

More recently the FAPL has become much more controlling in its approach to research such as this. In the last years of our research for them it was much more guarded, for example, about even launching the findings in case it attracted 'bad' publicity for its member clubs. It now has a Customer Care Unit, which seems much more interested in a narrower 'market research' to be used for PR and internally by clubs. We really couldn't work with them anymore, so are no longer doing the research, which I expect to take a very different tack in the future.

(via email: 25–30 September 2002)

Thus, the imperatives of corporate publicity will swallow, and eventually spit out, academic research on football and social exclusion. The previous February the Centre had announced to the press the results of their latest survey, the gist of which was that most supporters of Premier League clubs were 'still white and wealthy' (Chaudhary, 2002a).

The official version: social exclusion, football and 'New' Labour

The concept of 'social exclusion' has a special place in the lexicon of the contemporary Labour Party and, in this context, its meaning is both more specific and elusive than that adopted hitherto in this essay. The specificity of the term cannot be found, however, on the website of the government's Social Exclusion Unit, set up in 1997 and located since May 2002 in the Office of the Deputy Prime Minister, which cuts across several government departments. Here 'social exclusion' is described, with noticeable vagueness, as

a shorthand term for what can happen when people or areas suffer from a combination of linked problems such as unemployment, poor skills, low incomes, poor housing, high crime environments, bad health and family breakdown. The Social Exclusion Unit was set up ...

to help improve Government action to reduce social exclusion by producing 'joined up solutions to joined up problems'.

(http:// www.socialexclusionunit.gov.uk/, accessed 29 February 2003)

Talk of 'social exclusion' began in earnest in Labour Party circles in 1992. In the wake of the party's defeat in the General Election of that year, its leader John Smith set up a Commission for Social Justice. This reported two years later (Commission for Social Justice, 1994) and thereafter Tony Blair, the new party leader following Smith's death in 1994, made frequent public allusion to the notions of 'social exclusion' and the 'stakeholder economy' (Blair, 1996).[6] The report was welcomed on the centre left, for which Blair and 'New' Labour have always presumed to speak, and in particular found favour among those intellectuals who had identified 'New Times' in the 1980s. Anne Showstack Sassoon, for instance, wrote:

> The report talks about an intelligent, flexible welfare state to help people into work and to enable individuals to change jobs 'upwards' rather than be trapped in low skill, low pay jobs or no jobs. The object is not to eliminate uncertainty, which is inevitable, but insecurity, deskilling and long term unemployment.
>
> (Showstack Sassoon, 1996: 160)

The outcome for Labour both in opposition and, since 1997, in office has been a concerted effort to square the ideological circle. Blair's political coterie, whose members have been styled almost universally as 'modernisers', and which has included political strategists such as Peter Mandelson, pollster Philip Gould and the sociologist Anthony Giddens, has consistently argued for a 'third way' in politics. The 'third way' purportedly reconciles an 'open, competitive and successful economy with a just decent and humane society' (from Blair's speech in Malmö in 1997, quoted in Driver and Martell, 1998: 7). This has centrally involved the claim that the social and political times have changed and that the Labour Party's policies must change with them; Labour's *values*, however, will remain. These values have been distilled into frequently reiterated concepts, among which 'community', 'social justice', 'social inclusion/exclusion' and 'stakeholder' are central (Driver and Martell, 1998: 26–30, 54–9). To a significant extent these notions exist only at a level of rhetoric and subjectivity. Labour politicians, for example, may invoke a 'sense of community' and individuals may feel that they are 'stakeholders' in society, but this involves no government enactment to change their material circumstances. These ideas are promoted in the context of a free market with all the vicissitudes that that entails:

Workers no longer have a secure job for life but need to adapt and retrain between many jobs they will hold during their working lives. Rather than fighting this or living in a protectionist industrial world which has long since gone, post-Thatcherite governments should accept this scenario and make the best of it. ... Without help, flexibility, insecurity and rapid technological change may lead to the exclusion of workers made unemployed or with out-of-date skills and hence to lack of social cohesion.

(Driver and Martell, 1998: 55–6)

'Social exclusion', therefore, in its current political formulation, is defined principally in relation to the labour market. People may need help making their way in, or onto, or back onto this market and the government may fund projects to these ends. 'Social exclusion' is, thus, defined primarily in terms of life chances and not in terms of actual material circumstances.[7] More substantial programmes for the redistribution of wealth or the combating of poverty have been deemed to be incompatible with 'modernisation' – in the conventional vocabulary of British political life at the turn of the century, very 'Old Labour'.

All this has important implications for the British football world. In particular, given the central place of the word 'community' in contemporary political rhetoric and given, also, the relentless invocation of football as the people's game, the relationship between football and community has been thrown into sharp relief. I want, in concluding this chapter, to consider two dimensions to this relationship. These are, first, the role played by football, and football clubs, in the tackling of 'social exclusion' and, second, the grassroots campaigns to save football clubs which have, in many cases, caused campaigners to press, and to mobilise, prevailing interpretations of the word 'community'.

Game plan: the mission statement position

In September 2002 the Blair government published its latest policy document for sport. Called 'Game Plan', this sets out two principal objectives recently determined by the government's Strategy Unit. The first is 'a major increase in sport and physical activity, primarily because of the significant health benefits and to reduce the growing costs of inactivity'. The second is the promotion of 'sustainable improvement in international competition, particularly in the sports which matter most to the public, primarily because of the "feelgood factor" associated with winning'. It calls for greater grassroots participation 'with a focus on economically disadvantaged groups' and for organisational reform in the 'delivery' of these objectives. It further recommends that bodies such as Sport England and UK Sport be slimmed down. Greater scope, they say, should be accorded to other funding organisations, drawn from 'the voluntary and private sectors' subject, of course, to the appropriate 'performance indicators' ('Game Plan': Executive Summary, Points 2, 31 and 32, http://www.strategy. gov.uk/2002/sport/report/sum.htm, accessed 3 March 2003). Thus, Sport England, for example, devolves money to grassroots football projects via funding bodies such as the Football Foundation. The Foundation is based on a funding partnership between, among others, the FA Premier League, the Football Association, the government and Sport England. Its Community and Education Panel undertakes to 'enhance further football's role as a positive force in improving social inclusion and as a means of raising educational standards' (http://www.sport england.org/lottery/funding/football_found.htm#cep, accessed 3 March 2002). The combating of 'social exclusion', therefore, is a key part of the brief of this, and other, funding bodies and, thus, an inevitable indicator of its performance.

Football provides the terrain upon which the government's two principal objectives are most likely to be met. It is, as I've observed, a sport which captures the popular imagination more readily than ever, at levels both of participation and spectatorship. This applies most especially to the 'grassroots' of society, widely invoked in official documentation, and, since it's still a sport in which England retains a global credibility, it carries more promise than most sports of the hoped-for 'feelgood factor'. Besides which, as Neil Taylor makes clear elsewhere in this book, football clubs may be willing to involve themselves in community football projects, if only from the standpoint of corporate public relations – that is, to promote the notion that conspicuously well-off football people are 'putting something back'. Youth and grassroots football, moreover, offer opportunities for corporate sponsorship, since companies are always willing to be seen watering the green shoots of the people's game. Coca-Cola's involvement with FIFA would be the best example here (Sugden and Tomlinson, 1999: 58–63). In this country McDonalds (who signed a £30 million deal with the FA in 2002 to promote community football), Barclaycard (through their current 'Free Kicks' programme) and Nestlé, among other companies, are sponsoring grassroots football projects.

Actual grassroots experience of these community schemes however, implies a more complex and baleful political reality than government websites and apparent corporate munificence may suggest. I offer a brief case study.

Lambeth Town Hall, 6 August 2002

Lambeth Town Hall is in Brixton, London SW9. Although this area has sizeable Portuguese and Irish communities, it's generally seen as having a Caribbean identity. The name 'Brixton' is synonymous with inner city social exclusion, and has been associated in the public mind with urban disorder and police harassment of black people since the riots there in April of 1981. The Lambeth Football Forum is convened by the Martin King Shaw Trust, and is to report on twelve years of running football projects in the inner city. The evening has a Caribbean feel. The chair, the main speaker and most of the audience are from Caribbean families, there are various dignitaries from the black community, and the event celebrates forty years of Jamaican independence.

The Forum starts around 7.30. Some four hours later, with many 'grass-roots' members of the audience visibly drooping, very few of them have had a chance to contribute. This is because there are so many invited speakers, which in turn reflects the large numbers of organisational bases that those staging the evening have had to touch. Black ex-professionals talk about the need to convince young black lads that, even if they don't make the grade at a League club, they should still stick with their education. There is a representative of the Kick It Out campaign against racism in football and a video is shown of a young local girl practising her football skills. Her father, his dreadlocks packed into his bulbous leather hat, speaks eloquently of the equal right of women to play the beautiful game. But most of the time is taken up by speakers from the numerous funding bodies that now occupy the political-bureaucratic space created by 'New' Labour's Game Plan. Representatives of the Football Association, Fulham Football Club's outreach scheme, Lambeth Sports Development team, Positive Futures, the Home Office, the Football Foundation, Sport England and SRB6 are all represented here tonight. Many of these have funded the MKST and they come one by one to the microphone to tell the gathering about various programmes and initiatives and the criteria which govern the distribution of monies. The main speaker, Colin King (a contributor, coincidentally, to this book), has produced a report for the meeting and it is, in essence, an audit of the Trust's activities – a formal affirmation that it has had the now-mandatory business plan and carried it out (Martin King Shaw Trust, 2002). Colin tells the audience that managing these schemes is an exhausting business. A portion of his time is spent running them; the rest is spent at his laptop, writing bids for further funding. These bids are complex and time-consuming and it may sometimes be necessary to employ a consultant to advise on the wording of them. (Such a person might, for example, suggest the most promising way in which the prospect of 'social inclusion' could be invoked.) He doesn't know how much longer he can carry out this work.

This experience shows government policy in a different light. While real inner city kids do get to participate in real community football projects, the circumstances in which they do so are dictated by the priorities of government in the era of neoliberalism and capitalist globalisation. The Blair government, like its immediate predecessors and numerous other governments around the world, has opened up many public services and functions to the market. However, successive British governments have sought to ease the passage of these apparently unpopular policies by the felicitous use of language. In 1990 the sociologist Peter Golding discussed the apparent merging of state politics and public relations, so heavy had government expenditure on impression management and publicity advice become (Golding, 1990). Thus postmodern government produces strategy, detailed documentation and sanctioned language in relation to a particular area of policy. Monies are then released to those people who make the best pitch, based on the correct invocations of the government's stated priorities and mastery of the currently favoured terminology. Funding will be hard-won and short-term (twelve months is common) and numerous business plans, balance sheets, brochures, progress reports and public meetings will have to be produced to show how it has been spent. Much money goes on applying for money and on showing that it has been properly disposed of. Thus ideas of social exclusion, community and football for the disadvantaged are assimilated to the working of the 'public relations state' (Golding, 1994: 476) – and therefore to the state rhetoric and apparatus of strategy, accountability and performance indication. Moreover, through 'partnership' with 'private and voluntary bodies' the government provides a platform, via sponsorship, for the pursuit of corporate public relations strategies. Put plainly, people with social problems are delivered to companies, for the use of those companies in the fashioning of advantageous corporate presentations of self. These may, as in the case of Nestlé and McDonalds, be companies who have faced international criticism for their interventions in young lives – Nestlé for their aggressive marketing of powdered baby milk to breastfeeding mothers in developing countries in the 1980s, McDonalds for their exploitation of young workers and their dubious nutritional contribution to children's diets. Now they can mitigate such criticism, by financing the access of deprived youngsters to the people's game, thereby, apparently, facilitating 'social inclusion'.

Of mice and men-in-suits: community, the market and the fight to save the smaller clubs

I've argued, then, that the terms 'social exclusion' and 'community' have become central to the institutional presentations of self that the Blair government, football's major clubs and governing bodies, and interested corporations make to the world. They feature prominently in myriad mission statements. In these contexts a crucial part of tackling 'social exclusion' consists in asserting – in official documentation and on official websites – that it is being tackled, is given a high priority, and so on. Similarly, there has been widespread adoption of the word 'community' in the official discourse of the football world – aside from the pervasiveness of 'Football in the Community' schemes, the FA's Charity Shield (contested by the Premiership champions and the FA Cup holders) was renamed the 'Community Shield' for 2002. And among the current Premiership clubs Sunderland, for example, state in their customer charter[8] that it places its community operation 'at the heart of the club' and that one of its key objectives is the 'fighting of social exclusion across the North East' (Cope, 2002: 2). But, in the leagues beneath the Premier League, the 1990s were a turbulent decade during which a number of campaigns in British towns and cities were mounted to maintain a League football presence in their locality. These campaigns now have their own literature (see for example North and Hodson, 1997; Watkins, 1999). Here, once again, popular notions of community have confronted the market, but this time a different dimension of the contemporary politics of community came into play, as the remainder of this chapter shows.

The sports journalist Jim White wrote recently about the struggle of Wimbledon supporters in southwest London to prevent the club from moving to Milton Keynes. Describing how, in 2002, Wimbledon supporters, rather than countenance the relocation, set up their own club, AFC Wimbledon, in nearby Kingston, White writes:

> The story … involves stubbornness, betrayal and – naturally enough – money. But it is also a morality tale, one that suggests there is still an area of life in which big business interests have failed to bulldoze the little guy. The Wimbledon story has all the ingredients for … an Ealing comedy. This is the story of the mice that roared.
>
> (White, 2003)

'They wanted to steal our club', a member of Wimbledon Independent Supporters' Association tells White. 'Nick it and move it 70 miles north. That's what it is: nothing short of theft'. White also quotes Labour peer Lord Faulkner, formerly of the Football Trust and a Wimbledon supporter for thirty years, who told the House of Lords: 'A club remains the property of its community and its fans' (White, 2003: 28, 30). Literally, though, this is, of course, not the case. Clubs are the property of their owners and are theirs, therefore, to dispose of as they please. Across the country, supporters became indignant when historic grounds were sold to developers by chairmen often of recent vintage and regarded as unscrupulous.

'They just want to get their hands on the deeds', John Baine told me when I was researching a documentary for BBC Radio 5 Live in 1998. Baine helped to revive Brighton and Hove Albion when their ground, which is now a retail park, was sold in 1996. Half a dozen years on, similar campaigns were being conducted, notably around the Staffordshire club Port Vale, York City, whose chairman formed a holding company which bought the club's ground Bootham Crescent and then sold it to housing developers, and Brentford in west London. I attended a meeting of Brentford supporters one Sunday evening in the autumn of 2002.

Brentford: 6 October 2002

We are in the back room of the Princess Royal, a dingy pub beside Brentford's ground Griffin Park, which is to be sold, once again to a housing developer. The occasion is the premiere of a video made by journalist Adrian Goldberg (Goldberg and Lowe, 2002) about how the supporters have recently formed a political party (the A Bee C Party) and fielded fourteen candidates in the Hounslow council elections. Adrian introduces the video with a joke. 'How many Manchester United fans does it take to change a light bulb?' he asks. 'Answer's three. One to change the light bulb. One to buy the video of the last time the bulb was changed. And one to drive the car back to Surrey'. This triggers laughter and cheers in equal measure, releasing clear resentment of the clubs who are now global brands and face none of the problems being aired here tonight.

The film shows that one A Bee C candidate gets elected: Luke Kirton, an office worker living locally, takes Brentford ward after a recount. His agent, Steve Cowan, is a political veteran, who has stood for Labour in three general elections. However, as he tells the camera, the Labour Party 'has ceased to represent anything that me and my family represent'. He says the club should be a 'more modern community area'. After all, the club's been a 'major focus for this area – probably since the 1880s'. An elderly man with a Labour rosette is unimpressed – 'How can you let someone represent just Brentford football ground?'. But the Labour candidate, Patrick Edwards, Communications Director at University College London, when asked what he makes of the supporters' campaign, offers earnest vacuities. He is asked what he makes of the supporters' campaign. His reply – 'I, I, I, I, I, I make an awful lot of it … I mean, I think it's good … I think the fans are passionate about football and passionate about Brentford and that's absolutely fantastic' – brings the house down. The Tory candidate is also sympathetic.

'The football ground', says Luke's mum pointedly, 'once that goes, well there isn't that much left in Brentford'.

Local mobilisations and political intervention of this kind have apparently obliged sections of the Blair project to go beyond mission statement and corporate partnership. As I argued earlier, by the 1990s, most people in British public life were anxious to proclaim their love of football/the local football club. The game became an important element in 'New' Labour's politics of identity and, as such, it now became a permissible area for qualified challenges to the market. So did the fact that many clubs threatened with bankruptcy in the new 'winner-take-all' football market were situated in 'heartland Labour seats' – a situation accentuated after the collapse of ITV Digital (Denny, 2002).

Besides, 'community' was a designated keyword in the lexicon of 'New' Labour and should not be abandoned to the (now largely extra-parliamentary) left. The Wimbledon struggle, for example, came to the notice of the Socialist Workers Party. A letter to their newspaper in December 2001 pointed out that the Wimbledon Independent Supporters Association were defending 'values which are held dear by many socialists' (*Socialist Worker*, 15 December 2001, 6) and in *Socialist Review* the following year the columnist Pat Stack, while allowing that '[t]here are many who believe that under socialism there will be no competitive sport' nevertheless endorsed supporter opposition to the business values sweeping the game. 'Many of those who have loyally supported and felt part of their local football team feel as if it is being stolen from them. In the case of Wimbledon it practically has been' (Stack, 2002).

By then the Department of Culture, Media and Sport had instituted Supporters Direct, a scheme to help supporters to gain a greater stake in the running of their favoured clubs. Chris Smith (the Secretary of State between 1997 and 2001) recalled: 'Who was buying football clubs was a constant worry at the DCMS. It gave added urgency to the need to help fans regain control'. Now came a rash of supporters' trusts, one of which bought a controlling interest in Lincoln City in 2001. Some of those involved were at pains, however, to downplay any thought that these interventions should be thought politically radical. Brian Lomax, who became the Britain's first 'supporter director' (at Northampton Town in 1992) said later:

> The [football] authorities were initially very hostile to the notion of Supporters Direct. I think it was a fear of the unknown. They thought it was some kind of socialist takeover … [but] I'm not trying to be

Lenin or Trotsky here. My objective is to help supporters gain for themselves a full and proper say in the running of their football clubs.

(Palmer, 2001; see also Lomax, 1999)

This, perhaps knowing, adaptation of Clause 4 of the Labour Party's constitution (abandoned in 1995) took its place in a growing debate about football and the market. There were calls for football to be regulated (Hamil, 1999; Taylor, 2000; Clark, 2002) and for football clubs to do more than simply trade on the convivial term 'community'. Sean Hamil, for example, a leading architect of the 'Whose-game-is-it-anyway?' paradigm and now running a centre for research into football governance at London University, suggested that:

Football trades heavily on its community involvement, so it has more responsibility than other businesses to give something back. But most clubs do relatively little, and only when it's forced upon them.

(Cope, 2002: 2)

There was criticism of the lack of statutory powers accorded to the Independent Football Commission in 2002. It would be unable to force changes to market practices (e.g. to ticket prices) and, in any event, supporters were told, in the first instance, to take their complaints to the clubs concerned (Chaudhary, 2002b). And the Labour MP Andy Burnham, a former advisor to Smith and chair of Supporters Direct, called for the people's game to be returned to the people. 'Market forces have been corroding football's soul for years', he wrote, and the way forward lay in football trusts (Burnham, 2002).

As it stands, though, all this is perfectly in keeping with the 'New' Labour project, its strategies, stated philosophies and objectives. It is true that Chris Smith and his Sports Minister, Kate Hoey, both lost their jobs when Blair's Labour won their second general election in 2001. Both were rumoured to have been too sympathetic to the rank-and-file consumers of sport for the party leadership, and insufficiently responsive to corporate interests. Moreover, Smith's successor, Tessa Jowell, made it plain that there would be no financial assistance from government for clubs reeling from the collapse of ITV Digital. The market would decide the economies appropriate to clubs' new circumstances and a lot of professional footballers would be heading, in due course, for their local job centre. Besides which, the government has acquiesced in the big clubs' resistance to calls for regulation (Bower, 2003). Britain's leading investigative business journalist recently described British football as 'unique – it is effectively lawless' (*When Saturday Comes*, April 2003, 26).

But modest monies to sustain clubs that were not commercially attractive and to help procure the involvement in these clubs of dedicated local people whose voluntary efforts would keep them afloat, was quite compatible the ethos of 'New' Labour. After all, in this context, 'community' was to be based on a feeling of belonging that provided an emotional bulwark against the rigours of an increasingly globalised and competitive market. Football provided this, along with the promise of periodic local 'feelgood factors', which also had their place in the government's mission statement. This, then, was football's version of the 'third way'.

However, beyond a certain point football cannot meaningfully address 'social exclusion' nor sustain 'communities', either by corporate gestures or by the promotion of supporter involvement in clubs. The problems of 'social exclusion' lie, adapting 'New' Labour's own definition, in lengthy hospital waiting lists, schools with inadequate resources, poor pensions, 'sink' estates, decaying public transport infrastructure and so on. These problems cannot be solved by three points for the town's football team on a Saturday afternoon; nor by the democratising of football clubs; nor by a shirt autographed by a famous footballer; nor by a series of noble undertakings on a club's website. Football cannot be expected to mitigate the effects of the market; on the contrary, it is governed by dictates of that same market. A winner-takes-all arrangement, in football as elsewhere, means what it says. To adapt a phrase popular among British sociologists in the much-derided 1970s, football cannot compensate for society.

Notes

1   I'd like to thank Tim Crabbe, Peter Golding, Stephen Hopkins, Jonathan Horner, Paul Norcross, Neil Taylor, Rogan Taylor and Ian Wood for help in putting this chapter together.
2   Roehampton University
3   Pierre van Hooijdonk's remarks appeared in the *Observer Sport Monthly*, no. 37, March 2003, 4.
4   The article referred to the paper 'One David Beckham: celebrity, masculinity and the soccerati' by Andrew Parker and Ellis Cashmore, which was to be presented at the conference *Sporting Icons: Media, Celebrity and Popular Culture*, Centre for Research into Sport and Society, University of Leicester, 7 February 2003.
5   I've reviewed the Brimson books in the *International Review for the Sociology of Sport*, 35/3, 2000, 405–9.
6   For example, in a speech in Singapore on 8 January 1996.
7   For an exposition of the concept of 'social exclusion' as part of the 'third way', see Anthony Giddens, *The Third Way: The Renewal of Social Democracy* (Cambridge: Polity Press, 104–11). The most convincing intellectual and political challenge to

this 'third way' is Alex Callinicos, *Against the Third Way: An Anti-Capitalist Critique* (Cambridge: Polity Press, 2001).

8   Every Premier League club published a customers' charter at the start of the 2000–1 season, following a recommendation of the Football Task Force in 1999.

2

'You're not welcome anymore': the football crowd, class and social exclusion

TIM CRABBE and ADAM BROWN

Introduction: back to the future?

Edgeley Park, Stockport, 2001

With no room left on the open terraces themselves I am left standing in the aisles, the 'civilised' desire for personal space abandoned as bodies crush against friends and strangers alike, with the stewards redundant in the face of the packed adrenaline-charged crowd. Transistor radios are pressed to ears relaying scores from Huddersfield, Grimsby and Portsmouth as the ball is hooked forward hopefully before finding Freedman who goes on another weaving run towards the goal which sits invitingly before us. Whilst the clock continues to tick away, time is slowing down as the ball moves across each blade of grass and the crowd moves forward in anticipation, every face a picture of suspense. Another dummy, a jink inside, and the ball rockets into the roof of the net ...

The celebratory roar is too loud to hear, but fuels the emotions as bodies collide, falling into and over one another in an ecstatic explosion of joy, hugging, kissing and virtual loss of consciousness. Anyone will do, as countless fans now stand between me and the friends who have similarly been carried away in the crowd. Whilst we fall back into the vacuum created by the surge, the players are still celebrating as they are mobbed by fans moving onto the pitch, dancing, jumping, oblivious to the stoic behavioural conventions of contemporary football stadia. As the reality of the goal sinks in, a gradual return to the terraces is facilitated by obliging stewards before the final whistle precipitates another pitch invasion and twenty minutes of incessant singing before Palace's First Division survival is confirmed and the players re-appear to receive the crowd's adulation.

As we make our way contentedly out of the ground into the Stockport back streets and a more aggressive roar goes up as rival fans engage in ritu-alised physical confrontation, a terrace wag suggests that we are back in the

1970s: 'All we need is Dennis Waterman to add a commentary.'

This scene, drawn from one of our recent ethnographic research experiences, took place in the year 2001.[1] Yet even the 1970s were never characterised exclusively by such spontaneity, physicality or raw passion, for it is in the liminality of such moments that people fell and continue to fall in love with football clubs. Indeed Sam Hamman, Chairman of Cardiff City Football Club, seemed to recognise this point when he stoked up the atmosphere for the third round FA Cup clash on 6 January 2002 between Second Division Cardiff City and Premiership title-chasing Leeds United (see also Pat Slaughter's chapter in this book). Towards the end of the match he walked around the touchline whilst performing a head-slapping ritual, colloquially known as the 'Ayatollah', before standing behind the Leeds goal where Cardiff's winner was scored and running on to the pitch waving a Welsh flag, ultimately being carried off by jubilant fans.

Such spontaneous and passionate outbursts often go entirely unreported in the mainstream mass media, lying, as they often do, outside the focus of cameras and journalists. During one, somewhat run-of-the-mill, mid-season game in 2002 at Pride Park between Derby County and Manchester United, there was an explosion of singing, dancing and drinking under the stand during the half time interval – an occurrence that seemed entirely out of step with the previous forty-five minutes' of football. Several hundred Manchester United fans danced on each other's shoulders as beer was thrown across the concourse, a deafening 4/4 banging started on metal shutters and one song rang out *ad infinitum*:

> My old man said 'be a City fan' and I said 'bollocks, you're a cunt'
> I'd rather shag a bucket with a big hole in it
> Than be a City fan for just one minute.
> With hatchets and hammers, Stanley knives and spanners
> We'll show those City bastards how to fight …

The song specifically recalls a much earlier era – one where violence, both actual and threatened, was more commonplace, but also one where Manchester City were fierce on-field rivals of Manchester United. Given that in 2002 City were in Division One and the chances of violence at the match slim (even with Derby fans who were not the subject of the song), its relevance seemed tangential at best. It did however raise important questions about authenticity and nostalgia.

What was clear in the midst of this mayhem was that this was an overt attempt by some of United's away supporters to recreate a (mythic) past where they felt freer to express themselves unconstrained by over-attentive stewards and all-seat stadia. In the concourse there were no seats, no barriers, and the 'ecstatic solidarity of the terrace' (King 1998) was re-created to the excitement of many fans: 'Madness! It was just like the old days before the Muppets.'

In these instances a number of debates emerge about the football crowd, about shared and constructed memories and identities, and about expectations of behaviour which invoke the notion of the 'real fan'. Indeed, these complex and often contradictory concerns with, and claims to, authenticity within contemporary English football culture, are themes which re-emerged during the 2002 World Cup finals staged in Japan and Korea (Crabbe, 2004). In this chapter we wish to consider the basis of such claims, as articulated by supporters, administrators, journalists and academic writers, whilst, at the same time, relating the analysis to broader shifts within the social, cultural and economic fabric of the game. In doing so we seek to consider the ways in which the construction of fan identities and their interpretation acts as an agency of inclusion and exclusion across the game's increasingly diverse sites of consumption.

A 'whole new ball game'? Continuity and change

The perception that English professional football has undergone some kind of all encompassing economic and cultural revolution during the last decade seems to have been embraced almost universally as a social fact amongst commentators on the game. Unsurprisingly, the revolutionary terminology has itself been related to a shift in the social class credentials of those running and watching the game. This was beautifully articulated by David Thomas in the *Daily Telegraph* when football was placed at the altar of capitalism during the 1994 World Cup finals:

> The mood of this World Cup has been quite unlike that of football as we have known it. And the reason, I would suggest, is that USA '94 took a working-class winter sport and turned it into a middle-class, summer entertainment. ... This has been a tournament of tactical subtlety and occasional flashes of brilliant movement. It has been a game best appreciated over a cool glass of white wine rather than a steaming cup of Bovril and gristle pie ... But will the brave new world of sanitised football be quite as enticing as it seems? A decade or two from now, the roar of the crowd may well have dwindled to an appreciative murmur as up-scale audiences applaud the subtle interplay of footballers moving with balletic grace. ... But as dusk approaches, the ghosts of footballing legends...will look down from on high. They'll remember the passion...They'll think of the steam as it rose from a pulsating, shouting, singing crowd, who watched hard men play a hard man's sport.
>
> (*Daily Telegraph*, Saturday 17 July 1994, 17)

Both in the run-up to and aftermath of this tournament academic writers on the sociology of football began to develop and re-focus an interest in these developments. From Ian Taylor's assessment of the relationship between these changes and the advance of market relationships within the game (1995) and Anthony King's thesis on the new consumption of football (1998) to Steve Redhead (1997) and Richard Giulianotti's (1999; 2002) concerns with post modernisation and the emergence of the 'post fan', this has proved fertile ground. Yet as Williams (2000) has pointed out, whilst also falling victim to the same pressures, in considering the very notion of a transformation there is a tendency within these accounts to seek out and establish dichotomies between what has gone before and what is now. There has been far less interest in the continuities within football culture than with the changes, and less concern with the purpose and *effects* of the search for authenticity than with Taylor's acknowledgement of the significance 'of new ways of being a fan' (1995: 29).

The argument that English football has undergone fundamental restructuring in the last decade and a half is based on a number of elements. The Hillsborough tragedy in 1989 and the subsequent report by Lord Justice Taylor in 1990 led to the introduction of all-seat stadia in the top two divisions of English football by 1994. This development is generally regarded as representing a watershed for English football (FTF Final Report: Report One: 6; Ian Taylor 1992; Williams and Wagg 1992) and led to widespread reconstruction of stadia and relocation of a number of club grounds. The main implication of this for match-going supporters has been the removal of large, cheap, terraced 'ends', traditionally the location of the most passionate and vociferous fans. The rebuilding has also allowed clubs to develop further their corporate facilities and family enclosures and to reconfigure the location of different social groups of fans.

For example, at Old Trafford, terraced areas on United Road, the Stretford End and the Scoreboard Paddock were converted to seated areas (Brown 1998: 61). King has referred to this as removing the opportunities for ecstatic celebration of fans of the kind referred to at the start of this chapter, by replacing 'an open space in which it was easy to create an ecstatic solidarity' with 'the panoptic isolation of the seat' (King 1998: 161). However, the replacement, particularly at the Stretford End, of 'popular' standing areas with executive and family seating has also been portrayed as symbolic of wider changes in football.

Following the popularity of the 1990 World Cup in Italy (Davies 1990), renewed pressure from the richest Football League clubs also eventually led to the formation of the FA Premier League which was inaugurated in 1992 (see Conn 1997). This was an historic FA-sanctioned breakaway from the Football League. Its primary effect was to change the political economy of the sport, breaking the solidarity, based on revenue sharing, between professional football clubs, and widening the division of wealth between the top division and the rest – a process which has since been repeated across Europe (see European Commission Com. 1999 644). This latter change was made possible by the securing of an exclusive television deal between the new Premier League and BSkyB.

Subsequent to the rebuilding of grounds, the formation of the Premier League, and the BSkyB television deal, a number of clubs decided to restructure and realise capital investment by floating on the Stock Exchange. This has been described as one element in the 'colonisation of football by capital' (Ronstein 2001). There is little space to go into these developments in detail here and they have been described extensively elsewhere (Conn 1997; Lee 1998; Hamil *et al.* 1999; 2000). However, it is undeniable that, for those clubs who decided to 'float', new obligations were imposed, including to the interests of large financial institutions who almost universally owned the majority of club shares. There were now obligations to pay dividends to shareholders; new forms of governance associated with Stock Exchange rules; and pressures to maximise revenue and minimise expenditure.

One of the ways in which clubs sought to maximise revenue in the 'new football environment' was by increasing admission charges to grounds. By 1999 the Football Task Force found that ticket prices had increased by over 300 per cent since the formation of the Premier League (FTF 1999: 19). This increase more than any other factor has been cited as the reason for the 'social exclusion' of football supporters, especially where the supply of tickets has been considerably less than demand (e.g. at Manchester United and Newcastle United). As Giulianotti writes: 'There have been persistent criticisms of this boom on the basis that established (but relatively poorer) football spectators are being squeezed out of any stakeholder position within their clubs, most notably the biggest ones, in exchange for wealthier new spectators' (2002: 25). Individual supporters, too, argue that the increase has excluded them on grounds of economic status or class location:

> Most of the people I started going with to football no longer go. They dropped out as it got more expensive and now can't.
>
> (Manchester United fan, interview with AB, 2001)

> For me it is quite simply a class issue in that the working class are being excluded from United so that big shareholders and [Martin] Edwards can profit. Football is a working class game, but they're being excluded. Lots of people have given their tickets to others or started sharing.
>
> (Manchester United fan, interview with AB, 2001)

At Manchester United, alternative uses for the stadium (e.g. concerts), have accompanied the sale of financial services to fans – 'whatever you're passionate about, MU finance could help … it's our turn to support you with a personal loan of up to £25,000'. Meanwhile, new commercial partners such as Vodafone offer new ways to consume the club: a text messaging service of 'ManU information' was offered as 'the next best thing to being here' next to a photo of an empty seat at Old Trafford. In this context it is difficult not to conclude that the leading clubs at least have undergone some fundamental change.

However, here as elsewhere, continuities are often concealed and it would be a mistake to regard the huge changes which have undoubtedly occurred in the 1990s as necessarily permanent. At the time of writing there is huge concern about the future value of TV rights and talk of a 'football recession' (*Guardian*, 11 January 2002). Furthermore, the lack of 'value' of clubs listed on the stock market may indicate that capital's 'colonisation' of football remains unfulfilled. In some respects it is remarkable what has *survived*, not least in England a unique, four-league professional structure of ninety-two clubs. Equally, King is correct to argue that even historically *any* static reading of football is a mistake:

> the different constituencies of the crowds in different decades really gave the game different meanings at different times, which reflected the state of the wider social formation. To suggest that football remained fundamentally the same throughout the century is an exaggerated essentialism, and such claims of traditionalism must be treated with scepticism.
>
> (1998: 164–5)

Thus, whilst we can see that significant change has occurred in the finance, structure and organisation of football and in clubs' relations with fans, we can also see that many of the processes which have led to these changes are long standing in football. Therefore, continuity as well as change is a key feature of football since 1990. However, competing and often diametrically opposed claims are made by academics, journalists, football authorities, government, and supporters and their representatives, about the effect and desirability of these changes. The ways in which these debates and discourses have been conducted, and the contradictions and complexities within them, tell us something about notions of exclusion, class and football crowds and the pressing need to rethink them.

Discourses of change: the institutional response and the social 'inclusion' agenda

BSkyB's declaration that the formation of the Premier League provided us with a 'whole new ball game' sums up the aspirations of football's governors to create a new 'product' which would be saleable to television consumers. Rupert Murdoch has made no secret of the fact that he regards sport and football in particular as the 'battering ram' to open the door to pay-TV customers (*Guardian*, 7 September 1998; Brown and Walsh 1999). Some, indeed, have argued that BSkyB would have folded without securing the Premier League contract in 1992 (Conn 1997).

However, for that strategy to be a success changes were needed in the marketing of the game. The FA's own *Blueprint for the Future of Football* (FA 1991), which outlined the Premier League plan, argued that there was a need to raise the average social class of football supporters to make the game more attractive to advertisers, corporate sponsors and their guests.

The pursuit of this agenda – often termed 'gentrification' or 'commercialisation' – is continuing, with Manchester United's Chief Executive and Group Marketing Director both referring to the need to 'monetise the fan base'.[2] This strategy is currently being pursued through a new merchandising agreement with Nike, in which Nike take over the merchandising operation, and the development of new products from the club. Further change is likely with the expansion of pay-per-view television, internet broadband delivery, SMS text messaging, WAP and other new modes of football consumption.

From the point of view of commercial interests, the changes which have occurred have improved the product (better football), improved the stadia (more comfortable, safe and secure), and changed the nature of the people who watch the game live (higher social class, more bourgeois behaviour, more attractive to advertisers). At the same time the new strategy has been presented as returning to, or based on the traditions of, the past. Also, in contradictory ways, the authorities have presented their policies as 'inclusionary' despite the *exclusion* of some fans and forms of behaviour.

The adverts for BSkyB representing the Premier League as being a 'whole new ball game' have at the same time appealed to 'tradition' and the game's existing supporters through advertisements which seek to align the company's own attachments to the game with the emotional bond experienced by supporters. Likewise, football's administrators have for many years made appeals to get football 'back' to being a family game. Whilst the myth of football as a family concern has become rooted within the discourses of football's administrators, clubs, commentators and even some fans, as Russell (1997) has argued:

Those propagandists who call for the 'return' of the 'traditional family' game, when fathers and sons attended together in large numbers, clearly know little about the history of the game before the 1950s.

(1997: 57)

Alongside the misplaced nostalgia – itself reliant on notions of an 'authentic' past – a number of initiatives aimed at including 'new' groups of fans, especially women and minority ethnic groups, have been launched. Whilst there is a strong market logic for attracting such groups (many clubs are situated in areas with a highly diverse ethnic make-up which might provide new consumers), there is also a more general attempt at an 'inclusionary' agenda. However, these efforts have been framed within the broader context of moves to alter the behaviour of existing fans, to apply social engineering to the composition of the football crowd and resist attempts by some fans to 're-create' some of the conditions perceived to have prevailed pre-1990.

Football's reputation as a site for the performance of racist behaviour has been a major focus for football authority and governmental agencies during the last decade. However, even in this it has been notable that the emphasis is overwhelmingly on the social control of fans. As has been argued elsewhere, less attention is paid to other forms of racism in foot-ball, particularly when located within the institutions of the game (see Back *et al.* 2001). Indeed, this emphasis has also been true of football fans themselves, who have undertaken a number of initiatives which over-whelmingly focus on the self-policing of supporters.

Furthermore, in the process of establishing Kick It Out, the organisation with responsibility for running the Lets Kick Racism Out of Football campaign, an *ad hoc* body was established which broadened the parame-ters of the campaign to include anti-social behaviour, swearing and abuse of a non-racial nature. This was called AGARI (Advisory Group Against Racism and Intimidation). Thus anti-racist campaigning in football, which had its roots firmly in the fans' movement, became an officially sanctioned response targeting what the authorities, rather than fans, felt were the priorities (AGARI Press Release 1995). Indeed, attempts by the Premier League to control swearing at matches were subsequently met with ridicule by many fans.

Following minor disturbances (accompanied by exaggerated media reporting) during the Euro 2000 championship finals in Belgium, attempts were also made to broaden the base of support for the England national team whilst at the same time attempting to exclude 'known trouble-makers'. Part of the logic presented for this move was the claim that football hooliganism was more of a problem with England's away fans than at domestic matches or club European games.

However, the response represented an attempt to re-construct the social make-up of that following in the hope that by introducing more women and ethnic minorities, other fans would behave 'better'. Quite apart from the patronising attitude this represents to those 'excluded groups', this exercise in social engineering of the England Members Club (or *englandfans* as it was renamed) was based almost exclusively on two considerations: one, a desire to reduce the numbers of white males aged between twenty and forty-five; and two, to exclude those who had recent criminal convictions, whether these were related to football or not. This move by the FA has been mirrored in the legislative sphere with the Football (Disorder) Act 2000. This Act was rushed through Parliament following Euro 2000 with the objective of giving the police powers to stop and ban from travelling to games, individuals who may never have committed an offence at a football match at all, on the basis of other convictions and/or undisclosed police surveillance material.

As such the strategy relied on a series of questionable assumptions about fans: that fans from minority ethnic groups were less likely to be violent; that the mere presence of women could exercise some sort of social control; that belonging to the male, white supporter group made you more likely to be violent; and that holding an unrelated criminal conviction would (presumably along with a third of the adult male population) make you a potential troublemaker. Behind these assumptions lies a desire to alter the basis of football fan culture through a bourgeois interpretation of diversity, family values, safety and risk aversion. Some fans have explicitly identified these moves as part of a policy which produces social exclusion, in which the travelling fan especially – those Giulianotti terms 'traditional/hot supporters' (2002: 30) – is denied basic liberty: 'if you're a football fan, expect to be arrested' (http://www. redissue.co.uk May 2002).

However, it is in response to the commercial developments that those fans most affected by the changes have been most critical. In this they often display similar attachments to authenticity and notions of class, although from a very different perspective, to those made by the game's authorities.

The people's game? Class, football fans and social exclusion

One of the interesting features of some of the collective fan responses to these developments has been the contradictory ways in which they have expressed concerns about exclusion in football. The Football Supporters Association (FSA 1999), in its second submission to the Football Task Force, described the role of clubs in very traditional, romantic and somewhat static terms:

fans support for their team is a lifelong and unchangeable commitment. ... At a local level, clubs are an integral and historic part of the lifeblood of local communities.

(FSA 1998: 1)

Whilst this point rings true in many cases, at other times supporter groups have sought a more overtly democratising agenda – 'we need ... to involve all sections of society in our game: women, the disabled, young people and families' (Coalition of Football Supporters – COFS – press release, 25 February 1999). This belies Taylor's (1995) criticism of them as culturally conservative. However, even where there is this commitment to diversity within football fan culture, which has rarely if ever been witnessed in practice, there is an underlying juxtaposition of the authentic/old supporter and the inauthentic/new fan or businessman

The central point of our argument, then, is that responses to the wider changes within the game are often couched within broader concerns with class-based notions of 'exclusion', 'tradition' and 'authenticity'. Within contemporary football discourse, dichotomies, or what Garry Robson (2000: 87) has referred to as opposing 'ideal-type taxonomic sets', have been constructed around notions of the 'authentic' and the 'inauthentic' football fan, which generally consist of the types of distinction shown in Table 2.1.

In revealing the limited generic validity of these classifications what interests us is their continuing resonance within a variety of football discourses. Increasingly the concern that working-class fans are being economically excluded from attendance at matches has been accompanied

Table 2.1 'Authentic' and 'inauthentic' fans

Authentic	Inauthentic
Loyal	Fickle
Long standing	New
Working-class	Middle-class
Local	Non local/global
Live match attender	TV viewer
Away match attender/traveller	Home matches only
Sits/stands at 'ends'	Sits in main/family stand/corporate box
Masculine	Gender blind
Passionate	Effete
Anti-commercial	Consumerist
Street wise	Gullible
Knowledgeable	Ignorant
Football centric	Ephemeral

by a critique of the bourgeoisification of the game and a shifting of the terms of football discourse. This latter aspect has been associated with the emergence of a metropolitan journalistic 'Soccerati', criticised for reacting against this nostalgia in class-specific terms. Crucially they have been accused of 'blaming one less powerful social group (the working classes) for the [historic] social exclusion experienced by others (ethnic minorities and women)' (Giulianotti 1999: 151).

The articulation of these less sympathetic readings of 'traditional' football culture can be related to new forms of inclusion and exclusion, which are operating at the level of behavioural norms and standards, and the 'policing' of these norms and standards within football stadia themselves. Many claims have been made that the introduction of all-seater stadia and commercial efforts to encourage a broader social base of supporters, along with a rise in ticket prices, has brought with it increasingly subdued and dispassionate forms of spectating. With fans attending games less spontaneously, in smaller groups, restricted to pre-allocated seats, in environments which are increasingly sanitised and monitored by sophisticated surveillance equipment, there is less space for the kind of collective forms of expression and physicality described at the outset of this chapter.

This discursive framework has also been routinely taken up by journalists who contrast the atmosphere created by the new, less passionate, fan to that of yesteryear, in this instance citing the fan's age, geographical origin, commitment, concentration and volume of expression. Crucially, the blame here is laid at the door of 'new' commercial interests:

> 'There's too many tourists at Old Trafford these days. You know, see Buckingham Palace, go to Madame Tussaud's and catch a United game,' the thirtysomething Manchester United fan groans. Indicative of the McFootball nature of the Old Trafford experience these days are the pre-match PA announcements, the majority of which are of the 'and a warm welcome to Michael from Donegal in Ireland who's making his first visit to Old Trafford today' ilk. There's little sense of a committed hardcore of vocal support. During the first half on Saturday, when West Ham dominated possession, there was barely a peep from the home crowd. Where, at most other grounds, fans would greet an 18-pass move by a visiting side by standing up en masse and encouraging their team to intensify their efforts to regain the ball, most United fans saw the passage of play as an opportunity to chat with their neighbour. In the vicinity of the press box I heard just one disgruntled United supporter moaning at his side. Roy Keane's infamous 'prawn sandwich' outburst certainly rang true on Saturday. Even three years ago a

visit to Old Trafford was a fearsomely noisy experience. But as the club has attempted to become the dominant global sporting brand, so its support base has become diluted and lost its fanatical edge.

(Paul Connolly, *The Times*, 10 December 2001)

Crude efforts to control supporter behaviour have always been a part of the game, with Russell arguing that 'as early as 1890 the Football League, quite possibly in a deliberate attempt to limit the access of poorer (and thus supposedly "rowdier") supporters, raised the minimum adult male admission price' (1997: 56). However, in Foucault's (1975) terms, supporters' behaviour is now increasingly 'regulated by the gaze of others and by the gaze of [their] own self reflection' (Rojek 1995: 6).

Rather than being seen in a simplistic one-dimensional fashion, the exclusive effects of this gaze need to be seen in all their complexity, simultaneously defining and reacting against the self-conscious presentations of a variety of social class fragments and consumer lifestyles. The concern with the exclusion of working-class fans and nostalgic lament for the loss of 'the people's game' sits alongside a bourgeois concern to control the forms of aggressive working-class masculinity often associated with the game. As such, the more detached 'new middle-class consumers' of football, famously derided for being more interested in eating their 'prawn sandwiches' than getting behind the team by Manchester United's captain Roy Keane, are similarly subjected to the critical gaze of others. Equally, the contrasting fascination with the exuberant embracement of the England team and its supporters by Japanese fans during the 2002 World Cup finals was arguably reliant on the peculiarity of these forms of behaviour within the context of a hyper-commodified and culturally contingent media spectacle.

Yet the current concerns with supporter behaviour and the continuing desire to broaden the base of football support beyond its 'traditional' constituencies also points to the limitations of any gentrification of football and universal exclusion of working-class fans. Indeed Robson (2000: x) has argued that football remains 'the practical medium par excellence of the continuing expression and celebration of the core practices and concerns of embodied masculinity in a specifically working class variant'. Even at Manchester United, the most heavily commercialised of the English clubs with the largest element of corporate hospitality facilities, there is little evidence of a new liberal bourgeois hegemony. It is a paradox that whilst Manchester United are derided by supporters of rival clubs for the inauthenticity, anti-charisma and globalism of their fans, there is an enduring commitment to the maintenance of a fiercely 'local' terrace culture at the club.

The following, which appeared on a Manchester United e-mail message board, criticises the placing of an 'out of town' banner over the top of banners expressing Mancunian pride and remembrance ('Republic of Mancunia', 'Flowers of Manchester'):

> Thursday, 06 Dec 2001 Chelmsford reds. ... that poxy excuse for a flag was again draped over the T2 banners last night. ... Educate or eradicate ? something needs doin pronto.
>
> (imusa@yahoogroups.co.uk)

Particularly when playing away from home, as we described earlier, Manchester United fans also provided some of the most vocal and passionate spectacles of fan behaviour during the 2001–2 season which other accounts have suggested died with the cash turnstile. In turn this has prompted increasingly harsh reactions from the police and ground security personnel, as well as intervention from Trafford Borough Council, who have threatened to close sections of Old Trafford in response to the issue of persistent standing in seated areas. Equally, this less passive section of support has provided a basis for resisting the perceived changes in supporter culture and reversing the direction of the exclusionary gaze towards those who do not conform to these styles of spectatorship. As *Soccernet*'s 'The Insider' put it after the club's visit to Middlesborough's Riverside Stadium:

> The final word should go to United's magnificent support. There wasn't many of them – Middlesborough cut the visitors' allocation because they had the audacity to stand up in the corresponding fixture last season – yet they made far more noise than the home contingent. Unlike the hordes of day-trippers and crisp munchers who visit Old Trafford and criticise when things aren't going to plan, it is only the real United supporters who travel away. In fact, perhaps if this so-called bad spell they are having is the cue for two or three lean years the fair-weather supporters – and there are a fair few – will go forth and multiply and support whoever else is doing well.
>
> (quoted on http://www.redissue.co.uk [17 December 2001])

Increasingly then, the football ground can be viewed as a site of cultural contestation where processes of distinction-making considered in Bourdieu's terms (1984) emerge as the effect of certain kinds of knowledge (Wickham 1992) about what is required to be considered a 'real' fan. Whilst acknowledging Russell's point that 'generalisations about the football fan have blighted debate about the game since the late nineteenth century' (1997: 58), we might connect these processes of identity or person formation with competing governmental projects. Following Foucault (1979) it is possible to see how fan populations are subjected to and implement strategies which seek to maintain existing or establish new codes of behaviour which are increasingly determined through diverse modes of consumption.

Sky's the limit? Social change, television and the new consumption of football

It might be useful here to consider these developments within the context of broader social shifts associated with the erosion of modernity. This erosion encompasses the decline of the manual working class, increased social and geographic mobility, the decline of mass political action, the emergence of more varied leisure pursuits and increasing primacy of consumer choice (Hall and Jacques 1990; Lash and Urry 1994).

For instance, in Manchester, the transformation of Manchester United from a major local and national under-achieving institution to a global sports brand has taken place within much broader shifts in the social and economic fabric of the city. The epochal shift from cotton and machine manufacturing to a post-industrial service industry, emphasising leisure-retail and entertainment, has been described elsewhere (Taylor *et al.* 1998). However, perhaps more than most 'second' cities, Manchester has relied on its indigenous popular cultural production and consumption to reinvigorate, re-image and regenerate the city, with a particular emphasis on fashion, sport and music (O'Connor and Wynne 1996; Brown *et al.* 2000).

City pride in this renaissance, which began at the end of the 1980s with the 'Madchester' popular music boom (Redhead 1990; 1993; Champion 1991), is depicted in the film *24 Hour Party People*. It is something shared by supporters of both of Manchester's clubs, despite the cultural contest over 'ownership' of, and belonging to, the city itself. However, there are also some neat parallels between these developments and the changes associated with football culture in the city, which have not been lost on these fans. There has even been some criticism that the development of a thriving night-time economy in the city centre has itself been 'too corporate'. Several notable locally owned bars and clubs were forced to close in the mid-1990s as new spaces were filled by better-resourced national and multi-national leisure companies, replacing for some an 'authentic', local and unique experience with corporate, bland, tourist-driven developments (*United We Stand, passim,* Cochrane, Peck and Tichell, 2002).

As a product of the modernist Victorian sports project, football has only latterly, if spectacularly, adapted to the individualised, consumerist terrain of contemporary social formations which these developments reflect, in which class and locality have become less significant determinants of identity and consumption choices. Just as the centrality of 'the local' pub and 'corner' shop within the social fabric of working-class neighbourhoods has given way to the city-centre bar and supermarket, so then have 'football clubs' now sought to transform themselves. In many cases this has involved football clubs being physically lifted out of those neighbourhoods and moved to new sites away from residential areas. Or it has meant the rebuilding of stadia according to new design aesthetics which reflect the more instrumental blueprint for the out-of-town shopping mall rather than the piecemeal expansion of the Victorian industrial landscape. In accordance with other elements of the leisure industry, these grounds are then themselves increasingly run as mediated 'pleasure palaces' where entertainment is 'produced' for a variety of 'consumers'.

The efforts of football clubs to satisfy an increasingly fragmented supporter base has also mirrored corporate efforts within the leisure industry to appeal to the nostalgic sense of lost community. This, even in the 'new' world of the corporate 'pleasuredome', has resulted in a search for the 'real' and 'authentic' in the form of 'old world' styled pubs and 'authentic' world foods, as found in Manchester's Arndale Centre Food Court. In the football ground we have seen efforts to introduce officially sanctioned 'singing ends' whilst those businesses which target Giulianotti's 'hot/traditional' supporter (2002) (including fanzines and clothing companies) trade on notions of a more authentic past. These include Arkwright Sportswear and The Old Fashioned Football Shirt Company (TOFFS) who promised an alternative to the artificial/'inauthentic' 1990s. Despite in fact selling 'new' copies of cotton football shirts, Arkwright advertised their wares in unashamedly nostalgic manner: 'authentic 1970s football shirts made from 100% highest quality heavyweight cotton … wicked 50s shorts as worn by Matthews … 60s tracksuit tops'. Nevertheless the success of these companies suggests there is a resonance in this nostalgia amongst football supporters themselves despite the 'inauthenticity of the search for authenticity' (Hochschild 1983).

Whilst these examples of 'corporate inclusion' are firmly located within a new consumerist framework which 'sells' football, the cultural contestation over the game has increasingly focused on the 'forms' of consumption. As Bourdieu argued, 'a class is defined as much by its *being-perceived* as by its *being*, by its consumption – which need not be conspicuous in order to be symbolic – as much as by its position in the relations of production' (1984: 483).

Perhaps the most significant development in the game in this regard has been the rapid expansion of television coverage since the creation of the FA Premiership in 1992, which like the live event, has widened some social cleavages whilst narrowing others. Although ostensibly representing a form of 'privatisation', for many, an unintentional consequence has been the creation of new communal forms of consumption. Furthermore, this has in many cases been prompted precisely by the economic considerations previously understood to have undermined this 'traditional' mode of consuming the game, due to the comparative cheapness of watching on a large screen at a pub rather than paying the cost of satellite and cable subscriptions.

For some, the pub creates its own version of 'authentic experience' – whether it is the fan who reported that 'you get a better match atmosphere down our local in Salford … you even see kids being passed over heads to the front', or a business recognising the market potential of such gatherings ('well over 75,000 hardcore Manchester United fans watch games from Manchester pubs … some believe that the atmosphere … is now better than being at the ground itself. BSkyB has already started exploiting the trend' [Rubython 1998: 70]). However, for 'new fans' it has allowed an introduction and entry to games which might otherwise have been denied or ignored. Through this exposure new fans are also introduced to particular versions of the cultural capitals associated with football fandom.

Nevertheless, whilst such developments may provide a context for the cultural forms increasingly excluded from football stadia themselves, the game's increasing appeal and attendant commodification has also led to further forms of pacification and distinction making through the emergence of the 'corporate football pub'. During the 2002 World Cup finals, the Oxnoble 'gastro-pub' in Castlefield, Manchester's regenerated and leisure-oriented canal basin, was taking pre-match table bookings for family groups, which guaranteed a seat and table to sit at for England's games as long as a meal was ordered as part of the package. Casual supporters who had no table bookings were turned away.

Football fans and the search for authenticity: resistance, cultural contestation and distinction making

We have seen that some supporters' organisations have taken up political positions against the football authorities, government and individual clubs on the grounds that they feel that these kinds of changes are creating social exclusion. In this they see that the increasingly corporate football business is producing effects (ticket prices, match schedules) which threaten their enjoyment or even participation (all-seat stadia, aggressive stewarding of behaviour). Further it is making in-roads in a way which increasingly means some spectators feel that they cannot attain the 'spontaneity, physicality and raw passion' which produces their pleasure.

However, whilst there has undoubtedly been an erosion of the kind of liminal experiences described at the start of this chapter, the continuing presence of such events demonstrates that the process is far from 'complete' or clear cut. As Fiske points out:

> Popular culture is made by the people, not by the culture industry. All the cultural industries can do is to produce a repertoire of texts or cultural resources for the various formations of the people to use or reject in the ongoing process of producing their popular culture.
>
> (Fiske 1989: 23–4)

Thus, whilst it is necessary to explore the shifts in football fan culture in light of the structural changes the game has experienced, we must also recognise that football supporters, like consumers generally, will use, modify and customise in order to satisfy their diverse subcultural needs. These needs can never be adequately met by the football industry.

Despite the growth of alternative consumption sites for football, for many fans, the live match continues to represent an ideal or 'authentic' type of football experience. However, as this is further restrained and regulated, fans seek ways of enhancing their cultural experience, through a variety of different strategies. The experience of Manchester United fans at Derby County described earlier is interesting. Fans found it necessary to create their own celebration, using the materials supplied by 'new football' (shutters, bars, concourse space designed for passive consumption of branded and expensive catering) away from the main spectacle in order to achieve the kind of experience they sought. In doing this they 'made over' (to use Fiske's phrase) the cultural artefacts they were presented with, creating 'their' popular culture.

In this sense one can see an openly rebellious attitude in which fans simply try to ignore the new conditions which seek to control their behaviour. However, in other instances we see fans grouping together to try and protect or recreate conditions which they see as preferable for their cultural expression and pleasure. The Independent Manchester United Supporters Association (IMUSA) was originally formed specifically around the issue of atmosphere at Old Trafford, and in particular the efforts made by the club to stop fans standing in seated areas, a dispute which has continued for more than six years.

In such instances we can see fans actually organising in a formally political and campaigning way, purely to combat what they see as restrictions on their pursuit of pleasure. At other times, fans will find new locations for the pursuit of their subcultural needs, away from the increasingly proscriptive and officially sanctioned arenas of the football industry. These include travel to European away games which, although at times curtailed by draconian policing (Brown 1994; 1997), often allows a freedom which is rarely available at 'home' matches. Even travel to domestic away matches is regarded as preferable:

> there's a much better buzz at away matches without the day trippers at OT and you can have a sing, a drink, a laff and stand up at most of them. You know, it's a better class of supporter.
>
> (Manchester United fan, interview with AB, 2001)

Here we see not only distinction being made between the atmosphere and enjoyment of 'away' matches over 'home' ones, but also between those who watch matches in these contexts, recognising the different (and arguably more homogeneous) constituency of those fans who travel. For others, this 'escape' from the restrictiveness of football's new conditions is to be found at other events such as cricket, international football and even other forms of popular culture. There was, for instance, the well documented intervention of former football hooligans into the acid house music scene of the late 1980s (Redhead 1991).

'Resistance' within the fans' pleasure seeking is, as Fiske (1989), Hall and Jefferson (1976) and King (1998) all identify, neither simplistic nor total. King talks of the compromise made by 'the lads' and the 'imaginary incision between club and team' made by many Manchester United supporters who declare that they 'love the team, hate the club'. These fans' support then, is both resistant and compliant at the same time. Also, it is notable here that the motivation relates to safeguarding or recreating the fans' *own*, ultimately individual, pleasure seeking rather than wider class or anti-authoritarian issues.

As we observed, Giulianotti's taxonomy of football fans refers to these spectators – loyal, travelling, with a 'long term personal investment in the club' – as traditional/hot supporters. However, within his categorisation he says these fans will invest in the club in market-oriented ways and that 'showing support for the club (including market ones) is considered to be obligatory' (Giulianotti 2002: 33). We would suggest that, based on evidence relating to significant proportions of both club and England national team supporters, this requires some modification. In particular some of Manchester United's hardcore supporters feel that their role of supporting the team as well as being able to enjoy themselves in their own way is undermined by the actions of the club hierarchy and that the club is only interested in profit and the market. As such, many of these fans will refuse to purchase any merchandise. Similarly, large sections of England supporters (particularly those who are willing to follow the side overseas into hostile environments) are distinctive precisely through their rejection of national colours and of the FA's own range of 'leisure wear', their preference being for designer 'casual' clothes. Here, there is a fundamental schism between club and football authorities and this constituency of fans in which the fans see themselves not only as the 'soul' of the club/country, but also as an opposition.

In line with Robson's work on 'Millwallism' and the assimilation of 'Junior Lions' (2000: 154–5), central to their attitude is a concern for the future and an anxiety to preserve the routes, pathways or subcultural 'ladder' on which they themselves have travelled. In numerous interviews (as well as in fanzines, on email lists, websites and radio phone-ins) fans talk of the need to maintain access for the young, so that there is a future generation of supporters, who share the same values and cultural forms. One of the interesting aspects to this is that the concern about future generations is not confined to football fans. It is also a concern for both commercial interests in football – in terms of future markets[3] – as well as for government and social regeneration agencies, who place the young at the focal point of debates and interventions around social exclusion (Collins with Kay 2003; Crabbe 2000).

For male fans in their thirties and forties the football ground often represented the principal readily accessible site for the public display of highly charged emotive feeling which could be contrasted with 'everyday' life. The 'sanitisation' of the match day experience has then been heartfelt for these fans and rare exceptions are seized upon:

NEWS ITEM 1: LET THE GOOD TIMES ROLL AGAIN

> Last night, for the first time in almost nine years, we went to a football game at Old Trafford, rather than a theme park. Happy Days …
>
>   (http://www.redissue.co.uk)

The author subsequently commented: 'It was the day after Derby at home. For once OT beforehand seemed like a football ground. There were none of the usual tourists and shite cos we were doing so badly what with the doom merchants etc.' (Manchester United fan interview with AB, December 2001).

However, for younger football supporters (more often cited as the victims of exclusionary practices) there may be less of an all-embracing concern with maintaining these traditions in the football ground. They are, after all, surrounded by a plethora of cultural resources with the potential for producing uplifting and emotive experiences in the broader leisure market. Football can be consumed on the TV at times of heightened interest such as the World Cup finals, whilst 'good times' with a 'tribe' of mates can be secured through the consumption of drugs at a night-club, 'hanging out' or through gang rivalries, reflecting Ted Polhemus's notion of the contemporary pic 'n' mix 'supermarket of street style' (Polhemus 1994: 128).

The 'exclusion' of younger 'working class' fans from the live match day experience might then be read along individualised economic-cultural lines whereby football no longer offers 'value for money' for the post-modern sensation seeker. For in the contemporary match day context, inclusion no longer brings with it the certainty of class-inflected notions of a 'good time', regardless of events on the field. In this context there might be no guarantees that a regular presence at games amongst younger fans would bring with it lifelong attachments in anything like the ways previously understood as 'authentic'.[4]

Football is clearly now part of a much more diverse leisure market. It is not the 'only game in town' and, moreover, the entertainment it provides is itself much more diverse, expanding into museums and visitor attractions, soccer schools, travel, and even financial services. Commercial interests in football have encouraged this process, generating new income streams as well as creating different types of club experience. Indeed, despite the contemporary proliferation of leisure opportunities, football has retained some sense of hegemonic authority through its ubiquitous appearance in everyday culture, which ranges from advertising through to the public declaration of footballing affiliations by politicians. The irony here is that the one thing which made (and still makes) the football experience unique, and as such a central part of many spectators lives, may be lost as the liminality of experience and escape from 'reality' becomes less clear and certain.

What is interesting for us about the attitude of the authorities and TV companies in this context is that, despite their protestations that post-1990 football is a 'whole new ball game', they have had to evoke their own notions of authentic football tradition in order to convey images of what football 'means' and what a 'true fan' is. In this regard, we are following Bourdieu's recognition that

> principles of division, inextricably logical and sociological, function within and for the purposes of the struggle between social groups. ... What is at stake in the struggles about the meaning of the social world is power over the classificatory schemes and systems which are the basis of the representations of the groups and therefore of their mobilization and demobilisation.
>
> (1984: 479)

Whilst we have tried to expose some of the complexities and contradictions within discourses of exclusion and authenticity we also recognise that the exclusion of some fans, or of some forms of behaviour, will have certain effects which will ultimately undermine elements of football's market value at a time when there are numerous alternatives for thrill/risk seekers to pursue.

Notes

1　This chapter presents a synthesis of the findings of ethnographic research carried out independently by Dr Tim Crabbe (supported by Sheffield Hallam University) and Dr Adam Brown (for the Sport, the City and Governance project, funded by the Economic and Social Research Council). The opening scene was recorded by Tim Crabbe.

2　Peter Kenyon, interview with A. Brown (28 August 2001); Peter Draper, interview with A. Brown (23 November 2001).

3　Sir Roland Smith, then chair of Manchester United Plc, told the Manchester meeting of the UK Government's Football Task Force in February 1998 that they were concerned about the ageing fan base of the club. Since then, the club has made some limited attempts to attract young fans to Old Trafford.

4　We would offer the proviso here that a handful of 'youth gangs' have recently formed up around some clubs (Manchester United has both the 'junior boys' violence-oriented group as well as the more formally constituted Old Trafford Youth Commandos, whilst Cardiff City's Soul Crew is renowned for its large youth element).

3

'Giving something back': can football clubs and their communities co-exist?

NEIL TAYLOR

> Football clubs in England have deep roots in their communities. The club–community relationship has traditionally been based on mutual support. Football clubs draw strength from the good will of the local people, who have nurtured and supported them over the generations. Football clubs repay this by providing a community focus and [a] source of civic pride.
>
> (Football Task Force 1999: paragraph 2.1)

The assumption is often made that football clubs are intertwined with their local communities, and that clubs and communities have mutual and equal benefits for each other. This assumption is then often magnified, confused and perpetuated, not only by football clubs themselves, but by bodies such as local and central government agencies, and commercial organisations, all of which have wider political, corporate and social agendas to pursue.

The initial purpose of this chapter is to explore this notion of football clubs and their relationships with their communities. It then examines the reasons why football clubs are caught in a 'no win' situation by a combination of social change, outside pressures and the clubs' own structures of ownership, and why this has become an important issue. It also looks at how football clubs operate and whether they make good 'community partners'. The final part of the chapter discusses the role of external agencies in this process and offers case studies of innovative approaches being implemented.

However, before addressing the complicated and somewhat confusing relationships that football clubs sometimes have with their communities, it is worth detailing the internal factors that have made football clubs what they are now. As Theo Paphitis, the Chairman of Millwall Football Club, said: 'Without the community you haven't got a football club. It's about remembering your roots' (quoted in *When Saturday Comes* 2001: 25). Historically, it has been assumed that football clubs come from, reflect and represent their local communities. Examples are often given of how in areas of high industrialisation and high urban density football on Saturdays meant the release of working men from their everyday toil. The mood of individuals and of whole areas could be affected by a cup win or a relegation; whole towns would turn out for a parade by a local team with a newly acquired trophy. It is hard, however, to judge how accurate this picture is. In any case, it tends to be used to disguise much wider issues that underpin the roots of professional football, and explain why there is still friction between football clubs and communities. These are issues related to the ownership of football clubs.

There are very few examples of football clubs that were established on a mutual basis. Indeed, many came out of works teams ultimately run by factory owners. Certainly, by the time that football clubs had organised themselves and were sending teams to play in professional leagues, any sign of community democracy had been supplanted by the activities of paternalistic local benefactors, who saw opportunities to gain local and, to some extent, national prestige and recognition for themselves. The early owners and benefactors of football clubs knew what they were doing when they established the football clubs in law as private concerns with boards of directors. This legally protected structure, combined with the sometimes autocratic means used to acquire land on which to develop a stadium, calls into question the idea that clubs and communities are on an equal footing. One of the best examples of a club imposing itself upon a community is that of Arsenal. In 1913 the club moved from Plumstead in south London to Highbury in north London: as Simon Inglis has pointed out, at that time it 'faced no costly planning enquiries, but stitched up a deal for the land, then owned by the Church of England, for £20,000, promising not to play on Sundays, Good Friday or Christmas Day' (Inglis 1986, cited in the *Independent*).

However, although the ownership of football clubs has contributed to inconsistent relationships with communities, several external factors that have affected football clubs' ability to develop over the past 70 years have been of even greater significance. The three major external factors, which clearly intertwine, have been the shifting economic and social circumstances of inner-city communities; the 'Sky-ification' of football; and the greater political pressure from external agencies, especially central government.

Shifting economic and social circumstances

The combination of a dwindling manufacturing base, movements of people out of inner-city areas, and changes in cultural and social activities has left many football clubs exposed. The predominant white working-class culture used to be clearly and simply defined: now communities are far more diverse and 'community representation' has become more complicated. New communities, predominantly from South Asian, African and Caribbean backgrounds, have moved into inner cities, while much of the white population has moved out to suburbs, or even further afield. The effects are often quite striking. For example, seven of the 92 professional football clubs in England are now based in areas where more than 20 per cent of the local population belong to ethnic minorities. West Ham United leads the way, with 42 per cent, followed by Leicester City, with 28.5 per cent, and Leyton Orient, with 25.6 per cent (Bradbury 2001). Football clubs based in such areas now find it very difficult to make sense of their neighbours and, thus, to relate to these new communities. More broadly, ethnic minorities pose several challenges to football clubs, including finding ways of gaining their interest and support.

Research undertaken by the Sir Norman Chester Centre for Football Research at Leicester University found that football clubs were no better at recruiting staff, players or managers from ethnic minorities than they were at working with their immediate communities. The research found that:

> Nearly two thirds (65 per cent) of respondent clubs claim that they already appeal to all members of the community and one third (33 per cent) of clubs feel [that] they are already 'successful' in attracting black and Asian fans to matches. However, according to supporter surveys, the actual level of 'active' minority ethnic support for most football clubs in England is probably between 0 and 2 per cent of the total crowd. Most clubs which are sited in areas with substantial minority ethnic populations have very low proportions of these populations represented in their 'active' support.

More damning was the fact that:

> Sixty per cent of clubs in areas with large local minority ethnic populations admit [that] they have not been successful at attracting minority communities to matches. Claims for 'successful' recruitment of minority ethnic fans on the part of some clubs seem to us to reflect more a relative lack of ambition among clubs on this score rather than real successes in this respect.
>
> (Bradbury 2001)

On the other hand, some areas have experienced patterns of gentrification, in which well-organised and vocal residents' groups, critical of their local clubs, have emerged, most notably in parts of London around the home grounds of Arsenal, Chelsea, Queens Park Rangers and Fulham.

Contrary to the view expressed by the Football Task Force, that communities and football clubs are mutually supportive, it is often the case that the interests of a community are not the interests of a club. The classic friction develops when a club seeks planning permission to redevelop its ground and community groups feel that they are fighting a losing battle against a powerful neighbour. The recent campaigns against both Arsenal's and Fulham's plans for redevelopment testify to the work of organisations such as the Federation of Stadium Communities (FSC), which acts as a mediator and looks to find ways in which clubs can 'give something back' to communities.

At the same time as all these factors are coming into play, football clubs are facing another threat – the ageing of their once homogeneous fan bases – and have become more and more dependent upon third and fourth generations of fans. However, these younger fans have less and less connection with, and little interest in, the local communities with which the clubs were originally connected. This in turn has led to the development of a notion of 'fan communities', as opposed to local communities. In essence, this term refers to groups of fans who associate with a football club and, on the whole, feel some allegiance to the team, the club and, although more loosely and questionably, the area in which the club is based. The role of 'fan communities' has been intensified by the part that BSkyB's television coverage of the Premier League has played since 1992 in reshaping English football culture.

The 'Sky-ification' of football

The other major change that has affected football clubs in the past 50 years has been in the game itself. Although the majority of professional football clubs are still privately owned and still attract local benefactors, a new breed of football club owner has emerged. Football has become another leisure commodity, especially since BSkyB began to influence and reshape English football. As a result of the 'Sky-ification' of football, clubs lead a paradoxical existence, balancing their 'proud history' with the fact that the 1992/93 season, when the Premiership began, has come to be seen as a 'year zero' for the contemporary game. Fans are no longer expected either to live close to a club or to attend matches in order to feel 'part of the club'. In turn, the clubs' dependence on television revenues, and the higher stakes involved in winning and losing, have led the 'fan communities' to add their own pressures on their clubs to succeed. This in turn has led to higher turnovers of team managers and also of owners.

In addition, more and more clubs have become limited companies and had their shares floated on the stock market, and media companies have been buying up to 10 per cent of the shares in leading clubs. This has further added to the confusion about what football clubs are for and whose interests they serve. For many clubs whose reach is not confined to specific areas the question has become: who constitutes our community, the rest of the country or the rest of the world? Owners and players in particular have very little connection with the communities in which their clubs happen to have their home grounds. This has all made a major impact on how clubs, whatever their size, interpret, interact with, and attempt to represent 'their' communities.

External influences

As I have suggested above, football clubs have come under increasing external pressure to develop relations with their communities. This pressure has come from a range of agencies, including central government, local authorities, private companies such as BSkyB, and organisations in what is now known as the voluntary and community sector. Although these are all important sources of influence, since 1997, when 'New' Labour took office, the main one has been central government. Several initiatives, reports and recommendations have flowed from various government departments. These have included reports from bodies such as the Football Task Force and initiatives such as the Playing for Success project, launched by the Department for Education and Skills (DfES, formerly the Department for Education and Employment), and directly focusing on football clubs.

In 1998 the Football Task Force investigated the role of football clubs in their communities. In its report, published in 1999, it concluded that:

- 'Football in the Community' schemes should be supported financially by the clubs, especially those in the Premier League;
- opportunities should be developed for players to act as role models;
- a major investment should be made at the grass-roots level, in football specifically and in community projects more generally; and
- supporters should be encouraged to get more involved in the running of their clubs.

Many of the Task Force's detailed recommendations, based on these broad conclusions, have since been accepted and implemented.

The government has also taken an interest in the ownership of football clubs, especially in the aftermath of the attempt by News Corporation, the parent company of BSkyB, to buy out Manchester United in 1998. The government now supports and funds Supporters Direct, an organisation that seeks to develop and increase the number of 'fans' trusts', and to enhance the representation of fans on the boards of directors of football clubs.

The creation of the Football Foundation during 1999 has also proved to be a clever move on the part of the government. The government managed to extract 5 per cent from the proceeds of the Premier League's television deals and match it with funding through the Department for Culture, Media and Sport (DCMS), along with money from Sport England and the Football Association (FA). The football clubs cannot now use lack of funding as a pretext for not undertaking 'community-based' activities.

However, most of the emphasis from central government has been on how football clubs can play a part in tackling 'social exclusion'. Sport in the broadest sense is viewed as a 'good thing' and hence as having potential to 'make a difference'. The government's view and its subsequent funding initiatives stem from a report published in 1999 by the DCMS, which explored how sport could make a positive contribution towards 'social inclusion'. It urged Sport England and sports governing bodies, including the FA, to develop initiatives and projects around this issue. Plans, documents and strategies have been emerging from Sport England and, latterly, the FA ever since. In some of these documents football and especially those football clubs that have proactive community programmes have been cited as the way forward in tackling the issue of social exclusion.

The volume of resources that sport is now receiving to tackle this issue is unprecedented. At every level, from schools through to diverse communities, including refugees, those at risk of offending, those suffering from bad health or those who wish to improve their skills, sport and activities related to sport are being championed. Because of their locations some football clubs are in ideal positions to get involved and to use these resources in positive ways. For those administering football clubs initiatives such as the New Deal for Communities, the Neighbourhood Renewal Fund, the New Opportunities Fund, Education Action Zones, Health Action Zones and Positive Futures, as well as the sport-specific funding opportunities from Sport England (all now finished) all offer comprehensive opportunities for engagement. In addition, local authorities, through departments such as sports, education, housing, regeneration, youth services and drug action teams, have also become involved in implementing this influential new agenda, alongside other leading 'community' organisations such as housing associations. They take the view that sport has a major role to play in helping them to achieve greater 'social inclusion'. The potential is therefore massive for football clubs to get involved and to begin to tackle, or at least usefully appear to be tackling, social problems beyond their own immediate sphere.

With initiatives and funding coming from different parts of central government, local authorities, autonomous agencies of the state, and 'community'-based agencies and trusts, all claiming to be focused on tackling some of the social and economic problems prevalent in urban and rural areas alike, it is clearly imperative that the right 'delivery agents' be found. The consensus among fund-givers is that these should be people or groups who already have credible records in acquiring funds and running projects; employ high-quality, dedicated staff; achieve transparency in the management and funding of projects; make a real commitment to working in difficult areas or with difficult client groups; win the trust of local communities; and, above all, develop long-lasting links with a variety of partners and community groups.

The challenges for football clubs

What are football clubs at the beginning of the twenty-first century supposed to make of these developments? In broad terms, each professional football club is caught between two definitions of what 'its' community is: where the club is physically located or where the majority of the fan base lives. Understanding these definitions enables the football clubs to position themselves accordingly. However, as will be explored below, getting the balance right is difficult.

Many football clubs based in inner-city areas face challenges over their own identities and their relations with the communities that they purportedly serve. Depending upon their league position and traditions, they often attempt to appeal to both definitions of the community. Clubs have also devised a variety of ways of interacting with communities. Before these are explored in greater detail, however, it is worth considering why football clubs feel obliged to show any interest in their communities at all.

There are several factors that come into play here, most of which are interlinked. As football clubs are in effect private companies, their first concern tends to be with profits, and an important way of increasing profits is by having a strong public image. In a period of public debate about 'corporate governance' and 'social responsibility' the more forward-thinking and/or publicity-conscious clubs see some merit in acting as good 'local citizens', whether by establishing good relations with their neighbours on issues such as redevelopment of their grounds, or as a means of attracting new sponsors. 'Community' has become a very useful term for clubs to exploit whenever they want to demonstrate their credentials as good corporate citizens. In effect, they are 'playing the game' prescribed by outside agencies, including central government. The definition of 'community' is left very vague and very superficial, but in one sense that does not matter so long as there is local and national media interest in, for example, well-known players 'doing their bit' with disabled young people, or helping children with their school work.

As football clubs have invested more in public relations and marketing it has become clear that there is some mileage in their promoting themselves as 'community-friendly' and 'family-friendly'. Of course, some football clubs do this chiefly in order to survive, as their traditional fan bases decline and the need to attract new fans becomes paramount. Other, larger clubs that do not need their local communities to survive still like to project an image of 'doing their bit', either by supporting local charities or by opening up their facilities for (limited) community use.

In this context, the two biggest levers that local authorities can operate in relation to clubs are the lease agreements for the clubs' grounds, in those cases where clubs do not own grounds outright, and, for all clubs, the requirement to seek planning permission for new developments. Many clubs now have a 'community commitment' written into their lease agreements, as well as an obligation to provide 'community access'. Through the planning process local authorities can use what is known as 'section 106' to compensate local communities with improved facilities whenever private companies develop areas. Football clubs therefore have to contribute funding as compensation. In turn the clubs highlight their 'community work' in their attempts to improve their chances of gaining leases and/or planning consent.

As well as seeking to improve their relations with local authorities, central government and corporate sponsors, football clubs have other motives for tapping into the 'community'. The most obvious are to discover new players and to attract new fans. Every professional football club in England now has either an 'academy' or a 'centre of excellence' to pool young talent and develop it further. The FA and Sport England have driven both of these initiatives, stipulating that the boys (and, in 32 cases, girls) must not travel distances that take more than 90 minutes to traverse. This implies that the players recruited for these centres should come from each club's local community. As for the issue of the fan base, very few clubs can claim to have a national reach, let alone an international one, and most therefore need to target fans more locally or regionally. Some clubs have devised imaginative marketing initiatives to attract more local support. As the Sir Norman Chester Centre found:

[Community] schemes at these football clubs are providing enormous net commercial gains in terms of recruiting new fans to their football clubs. In fact, nationally, attracting close to 7 per cent of the home fans each week is probably worth around £20,000 per club per weekend on average, or £400,000 to £500,000 per club per season, or close to £10 million in gate receipts alone in the FA Premier League every year.

(Evidence to Football Task Force 1999)

A report on the radio programme *On the Line* (BBC Radio 5 Live) also demonstrated the potential financial gains for football clubs. Wolverhampton Wanderers FC was highlighted as one club that worked well with its community. However, in a subsequent interview with the club's chairman it transpired that the underlying motivation for working with young people was the club's desire to exploit their potential to become loyal fans and the income that could be generated over 50–60 years.

It has to be pointed out, however, that very few 'community' initiatives have come from football clubs. Central government, local authorities and, in particular, the Professional Footballers Association (PFA), through the Footballers Further Education and Vocational Society (FFE&VTS), have been the main actors in promoting change. In addition, organisations such as the Football Foundation (formerly the Football Trust), Sport England and individual government departments have now begun to influence the ways in which football clubs interact with communities.

'Football in the community' initiatives

All professional football clubs in England and Wales, along with a few non-league clubs, have set up 'Football in the Community' schemes, most of which are supported by the FFE&VTS. Originally set up in 1986 in partnership with the former Manpower Services Commission's Community Finance Scheme, the programme was expanded in the early 1990s.

Perhaps one of the main reasons why football clubs community work has been so centred on football clubs is that the lead came from the FFE&VTS. The original aims, as set out in 1986, were:

- to provide employment and training for unemployed people;
- to promote close links between professional football clubs and the community;
- to involve minority and ethnic groups in social and recreational activities;
- to attempt to prevent acts of hooliganism and vandalism; and
- to maximise the use of the facilities of the football clubs.

These aims were pioneering at the time: they clearly represented an attempt to take football clubs in a new direction. However, in 1991 the aims were revised and somewhat watered down. The new aims were:

- to encourage more people, especially children, to play football;
- to encourage more people, especially children, to watch football;
- to encourage more people to become interested in and to support their local football club by forging closer links between them;
- to improve the image of the game;
- to improve the atmosphere at matches; and
- to improve the behaviour of players and spectators.

Following further revision in 1997, some of the original spirit of 1986 returned, with two additional aims:

- to maximise community facilities and their community usage at football clubs; and
- to provide temporary and/or gainful employment and training for unemployed people.

                                    (FFE&VTS, cited in *Football Insider* 1999)

In the main, each club employs a few 'community officers' who run football-based activities both inside schools and during school holidays. The schemes are predominantly aimed at young boys who, more often than not, are fans of the club. These schemes also run advanced soccer schools, which have links with the academies and centres of excellence mentioned above. Match day activities are also part of the portfolio, as are children's birthday parties. The focus is very much on the club and on promoting a positive image. Some football clubs also aim to increase attendance at matches by offering discounted or complimentary tickets to local school children, as well as to disabled people's groups. Within this narrow focus some football clubs have become good at providing match day facilities for families and those with disabilities, and at creating junior sections through which children can become members.

    In line with the revisions made in 1997 some football clubs have also opened up their facilities for 'community use', mainly to groups of old-age pensioners, as well as hiring out their bars, restaurants or meeting rooms for conferences and meetings of local businesses. Here again we see external influence and pressure being placed on football clubs to do more with 'their' communities. In the realm of education the most important initiatives have included the 'Playing for Success' (PFS) projects, established under the auspices of the DfES at 53 professional football clubs. Similar initiatives have been set up around the theme of anti-racism. These include Sport England's Asians into Football project, based at West Ham United; Kick it Out, a national campaigning agency; Football Unites Racism Divides (FURD), based at Sheffield United; and Charlton Athletic's Racial Equality (CARE) programme. There are also schemes intended to deter people from drug abuse and crime, through the Probation Service and the National Association for the Care and Rehabilitation of Offenders (NACRO), at Leyton Orient and Colchester United. In addition, other agencies, such as 'community regeneration' and youth organisations, have also developed projects at football clubs.

Have these schemes proved effective and are football clubs working more closely with their communities? The superficial answer would be Yes, especially as external agencies have brought with them funding that has created full-time posts for people employed to 'deliver' the projects. However, there are some inherent challenges that face organisations willing to work with football clubs. As has been highlighted above, this issue is complicated by a series of internal factors, such as the ownership of each club, as well as the external expectations and pressures brought to bear on the clubs. Taking time to develop a business plan, and a long-term strategy to recruit and develop a new fan base, is not usually high on a club's agenda, although both are widely recognised as important. Very few clubs are in a position to take the long-term view. Most cannot or will not undertake such exercises, because 'communities' are very complex and confusing entities to get involved with. Football clubs therefore do not tend to invest time or recruit high-quality staff if such investments are seen as confusing or offer little obvious reward. The process of 'community engagement' is time-consuming and expensive, and, more often than not, it brings a club no tangible result or benefit. What is the point of working with a tenants' group on a housing estate, involving hundreds of church hall meetings, or working with people who are on probation or are homeless, if they then fail to buy replica shirts or to become season-ticket holders?

Even when football clubs do invest in 'community officers', these officers, if they work effectively, soon find themselves living contradictory lives as they try to meet the perceived needs of both the community and the club. If a club's management believes that community work is just an extension of the marketing department, then the community at large may well begin to wonder why the club's community officer is involved, what his/her motive is and how long they will be around for.

It is, then, no surprise that many football clubs like to play safe with their definition of 'community', and to operate within parameters that they can understand and hope to control. This means that they concentrate on match days or, at most, football-related activities that predominantly serve their own interests. Football clubs are aware that they need to engage with organisations such as the FFE&VTS, community and voluntary organisations, Sport England, and government departments, but they do not have the means or time to do it properly. Yet there are real dangers for clubs that decide not to 'engage with the community' in any meaningful way. The most obvious danger is that local people may view the club as being irrelevant, since it does not improve the quality of their lives or offer them anything that is different from what any other private company offers. Cynicism and distrust have the potential to undermine football clubs. Many clubs are located in areas separated from where most of their fans now live. Over one or two generations those clubs that do not belong to the very small elite of national and international football may have to face either extinction or migration to the areas where their fans now live. It follows that clubs must recognise the real needs of their diverse communities, and try to find ways of communicating and working with them that are meaningful and can engender trust. The days when a football club could convincingly claim to be at the heart of 'its' community are over; the issue is far more complex and muddled nowadays. The challenge for clubs and their owners is to find ways to overcome distrust, rather than simply to assume that loyalty comes naturally.

A way forward

The football clubs' 'funding partners', perhaps especially central government, are very keen for the clubs and the wider football industry to play their part in addressing the 'community and social agenda'. They have taken proactive measures to ensure that the clubs that they have highlighted as being good 'community partners' really can put their stated intentions into practice. Although there may seem to be a huge gap between the government's aspirations and the practices of football clubs, some changes are taking place. These changes could be said to follow a 'third way', indirectly enabling football clubs to 'give something back' to their communities.

   In the attempt to avoid the perceived shortcomings of football clubs (as outlined above) and to address the needs of 'communities', as well as wider social policy agendas, the consensus among the fund-givers is that financially independent professional and managerial organisations are required to undertake this work. The crucial balancing act is to associate such organisations with clubs but not to make them dependent upon clubs for survival.

What has emerged since 1997 is a range of organisations and projects that are neither affiliates of clubs nor offshoots of the statutory sector, but are community and voluntary bodies, which can act as bridges between the clubs and the funders, as well as between the immediate community and the larger communities of which it forms a part. Across the country there are now growing numbers of projects based at football clubs but not run by them. These are making a real impact on their immediate local communities, and also fit with the government's wider social and political agenda. These projects tend to fall into one of the following three broad categories:

- 'football in the community' schemes that have become charities;
- partnerships based at football clubs; or
- central government initiatives based at football clubs.

'Football in the community' schemes that have become charities

As has been mentioned above, each professional football club has a 'football in the community' department, generally employing a few people who carry out football-based activities in the local community, mainly in schools. However, the conventional mould for these departments is beginning to be broken by some of their leading officials, who want to create projects that go beyond providing benefits for the clubs and can have real effects on local communities. A number of club-based community schemes have sought independence from their clubs by becoming registered as independent charities. The reasons for this move are varied, but they usually centre around the hope of sustaining a project by recognising its funding potential, and the need for total transparency when dealing with funders, 'partners' and the community. There is also usually the linked realisation that, despite all the platitudes expressed by football clubs about their commitments to local communities, the first casualty of a club's financial plight is generally its community work. It is also becoming clear that some clubs, as well as the FFE&VTS, view any such move to acquire charitable status as a panacea and assume that new sources of funding will automatically be found. In fact, running an independent charity successfully requires skilled and experienced development staff, and simply changing the legal status of a project does not guarantee that any other changes will follow.

According to data compiled by the Charity Commission, there are currently 21 'Football in the Community' schemes registered as independent charities, at Birmingham City, Bolton Wanderers, Bristol City, Bristol Rovers, Burnley, Colchester United, Everton, Hull City, Ipswich Town,

Kidderminster Harriers, Leyton Orient, Manchester City, Millwall, Northampton Town, Norwich City, Notts County, Port Vale, Southampton, Sunderland, Walsall and West Bromwich Albion. Leading the way throughout the period since 1997 has been the Leyton Orient Community Sports Programme (LOCSP), operating from offices at the grounds of Leyton Orient FC, which is currently in Division Three of the Nationwide Football League. (At this point the author should declare his interest: he is currently the LOCSP's Strategy Development Officer.) The LOCSP was initiated in May 1989 as a three-way partnership between the club, Sport England, and the Arts and Leisure Department of the local authority, the London Borough of Waltham Forest. For the club involvement in the LOCSP was a response to the problems of anti-social behaviour associated with football and to the dwindling attendances at its matches. For the local authority and Sport England it was an attempt to tackle the inequalities in levels of participation in sport among local people. It had long been recognised that members of specific social groups – such as children and young people, girls and women, people with disabilities, or ethnic minorities – were (and are) under-represented in mainstream sport.

In 1992, when money was first made available for all professional football clubs to develop community programmes through what was then the Football Trust, Leyton Orient expanded its activities into the London Borough of Hackney. By this time the LOCSP was operating an extensive community sports development programme targeted at those considered least likely to be involved in sport, many of whom were living in some of the most deprived areas, not just of the two neighbouring London boroughs, but in the entire United Kingdom: Hackney in particular is still known, on the basis of census results and other statistics, as the poorest local government district in England. The LOCSP was consistently recognised as being at the forefront of community football development, culminating in its receipt of an award as Football Trust Community Club of the Year in 1995.

At the same time the LOCSP also began to work in another northeast London borough, Tower Hamlets, on a project-by-project basis, first in Shadwell in Wapping, then at Aberfeldy and Teviot in Poplar, and then on the Isle of the Dogs. At that time the LOCSP was being managed by representatives of all the funding partners as an unincorporated association. This was proving problematic when it came to attracting new funding in order to develop certain projects. For example, many of the programmes that were being devised for inner-city housing estates needed large subsidies to overcome the two major barriers to participation: affordability and access. It was becoming apparent that if the LOCSP was to obtain funding from both commercial and charitable bodies it would have to change its legal status.

This was agreed by the funding partners then in charge and in September 1997 LOCSP became a not-for-profit company limited by guarantee, with eight independent trustees. In the following September it was granted charitable status, reflecting the Charity Commission's assessment of the work that it was doing.

The partnerships that then existed were dismantled and reconstructed to fit the new aims of LOCSP. The new arrangements built on much of what had been successful in the past, but with increased emphasis on targeting those who were socially excluded from mainstream provision. In practice, this meant devising appropriate programmes of activity for children and young people living on housing estates, or for adults recovering from drug misuse or serving probation orders. It also meant linking the LOCSP in to other projects delivered by those concerned with crime, health, education or employment. The appointment of an education officer in 1997 was a step in this direction. It also meant thinking more strategically about how to fund the LOCSP's work, what it was hoping to achieve, how success was best measured and how the various projects could be sustained.

Between 1998 and 2001 LOCSP's annual turnover doubled; so too did the number of people it employed. It is now working on a number of projects with a number of partners, some of which are time-bound while others are not. The most ambitious by far is the Sports Club Orient (SCORE) project. SCORE provides essential new recreational, sports and community facilities for the benefit of all residents in the local communities of northeast London. The idea is to create a new split-site community venue opposite Leyton Orient FC's ground. A community building will house a variety of different activities, including child care, youth provision, meeting spaces for local groups, a community health centre, and access to training and employment services. There are also proposals for major upgrading and improvement of existing facilities for football, tennis and bowls, and the provision of a dedicated indoor climbing area, a multi-use games area and new children's play areas.

SCORE's roots lie in work undertaken in the area by a number of organisations, which together have identified a real need for better-quality community facilities, in accessible locations, for use by local people, community groups and football teams. The four key partners in the SCORE project have been the LOCSP, the Waltham Forest Housing Action Trust (WFHAT), O-Regen, which is a community regeneration agency, and the London Borough of Waltham Forest. These partners are all formally committed to developing this project with the community and for the community. The two major priorities for the partners are ensuring that all facilities and programmes are both affordable and accessible for local people.

Partnerships based at football clubs

Alongside community schemes that have made the bold decision to become stand-alone charities, several other agencies have recognised the potential benefits in being based at football clubs while working in more imaginative ways than simply for the clubs themselves. These have been led by local authorities in the main, but also by established community associations. The best example of partnerships based at football clubs is Football Unites Racism Divides (FURD), which is based at Sheffield United FC.

FURD began informally in the early 1990s, when a group of fans and youth workers got together to find ways of tackling the issues of racism in Sheffield and beyond. The organisation was formed in 1995, with the following aims:

- to ensure that people who play or watch football can do so without fear of racial abuse and harassment, in either verbal or physical forms;
- to encourage all those associated with Sheffield United FC to improve standards of behaviour, especially in relation to racial abuse, harassment and discrimination; and
- to create greater access for local black people through active and safe participation as players, staff and supporters.

FURD's aims were updated and expanded in 1999 to include:

- increasing the participation of young people from ethnic minorities in football, as players, spectators and employees, and significantly increasing the participation and involvement of young women from ethnic minorities;
- challenging racism through anti-racist education and reducing racial harassment;
- developing the work of FURD's Resources and Information Centre;
- increasing the participation of volunteers in the work of FURD, especially young people aged between 16 and 24; and
- developing regional, national and international initiatives.

The key to FURD's success has been its ability to develop strong partnerships with, among other bodies, Sheffield United FC, the Hub African–Caribbean Centre, the Abbeydale Asian Youth Project, Sheffield Wednesday FC, Sheffield Race Equality Council, the Sheffield Youth Service, Somali Blades FC, and the Sheffield and Hallamshire County FA.

After bidding for and receiving funding from the European Commission FURD appointed its first full-time officer and the partnership was officially launched early in 1996. More funding and more partners were attracted to the project, including the South Yorkshire Police Service and various regeneration projects based in Sheffield, as well as the Home Office. In 1999 an educational dimension was added to the partnership, which then evolved as an educational trust. The trust has been able to develop steadily and bid successfully for National Lottery funding, as well as for more money from the European Commission to design and maintain a website for Football Against Racism in Europe (FARE).

FURD now delivers a range of social, sporting and educational projects and programmes, including coaching sessions for boys and girls; support for people from ethnic minorities aiming to become qualified as football coaches; and support for the formation of football teams from among ethnic minorities. FURD also encourages Sheffield United to become more community-focused and has developed a comprehensive football-based anti-racist education programme in schools, colleges and youth centres in and around Sheffield. Its links with similar fan-based projects across Europe have been particularly focused on the development of the FARE network.

Central government projects based at football clubs

The final category of third-party agencies now working at football clubs comprises government-funded projects, of which Playing for Success is probably the best-known. Following 'New' Labour's election victory in 1997, Playing for Success was developed on the basis of the belief that football clubs could contribute greatly to the education of disaffected young people. It has also enabled the government to encourage football clubs to take a more direct and substantive interest in their communities.

However, the DfES was very shrewd in its initial assessment that football clubs should not be given state funding to develop their own projects. Instead clubs have been tied into rigid three-way partnerships, through which the DfES and local education authorities (LEAs) provide funding, staff and resources, and the clubs provide space. The DfES and the LEAs have also insisted that high-quality teachers be seconded to manage these projects, which usually means that they are deputy heads or even heads of schools. These arrangements have shifted some of the power within the clubs and given the projects a very good chance of sustaining themselves. The staff delivering the schemes are perceived as being on an equal footing with the clubs' officials, or at least as not to be undermined, since both the LEAs and the DfES have an interest in supporting them.

Playing for Success is aimed at improving disaffected young people's literacy and numeracy, increasing their motivation, and helping them to become independent learners. The centres have strong links with schools, are equipped with first-class IT facilities, and operate after school, at weekends and in school holidays. According to the DfES's own promotional material, the centres offer a range of activities, including:

> literacy and numeracy sessions; opportunities to do homework with all the necessary facilities available – including CD-ROMs and internet access; training in improved study skills; and using football as a route to other knowledge, skills and understanding (e.g., statistics, geography, history, science, etc.).

The programme now involves 57 clubs: Arsenal, Aston Villa, Barnsley, Birmingham City, Blackburn Rovers, Bolton Wanderers, Boston United, Bournemouth, Bristol City, Burnley, Carlisle, Charlton Athletic, Coventry City, Crystal Palace, Derby County, Everton, Fulham, Grimsby Town, Hartlepool, Huddersfield Town, Hull City, Ipswich Town, Leeds United, Leicester City, Leyton Orient, Liverpool, Manchester City, Manchester United, Mansfield Town, Middlesbrough, Millwall, Newcastle United, Norwich City, Nottingham Forest, Oldham, Oxford, Port Vale, Portsmouth, Preston North End, Queens Park Rangers, Reading, Rochdale, Rushden & Diamonds, Scunthorpe United, Sheffield United, Sheffield Wednesday, Southampton, Stockport County, Stoke City, Sunderland, Swindon Town, Tottenham Hotspur, Walsall, Watford, West Bromwich Albion, West Ham United and Wolverhampton Wanderers.

To ensure that the centres are sustainable and can make a wider impact many are diversifying into other areas, including adult education, and opening up their facilities to other users, including local colleges, job centres, social services departments and community organisations. New and diverse groups, which would not have gone anywhere near football before, are thus coming into clubs from their immediate communities. At least in the eyes of the government's supporters, the size, scale and sheer cost of the programme reflect the government's commitment to improving disaffected young people's opportunities for educational development and to getting football clubs to engage in meaningful ways with groups that are difficult to reach. On the other hand, as critics have begun to point out, the projects still have a long way to go in their development and there are serious doubts over their sustainability, especially as government funding is slowly being withdrawn, and the projects are being compelled to seek alternative sources of finance and support. Nevertheless, whatever the future holds, it is already clear that Playing for Success has brought significant benefits, and not only to the young people whom it is primarily aimed at.

Conclusion

Are football clubs any closer to 'their' communities, or making any more of a real impact on their immediate neighbourhoods, than they were before the initiatives described in this chapter were launched? Progress, of sorts, is being made and certainly more is happening now than, say, ten years ago. However answers to the questions of how effective these projects are and what impact they have made remain elusive. Despite the good intentions of the external agencies, there are still grounds for inferring that, left to their own devices, football clubs would take very little interest in putting themselves out for their communities.

Despite the professionalisation that has affected many football clubs, in line with improved public relations and marketing strategies, the shift in ownership towards media/sports management and promotion companies, and the move to public flotations, clubs continue to have many shortcomings when it comes to forging partnerships outside their immediate ken.

On the other hand, it can be argued that external agencies are expecting too much of these clubs and operating on the basis of an exaggerated view of the role that football plays in English society. Would they ask the same questions, or be equally sceptical, about any other private companies, especially in the leisure industry? The main difference seems to be that other companies rarely promote themselves as being 'community-based', or as attempting to represent local people. It appears that football clubs themselves have entered a vicious circle: they have created and perpetuated myths of community ties, and then been surprised when others seek to hold them to the commitments that these myths imply. This contradiction has been magnified as demographic and economic changes have altered the landscapes of inner-city areas. These changes have added to the problems facing some clubs and have made them feel more insecure. Add to this the increased pressure that has been exerted on football clubs by central government and local authorities, as well as by pressure groups, community organisations and the media, all of which claim to expect clubs to be good 'community partners'. Can it really be a surprise that some clubs become defensive and fail to be effective? Both the expectations and the funding opportunities for football clubs have been enhanced in recent years. The wider agenda now promoted through the government's 'social inclusion' policy depends on football clubs, among many other institutions, to respond effectively. Third-party agencies have developed and strengthened their positions in relation to football clubs primarily on the basis of this agenda, acting as bridges between the football clubs and the outside world. However, despite the efforts of the government in its various guises and through its pioneering projects, the overall effects remain limited and uneven.

What, then, is the future for football clubs in their relations with their communities? There can be little doubt that, as long as there is no major economic downturn, there will be more initiatives and funding from central government, aimed at football clubs and the governing bodies of the game. This will inevitably mean more projects and more opportunities for those who are involved in this work. The challenge for all concerned, however, is to make these projects stronger, more effective and more sustainable. Everyone with a vested interest, including the clubs, the PFA and other external agencies, will have to be prepared to look outside the realm of football, and reflect on what the real needs of their immediate neighbourhoods are. How can they offer comprehensive packages of support and investment? Doing so successfully will mean a sea change in how football clubs operate and how they relate to external bodies. It will also mean building on the projects already established by third-party agencies, and finding innovative ways of supporting and developing such programmes and partnerships.

Above all, there is a pressing need to get these projects right, so that the clubs have no excuse to give up participating and communities have no reason to become disillusioned. This is the difficult part, especially as the work is hard, unglamorous and, at times, very unrewarding. It is crucial that the third-party agencies are supported effectively, and developed and sustained so that they can fulfil their potential. It is not enough for some of the existing 'football in the Community' schemes to become registered charities if they do not change their focus, and employ staff with community and partnership backgrounds. If all that changes is the legal status then it is not worth doing. It is incumbent on those who purport to support these initiatives to take on far more facilitative and supportive roles. Without such changes cynical communities will continue to live alongside cynical football clubs.

4

A day out with the 'old boys'

PAT SLAUGHTER

Excluding 'hooligans'

**** seldom gets a chance to watch Nottingham Forest play since he started his new job at a sports media company: he spends most match days editing the highlights of high-profile games in the Premiership or the Champions League. A pre-season friendly at Peterborough offered him a rare opportunity to cheer his side on. Meeting friends in a pub in the centre of Peterborough before the game, **** sensed an uneasy tension between the locals and the various groups of Forest fans dotted around the pub. As the Forest fans left the locals attacked them in the street outside. **** was slightly ahead of the main group of fans and managed to avoid the confrontation. Two months after the Peterborough incident **** attended a midweek Worthington Cup game in Nottingham. Taking his new Japanese girlfriend to her first football game, he assured her that she was unlikely to see any of those football hooligans who intrigued her so much. At half-time the football liaison officer with responsibility for collating and disseminating intelligence on Forest fans approached ****. Taking **** by surprise by addressing him by his first name, this policeman explained that **** had been positively identified in CCTV footage of the fight in Peterborough. In friendly tones the policeman advised **** that it would be in his best interests to surrender himself to the Peterborough police for interview, rather than run the risk of being arrested in a dawn raid. After undergoing a lot of anxiety, and having taken the precaution of obtaining legal representation, **** attended a police interview at which a video was played, clearly capturing several men engaged in criminal activities and just as clearly showing that **** had not been involved in the violence. The police were eager for **** to account for himself during the short periods when he was out of shot, presumably in the expectation that he would confess his involvement in the fight.

We are living now in a time when the regulation of football fans can involve questioning supporters about their behaviour when the gaze of the

CCTV cameras is not upon them. It is also a time when a magistrates' court can order the destruction of an 'offensive' scarf:

> Ancient rivalries in the Northeast of England fell foul of the law yesterday when a pub landlady was convicted and fined for the unusual crime of displaying an offensive football scarf. Draped above the bar at the Adelphi in the centre of Newcastle, the knitwear announced neatly in the black and white of the city's Magpies football team: 'Sunderland are Shite.' . . . The magistrates fined Mrs Mann £400 with £180 legal costs. The scarf was forfeited as a threatening, abusive or insulting sign likely to cause harassment, alarm or distress, and is to be destroyed.
>
> (Martin Wright, in the *Guardian*, 3 September 2002)

It makes sense, then, to explore the ways in which this new regulatory environment affects football fans' match-day experiences.

Early in 2002 I travelled to South Wales to watch the team I support, Leeds United, play Cardiff City in the third round of the FA Cup. I went to the game with a group, some of whom were close friends of mine, others close friends or acquaintances of my close friends. The common bond in the group was that, to greater or lesser extents, our 'fandom' was informed and structured by a nostalgic allegiance to the memory of the 'football casuals' of the 1980s. Some months before this day out Stephen Wagg had approached me about the possibility of contributing a chapter to a book exploring the various ways in which processes of social exclusion manifest themselves in and around the game of football. My brief, we agreed, would be to comment upon the effects of anti-hooliganism measures on the popular culture of the 'rougher' elements of the football crowd. I had been recommended to Wagg by an academic colleague and friend as 'the natural choice' to write on the subject. I teach criminology at a university in London, I am familiar with academic debates concerning problematic supporters at football matches, and I have a grasp of intellectual concerns about the causes and effects of the politics of exclusion. In addition, I was convicted of 'conspiracy to cause affrays' in 1988 and jailed for four years, having come to the attention of the police during 'Operation Wild Boar', a covert investigation of organised hooliganism at and around Leeds United football matches (see Armstrong and Hobbs).

I appreciated my sponsor's logic, but for me this project has seemed anything but 'natural'. I feel uncomfortable writing sociologically about hooliganism. I have read the implicit assaults on character swapped by academics whose niche is this particular field. I feel vulnerable to charges of 'going native'. I also feel uncomfortable about writing about my friends. My wife feels uncomfortable about this aspect of her husband's past; and how will I explain it all to my daughter, now a baby, when she is older? However, I warmed to the idea that 'We are attempting to reach a wider audience, [producing] something not only for the academics but also for those who read *When Saturday Comes.*' In what follows I purposely avoid engaging with the literature and arguments that attempt to offer explanatory frameworks for football disorder. The account of 'our day out' is underscored by an analysis that fails the test of objectivity: it overtly comes from a personal history that is 'too close to the subject'. Yet in attempting to make some sense of everything that happened that day I have drawn upon some of the criminological literature relating to exclusion, risk, tolerance and anxiety.

I argue that during the 1990s moves to exclude 'hooligans' became particularly effective in 'disciplining' Premiership football crowds. This disciplinary project is resented by many supporters, who feel threatened and unwanted by the new orthodoxy in English football. This orthodoxy seems to derive from a wider political shift, resulting in a situation in which authority blames more and forgives less. Resentment of it causes individuals to form alliances with disenchanted others. From the early 1990s onwards a new football subculture became apparent: the 'old boys' are still passionate about their days out at football matches, but they are adamant that the experience is not as good as it was before.

The governance of behaviour in and around football stadiums has become an increasingly sophisticated and refined process. The bodies charged with regulating the various aspects of football fans' days out seem ever less tolerant and ever more zealous in their pursuit of unruly spectators. What occurs is the establishment of exclusionary mechanisms that target fans whose conduct is regarded as problematic. Individuals are identified and acted against; stewards eject over-boisterous supporters from grounds; clubs withdraw season tickets because complaints have been received that their holders refuse to refrain from vile racist language; the police apply to the magistrates' courts for banning orders because individuals have repeatedly been seen in the company of 'known hooligans'; courts imprison pugilists convicted of striking fans of opposing teams. Such examples describe the physical exclusion of people from the football environment. Sections of the football crowd sense that the prevailing atmosphere is becoming increasingly punitive. How does such a mood affect the rituals of 'the lads'? In what ways does it serve to discipline and moderate the behaviour of 'old boys'?

The focus of this chpater is on the ways in which the authorities' attempts to 'clean up football's act' have redefined the match day experience for many. In essence, I argue that, although a small number of fans have been physically excluded from the football-supporting domain, it is within football's newly established *cordon sanitaire* that we see the greater impact of the sanitising project. The popular culture of those who remain within the domain is increasingly informed and constructed by the threat of exclusion. For those supporters who perceive that they might be 'next on the list' the need to calculate the ever-increasing risks posed by football's brave new world is pressing if they are to survive. Risk calculation leads to adaptation. Fans who feel at risk adapt their supporting style in a way that accommodates the appropriate safety procedures as much as possible. If football fans are to be held to account for those fleeting moments when they are 'out of shot' the minimising of risk is a priority.

In following the experiences of a group of Leeds United fans as the events of 6 January 2002 unfolded, I place the emphasis on portraying the ways in which particular groups of football fans have adapted to contemporary circumstances. Portraying the ways in which they organise themselves around a particularly 'risky' fixture allows for an analysis that addresses the content and causes of actions. Which are rebellious and which are conforming? To what extent are they informed by the fear of exclusion? The fans in this particular group are among those who feel most keenly the breath of the excluders upon their necks. In offering an account of how such a group seeks to reduce risk and how it attempts to navigate on the safe side of football's inclusionary/exclusionary borders, it is possible to glimpse an emergent 'fandom' that sees its ancestry in the hooligan 'firm' of the 1980s, but adopts reasoning and behaviours that are determined by the contemporary threat of exclusion.

The magic of the Cup

Leeds United went into their third-round FA Cup tie with Cardiff City sitting on top of the Premiership pile. Cardiff's Second Division campaign had yet to live up to expectations. Premiership aristocrats versus lower league underachievers: a classic Cup encounter. The 'David and Goliath' headlines are an annual feature of FA Cup reporting. The weak upset the mighty. Such exploits offer relief from the monotony of Premiership certainties, which dictate that the strong will emerge triumphant. When Cardiff and Leeds came out of the hat paired together it was a draw to whet the appetite. To football purists it whispered the tantalising prospect of an upset. For certain sections of both sets of fans the magic of the Cup in this instance was more about realising a rare opportunity to test out the reputations of those who otherwise live in far-away leagues.

The reputations of both sets of fans are well-documented in the annals of football hooliganism. Leeds fans' capacity to grab 'the wrong kind of headlines' is long-established. The rioting in Paris that followed defeat by Bayern Munich in the European Cup final in 1975 was the first of a number of major incidents that marked out the Leeds following as being among the very worst. The 1980s witnessed the emergence of the self-styled Leeds Service Crew. Among the other 'super-firms' of the period the Service Crew was generally regarded as sharing parity with the Inter City Firm at West Ham United, the Headhunters at Chelsea and the Bushwackers at Millwall. The last time Leeds fans were castigated for their involvement in a major incident of hooliganism coincided with their promotion, as Division Two champions, to the old First Division. The scenes of destruction coming out of Bournemouth were taken as a omen by those who now had to play host to them in the higher division. After all, if these football fans could find it in themselves to unleash such violence on a sleepy seaside town, when it could reasonably have been expected that they might be in an altogether more celebratory and slightly less misanthropic mood, what might they do at Old Trafford on the wrong end of a 4–0 drubbing? Yet that was largely the end of the story of Leeds United as a focus for 'hooligans'. In more recent years there have been more incidents in which Leeds fans have been victims: some were stabbed in Rome and Milan, and two Leeds supporters were killed during skirmishes on the eve of Leeds's semi-final match against Galatasaray in Istanbul in April 2000. Although many observers remain sceptical, Leeds fans' predatory behaviour has given way to a sense of unease and vulnerability.

Cardiff's rise to infamy is much more recent. Somewhat perversely, their troublesome pedigree has been established in a period when hooliganism is generally regarded as being on the wane and is certainly less evident across the game as a whole. In a period that is regarded by most as being largely trouble-free, when the general belief is that most clubs' hooligans have somehow been tamed, especially in the higher reaches of the game, there are periodic reports that far-flung outposts (far-flung from the point of view of southeast England) are still experiencing trouble. Three clubs in particular have fans who seem insistent on resisting the trend towards pacification: Stoke City, Millwall and Cardiff. It is significant that the hooligan hierarchy has undergone the shift that it has. West Ham, Chelsea and Leeds have become permanent members of the Premier League, and neither the clubs nor the corporate interests that stand behind the reinvention of top-flight football want these clubs' followers to remain as

they were. The exclusionary mechanisms touched upon earlier are much
more intensive and effective at the top end of the game. In such a climate
many of the longer-established 'firms' find little opportunity to justify their
fading reputations. The fans of Premiership clubs do not talk about 'firms'
in the present tense any more; the fully functioning fighting gang belonged
to an age before the BSkyB circus hit town. Longevity is only possible for
a 'firm' if, like Millwall, the football club that the 'firm' is associated with
fails to scale the heights.

A match between Cardiff City and Leeds United was therefore a
prospect that mixed the old with the new. The past reputation of the Leeds
fans was challenged by a rare assignment outside the super-regulated
Premiership, to a club whose fans are very much the 'new kids on the
block'. The contest offered a contrast between a club enjoying the new
riches of football and swaggering under the weight of all the
accompanying baubles – an assertive corporate identity, its revamped
Elland Road ground and a conspicuous media image – and a club that
offered a ghostly vision of its past, run seemingly for the personal rather
than financial satisfaction of its chairman and based at a decaying ground,
offering plenty of unwanted space on the television gantry. The
fashionable set were coming to town, giving the poorer cousins an
opportunity to strut their stuff.

One Leeds fan, Dean, remembers how it was at an earlier encounter, on
10 September 1983:

> I remember when we got off the train in Leeds some lads told us that
> Cardiff had smashed the windows in the Prince of Wales and done a
> load of spray-painting about the Soul Crew. We'd never even heard
> of the Soul Crew then. We went down the Black Lion and everyone
> was saying 'Who the fuck are Cardiff City?' and 'Where are the
> cheeky cunts?' When we got to the ground Cardiff only had about
> 300 or so and from what you could see most of them were scarfers.
> We heard that they'd done a load more graffiti round Holbeck. After
> the game me and Gis got through the police and got on the bus taking
> them back to the station. There were only about 30 of them and most
> looked like they'd just come out the miners' welfare, all white socks
> and purple sta-press. There were a few younger ones dressed in last
> year's track-suits: Tacchini and Fila and that. Got talking to them and
> that and they were giving it 'Where was your famous Service Crew?
> We got here at three in the morning and didn't see anyone.' Me and
> Gis were pissing ourselves. They gave us these really naff calling
> cards: 'Congratulations you have just met the Cardiff City Soul
> Crew' and 'Government Health Warning: Cardiff City Soul Crew

can seriously damage your health.' We went to Jacomelli's after and told all the lads what the score was. They were all like: 'Yeah, they really came looking for a fight, didn't they?' You know, taking the piss out of the Welsh knobheads because we were the top firm then.

Setting off

'Dave' has organised the excursion. The party meets outside the Red Parcel depot at Kings Cross Station at nine in the morning. Supporters congregate in twos and threes, waiting for the coach to arrive. Dave moves furtively from one group to another. He explains that the coach driver is under the impression that we are going to Newport for a day's drinking. 'Best keep it quiet until we get a bit closer to Wales, we'll give him a bung to keep him sweet.' The need for subterfuge is justified by the belief that if the coach company were to know the true purpose of the excursion it might have declined our custom, and also in order to avoid any police interference. Dave seems pleased with his mastery of intrigue.

Kings Cross is the regular point of departure for home games for the Leeds United London Supporters Club. For the Cardiff game the members of the London branch are travelling by train from Paddington. Take-up for the official excursion has been disappointing by the usual standards. Many have been put off by the Welsh fans' reputation. The party travelling from Kings Cross this morning are doing so, in the main, because of that reputation. The coach arrives and Dave ushers us on board. Although many members of the group know one another, this is the first time that they have all travelled together. The London gathering of Leeds old boys sets off on its journey to South Wales.

Sitting on the coach

There are 35 of us on the coach. Twenty-nine members of the group are aged between 33 and 44, the majority of these being in their late 30s. The six younger fans are in their early 20s. Of the older members all except one have been attending Leeds games since at least the early 1980s. Fifteen of these older fans have always lived in London and the remainder were originally based in Leeds, or elsewhere in West Yorkshire, before moving to the capital. The six younger fans comprise two distinct sets of friends, one based in north London and the other in a commuter town 30 miles away. None of these younger fans originally lived in the North. Among the older fans whose support for the club is longstanding current patterns of attending games vary. Five attend all home and away games; eight attend games on a very casual basis, making the effort for the 'really big' home games but usually catching the team only when it comes to London; and the remainder attend games on a semi-regular basis.

A constant theme of conversations throughout the day concerned the justifications that individuals had for non-attendance: 'Just can't be bothered going all the time anymore'; 'The missus gives us too much grief'; 'Too much of a nightmare getting tickets'; 'I'm not travelling with those knobheads in the supporters' club'; 'It isn't as good as it was in the 80s'; 'I prefer to do a few lines of charlie and chill out in London'; 'The old Bill are too on top these days'; 'The atmosphere has gone'; 'Can't afford it'. Although the majority talked about not attending Leeds games as often as they once had, many reported that over the past three or four years they had begun to step up their attendance after a period of infrequent attendance or, in some cases, non-attendance. The reasons given for their renewed patronage included: 'Got bored of the dance/drugs scene'; 'A lot of the old boys are beginning to turn out again'; 'It's the best football Leeds have played for years'. The one older fan whose support is a more recent development is a season-ticket holder and attends most away games. The two younger sets both have one member who attends regularly, while the others attend the 'big' games.

For those on the coach who exercised choice in determining their attendance, there were, broadly, two criteria for 'making the effort', beyond the convenience and ease of watching Leeds whenever the team played in London. Most would travel to those games that were considered important in determining the fortunes of the club: the big European games, the 'glamour fixtures' in the Premiership and so on. A feeling of pride in the club and a desire to be present when something important for the club happened seemed to stand behind these decisions. Conversations rolled around the coach about how well 'we' played in Brussels, the 4–3 thriller against Liverpool, the joy of being there when 'we' got that last-minute winner against AC Milan. The second criterion gauged a game's attractiveness on whether or not the day would provide a 'buzz' for the fans. For example, a game against Chelsea would be attractive because a certain atmosphere would be generated and certain people were likely to be there. Fixtures that had a 'history' among the fans, where antipathies would be reproduced or local rivalries reinforced, always proved popular. Choosing to attend on this basis might lead to a fan attending a game that had little value for neutral football enthusiasts. Occasionally the reasons converged: nobody liked to miss Manchester United's visits to Elland Road.

Individuals have come on this 'old boy' outing with specific and contrasting histories of supporting their club. Only four of the group would be considered to have been active members of the Leeds Service Crew and now they all fall into the 'semi-regular' cohort. The five who attend all games regardless are well-known among Leeds United supporters for their 'loyalty'. Their attendance patterns have remained unchanged for more than 20 years. All of them were well-known to the Service Crew, having been popular 'straights' who occasionally found themselves caught up in 'the action', but were 'really there for the football'. The rest of the older fans on the coach, excepting only the 'newcomer', have all seen, or been involved to a certain extent in, the mass confrontations of the 1980s. For anybody who supported the club during that period it would have been difficult not to have. Some of these had been allied to supporters' groups that were unpopular with the Crew.

In particular, the Kippax supporters' club was viewed with disdain by the Service Crew, because they wore scarves, sang songs and 'made exhibitions of themselves'. They were regarded by members of the 'firm' as an embarrassing hang-over from the 1970s: they seemed not to understand the fashion and could not get their heads around what, in the 1980s, had been the new aesthetic. Barracked for being 'Christmas trees', they were thought of as chinks in the armour. Four of those who once travelled with the Kippax are now sitting on the coach with their old Service Crew adversaries, the details of past arguments long forgotten.

Three of the fans on the coach are active members of a small group of Leeds fans, about 50 in number, whose primary purpose in attending games is still to seek confrontation with rival fans. One of these three is an older fan, whose previous involvement, in the 1980s, had been very much on the fringe of things. Another is the 'newcomer', which for many of the older 'faces' is puzzling and a little absurd: 'You get to 28 and you think "Fuck it, I'll be a football hooligan." What's all that about?'. The third is one of the younger fans, who is only weeks away from an appointment in court to defend himself against an application by the police for a banning order (which is subsequently granted).

Everybody on the coach is in some form of paid employment, except one of the younger group, who is a full-time student. The range of occupations varies considerably: an actor sits next to a loss adjuster, behind a British Telecom engineer and a labourer, and so on. Occupational status is very much a non-issue in relation to the group dynamics. When I commented on this to one of the group some weeks later, he agreed with me that this was very much in contrast with the way in which the Service Crew tended to interpret the significance of someone's employment. Ordinarily, students and those holding 'middle-class jobs', meaning all non-manual jobs, would be regarded with suspicion and often subjected to ridicule. The old 'firm' was mainly made up of young men who had a trade, unskilled manual workers, petty criminals and school kids.

Making plans

From the moment the coach sets off, it seems as if at any one time at least five of the passengers are talking on mobile phones. Many of the conversations are with other Leeds old boys making their way to Cardiff. Messages are being relayed back and forth: 'Yeah, there's about 40 of us. We met at Kings Cross this morning . . . Yeah, yeah, they're all good lads.' The coach was kept constantly informed of other groups' progress: 'The Donny [Doncaster] lot got pulled over by the police as soon as they got on the motorway.' Dave, the coach trip organiser, is one of those who seems constantly to be either on his phone or communicating the content of his conversation. In a methodical manner he shifts from one seated pair to another, bending down conspiratorially with his hand across his mouth: 'I've just talked to Otley Pete and he reckons that it's going to get really lively.' The constant chatter is responded to in different ways. For some the updates are a source of humour, Dave being regarded as an overenthusiastic gossip. Others devour every morsel of information.

News come through from the travelling Yorkshire contingent that the plans have changed. Originally the arrangement was that the eight coaches carrying the 'old boys' to the game would converge in Newport at midday so that the fans could meet at a pre-selected pub. From there the combined group would have made the short train journey to Cardiff. The reasoning behind this strategy was informed by a number of different concerns. First, a social concern: the general consensus was that the Cardiff police were unlikely to allow the group to meet up or drink in pubs in the city centre, for fear that such a gathering would be targeted for attack by locals. Second, a representational concern: many felt that the reputation of Leeds fans would be compromised if they failed to 'turn out in force' for such a potentially volatile fixture. Third, a protective concern: the reputation of the Cardiff fans is such that the Leeds fans believe that if they were to arrive in the city in small groups they would be much more vulnerable. Somebody on the coach comments that if our group were to arrive unsupported by others it would be 'tantamount to committing suicide'. Finally, there is a concern for nonconformity: the 'old boys' relish the opportunity to demonstrate that they will not have their day out 'spoilt' or interfered with by the police, or anybody else.

The planned rendezvous is abandoned, however, after it becomes known (where this information comes from is not discussed) that the police are aware of the intentions of the 'old boys': they plan to intercept the coaches upon their arrival in Newport and ferry them immediately to Ninian Park. An alternative plan is now communicated over mobile phones. The coaches from Yorkshire will head for Hereford and the old boys will meet in a pub before catching a train to Cardiff. For the London coach party it is decided that a detour to Hereford would be time-consuming and inconvenient. Instead our group is now headed for Cwmbryn, which will allow us an hour or so for a drink before intercepting the train to Cardiff carrying our friends.

The coach driver has now been informed of the group's intentions. He seems satisfied by Dave's insistence that his passengers are 'all good lads' and that there will be no trouble. A whip-round has raised £75 for the driver and the group's members are conspicuously polite in his presence. Before reaching Cwmbryn Dave has passed around a bin-liner several times, commenting loudly that if we keep the bus tidy it will save the driver any extra work. We are dropped off at Cwmbryn Station just after noon ('Just in time for the pub') and the coach continues to Cardiff. Members of the group contemplate the confusion of the police as empty coach after empty coach approaches the ground. There is a general sense of satisfaction that things are going well.

The group finds a pub attached to a run-down shopping centre, on the other side of the road from a bleak and forbidding council estate: 'Nice round here i'n't it?' The pub is virtually empty. The barman looks nervous as the pub suddenly fills with strangers. A couple of teenage boys hover uneasily around a fruit machine. Four old men tend to their pints and seem unimpressed by the influx. The pub is soon filled with noise, and there is a sense of excitement and anticipation. Two of the group have joined the old men's table, and are laughing and joking with them. The fruit-machine players are now caught up in a conversation with four or five of the 'old boys'. The barman takes in good humour a barrage of sarcastic comments as to his inability to serve his thirsty customers quickly enough. Occasionally bewildered-looking locals stumble across the scene. The atmosphere is good-natured, spirits are high. Being in the pub represents some kind of victory for the 'old boys': 'Did you see the look on the barman's face when we first walked in?'; 'Those old fellas had a good crack with us, they knew we were all right.' On the one hand, the members of the group seem pleased that we have an intimidatory appearance; on the other hand, they are equally concerned that neutral outsiders appreciate the social qualities of 'old boys'.

We then make our way to the station *en masse* and find the platform for the Cardiff train. Many of us are carrying bottles of lager or pint glasses, our unfinished drinks from the pub. There are about 50 other football supporters on the platform as we arrive. The majority are in small groups, many wearing Cardiff shirts. As before, in the pub, our immediate arrival causes consternation. Those already on the platform initially look puzzled, but Yorkshire accents give the game away and they shuffle as inconspicuously as possible to the end of the platform. A policeman comes running on to the opposite platform, stops short when he spies us and runs back in the direction he came from. The 'old boys' split into groups and several begin to engage with the Cardiff fans: 'What do you reckon the score'll be?'; or, referring to Cardiff City's owner, 'That Sam Hamman's the best thing that ever happened to you lot.' The desire to be viewed as 'all right' surfaces again. Conversations among the 'old boys' are intended to legitimate the group's friendliness: 'It's not like it's their lads [i.e. their "firm"] is it?'; 'Can't wait to see this lot's fucking faces when they get on t'train and they find 300 Leeds psychopaths on board.' Ten policemen run dramatically across the bridge to our platform: 'Old Bill have sussed us, it's on top now.' When the police reach us they look slightly embarrassed and lost. The Leeds fans and the Cardiff fans stand drinking and chatting together, waiting for the train to arrive.

As the train pulls up to the platform it is immediately apparent that it is already full to the point of bursting. Faces are pressed to the window and other Yorkshire 'old boys' are waving to and cheering their London comrades. As we squeeze ourselves into already over-full compartments, pleasantries and banter are exchanged: 'No room for soft southern fuckers on this train, mate'; 'Good to see you, fella. I tell you what, mate, we've got a right juicy firm on board.' The police follow us on board, just about making it on, crammed up against the doors: 'Who brought fucking old Bill with 'em?' I notice that a number of the Cardiff fans remain on the platform. I am jammed up against a toilet door; occasionally somebody defies physics by making it through the crush to relieve a full bladder. Pushing the door open, they are rebuked by the four Leeds fans inside: 'Shut the door. We're doing a line of charlie in here.' One of the Yorkshire contingent comments to me that their group has 'been bang at it all day.' Pointing to his friend, he adds: 'This daft fucker has done two Es. Just what you need to be, all E'd up going to Cardiff.' His friend smiles at me.

At Cardiff Station the platform is lined by police. The Leeds fans are all shepherded to a side-exit. As we go through the exit the police have contrived a gauntlet so that we can go through only one at a time. A policeman points a video camera at the faces of the emerging Leeds fans. Many of the group make efforts to conceal their identities by pulling down their baseball caps, wrapping scarves (Burberry, Aquascutum or Daks, not Leeds United) around their faces, or pulling up the collars of their Stone Island jackets. 'Like the police won't be able to work out who they are if they wanted to', a more dismissive 'old boy' commented. We are held in the station car-park for about ten minutes. Taking stock of the combined forces of 'old boys', I estimate that they number about 250 in all. The police, who are dressed in riot fatigues, seem slightly to outnumber our group and make for an imposing sight.

As the convoy sets off with this escort five youths who have been waiting outside the car-park negotiate the police lines and join the group. Some shoving and pushing takes place before the five emphatically declare: 'We're Leeds. We're Leeds.' A tangible air of tension and nervous anticipation hangs over the 'old boys'. We are led through the back streets towards Ninian Park. Leading the escort are ten mounted policemen. The 'old boys' are penned in the middle of the road, police officers are two and three deep in front and behind us, and others are similarly arranged on the pavements either side of us. Every 200 metres or so the horses come to a halt and the group is made to stand idly until the police decide to move on again. A lot of the supporters ask 'Where are the bastards?' We approach a bridge: somebody announces that 'this is where they ambushed Millwall'. Some fans are bobbing up and down, trying to stare over policemen's helmets for any sign of activity. The streets we pass through are largely deserted. Some middle-aged women carrying Tesco bags pause on a corner to take in this unusual sight.

Then an Asian family, two young parents with three children, are spotted staring from an upstairs window at the strange traffic flowing below. A chant is taken up by 20 or 30 of the group: 'Lee Bowyer, Lee Bowyer, Lee Bowyer.' One of my neighbours comments: 'Well, we've got some right knobheads with us today.' I am not sure whether his disdain is because the singing contravenes the old 'casual' view that singing is something that 'woollybacks' do, or because of the implicit racist message that the chant communicates. Bowyer was convicted of affray in December 1997, after an Asian waiter was attacked in a burger bar. In 2001 he was acquitted of inflicting grievous bodily harm on an Asian student in Leeds city centre. Rightly or wrongly, stories have persisted in the football world that Bowyer holds racist views. I feel embarrassed and wonder how the two black 'old boys' who have travelled with us that morning feel now. In the 1980s, when racism at Leeds games was much worse, 'Salt' often came to matches wearing a National Front T-shirt. Some of his fellow-fans said, behind his back: 'He's all right, for a black bastard.'

As we get closer to the ground the 'old boys' become more relaxed. Some of them are on their mobile phones: 'I'm telling you, we've got a right firm today. Loads of old faces . . . no, no, I haven't seen a sniff of 'em – bottle-less bastards.' At the point of reaching Ninian Park a hundred or so teenage Cardiff fans, queueing at a turnstile, face us, and chant their threats of violence, and their claims of superiority and loyalty. We join other Leeds fans outside the away fans' entrance to the ground. The police are keen to get spectators into the stadium as quickly as possible. Before being allowed access to the turnstiles the Leeds fans have to present their 'Premier Club Cards' to the Leeds United stewards who guard the entrance. Such a procedure is nearly always carried out at Leeds away games, ostensibly because the club feels the need to vet its own fans, although many supporters believe that it has much more to do with the income that the £10 cost of the cards generates for the club. The 'old boys' mill around the entrance, displaying no eagerness to go in, some arguing that 'loads of our lot don't have cards'. Others are keen to see whether the Cardiff supporters are going to 'make a show' or not. Simultaneously the police lose their patience with those outside and push everyone forward. The Leeds stewards give up their task and wave everybody through.

We have got inside the ground at 2:30, an hour and a half before kick-off. The ground already seems half-full. This contrasts hugely with the normal Premiership match experience, where the majority of fans make their way to their seats minutes before the games commence. The Cardiff fans are in full voice. From every side of the ground they direct their chants at the Leeds fans, who have been allocated a corner of a terrace behind one of the goals. It is interesting to see the dynamics of who stands where and next to whom on the terraces. Coach-loads of the 'singers', resplendent in Leeds United shirts and some wearing scarves, make their way to the far end of our pen and start singing, in defiance of the Cardiff City fans who share our terrace but are separated from us by an open pen. The Leeds 'old boys' tend to remain in the corner area of our pen, which is bordered perpendicularly by a stand seating the home fans. The 'old boys' stand broadly together, but choices as to who stands immediately next to whom seem to be largely determined by more refined commonalities. The six younger fans who travelled with us from London stand with those of a similar age. Those who have never missed a match chat with other 'loyalists'. Former Service Crew 'activists' chat about the 'good old days'. The group who are still active press themselves close to the fence dividing us from the seated Cardiff fans. As more coach-loads of Leeds fans enter the ground the ranks of the 'old boys' swell. The ticket allocation for Leeds fans is a little over 2,000. By the time the pen is full the ratio of 'old boys' to 'knobheads' was roughly even: 'I can't believe what a mob we've got out today.'

As kick-off approaches the atmosphere in the ground becomes electric (it is a cliché, but some clichés fit). It seems that every Cardiff fan is singing, jumping, swearing, threatening. Again and again I hear Leeds fans saying: 'It's just like the 80s', or 'It's just like the fucking 80s.' At first there is just an occasional bottle or coin coming our way, but as the game begins the shower of missiles becomes more sustained. The Cardiff fans to our left raise themselves onto their seats: they taunt us, pointing to their bottles, pointing to us and then throwing the bottles at us. It is difficult to see exactly what is going on to my right, but an arc of missiles can be seen dropping onto the 'singers'. The more cautious among them are now edging away from the dividing fence and attempting to find some safe middle-ground. I can see a number of fans approaching the stewards and asking to be let out of the ground before half-time. This assault is greeted with incredulity by the 'old boys': 'I can't believe this. I 'aven't seen owt like this for years.' There is also some anger and scorn: 'Have you seen 'em? They're all little kids'; 'Where were they when we got into Cardiff, the soft bastards?' A few Leeds fans throw missiles back, although others comment: 'Wants to be careful, 'im. Can't he see copper wi' camera?' The police, on the other side of the perimeter fence, are all facing the Leeds fans; senior officers direct the cameraman, who had previously been waiting for us at the station, to film this or that particular group.

As the game draws to a close it looks increasingly as if the game will be drawn. During the second half the stream of missiles directed at the Leeds fans has intensified and the anger rises: 'I can't wait to get these fuckers back to our place'; 'D'you reckon they'll be so brave at Elland Road?' It is 1–1, with little time to go, when Cardiff's Chairman, Sam Hamman, comes on to the side of the pitch to urge his team and the club's supporters on. He makes his way around the perimeter of the playing field. He passes the Leeds fans and turns to face them: he raises his hands above his head and starts to clap. Some swear that he is sneering. Leeds fans surge forward, spitting and throwing coins at Hamman. A reasonably well-supported chorus goes up: 'You're just a club run by a Paki, a club run by a Paki.' Hamman's shaven-headed man-mountain of a bodyguard smiles wryly at the Leeds fans before taking his charge gently by the arm and leading him away to the other side of the terrace. A subsequent tabloid exposure identifies this bodyguard as a former leader of the Cardiff City Soul Crew. Hamman raises his arms to the Cardiff fans and the noise intensifies, with chants including: 'Outside it's a massacre' and 'We killed Millwall.' An occasional 'Ar-gen-tina!' confirms the anti-English sentiments.

Scott Young scores the winner. At the final whistle thousands of Cardiff fans run onto the pitch and Hamman is hoisted high on somebody's back: it is the magic of the Cup, an historic upset, the mighty have been slain. From the outset of the invasion the majority of those on the pitch surge towards our corner of the ground. The police initially attempt to charge the Cardiff fans away from our corner, but, hopelessly outnumbered, they determine to hold a line five yards or so in front of the fence penning in the Leeds fans. Police batons are flailing but the Cardiff fans keep surging forwards. A large number of Leeds fans now surge towards the fence and a few actively try to scale it in order to get at the Cardiff fans, but they are beaten back by a rearguard police action. More missiles than ever are now pouring into the Leeds section. Some Leeds fans, sensing that the Cardiff fans will imminently break in to the Leeds pen, head for the exits. Police reinforcements arrive and attempt to push the home fans away from the fence. The police strategy relies on dog-handlers setting their dogs upon the Cardiff fans. As the supporters back away police in riot gear plug the gap. Cardiff fans jump up and down, arms outstretched, baiting the dogs to 'come on!' Several dogs disappear from view in a flurry of kicks and punches.

As the Leeds supporters I am standing with survey the scene, 'Halifax Mac' comments: 'This i'n't how old script use to go, is it?' Tony, who is 40 years old, asks: 'Which one of them 16-year-olds is going to massacre me outside, d'you reckon?' Dean nudges me and points to an 'old boy' in front of us who is telling someone on his mobile phone: 'It's gone right off here. Are they showing it on telly?' 'Knobhead', Dean observes. The police are making slow progress in pushing the Cardiff fans back. The Leeds fans who had aggressively surged to the perimeter fence quite suddenly turn and rush towards the exit. While so doing those who have not already taken precautions quickly pull down their baseball caps, wrap scarves around their faces and pull up the collars of their jackets. Dean turns to the rest of our immediate group: 'Who they going to fight? All Cardiff lot are on pitch.' On the return journey to London one of the younger supporters on the coach described what happened outside the ground:

> Someone says the gates are open and we all made it outside to see if any of their boys were there. 'Black Stan' [the football liaison officer who monitors and collates intelligence relating to 'troublesome' Leeds fans] and a couple of other coppers were outside but we steamed through 'em and went running up the road. But there weren't no proper lads about so we came back in.

Meanwhile, as the pitch-invaders are gradually pushed back to the half-way line the majority of the Leeds supporters head for the exit. Their coaches are parked directly across the road from the away fans' exit gate. Hundreds of Leeds fans now stand around the coaches, waiting to see what will happen next. A senior policeman repeatedly urges them to depart: 'Gentlemen, can you please get on board your coaches?' Many of the fans are asking: 'Where are the bastards?' After ten minutes or so the police lose patience and set their dogs on to the waiting fans. Behind the dogs come policemen wielding batons. A group of fans attempting to escape the onslaught collapses in a pile when the fence they are crushed against gives way. Several 'old boys' standing at the back of the mêlée urge those at the front to 'stand', but the coaches are now filling up quickly. On television the following day a senior organiser for the Leeds United Supporters Club is to be seen on television sporting a badly mauled leg and complaining about heavy-handed policing.

On the coach back to London

Our coach driver is listening to *606*, a football phone-in show on BBC Radio 5 Live that is advertised as the programme 'where fans celebrate football'. He greets us with an ironic grin: 'Had a nice time lads?' We contemplate the police action: 'What can you do when t'police are on top like that?' Some are still curious: 'Where were the bastards?' The wailing of sirens and the flashing of police lights announce the progress of our departure from Cardiff. The long line of coaches loses its police escort as it spills on to the motorway and the conversation continues: 'They were all little kids'; 'Where were they before the game?'; 'There were thousands of 'em. If they'd really wanted to get at us they could've steamed t'police'; 'Our lot could have killed 'em'; 'Old Bill were out of order'; 'It were that Sam Hamman who kicked it all off.' The supporters are on their mobile phones again: 'No, we'd've killed 'em. Just little kids. Police were right on top'; 'No, love, we're all right. Don't worry. It looked worse than it was . . . No, no, everyone's all right . . . Yeah, I'll be back about midnight . . . Yeah, you too'; 'What did it look like on telly? They were nutters.'

The *606* phone-in is still on the radio and Leeds supporters are phoning in to condemn the Cardiff supporters.

'We've got Richard on the line on the M62. You're making good progress, Richard.'

'Couldn't get out of Wales quick enough, Alan. I haven't seen anything like that since the 80s. I thought we were going to get murdered.'

The passengers let out a collective groan and some dark mutterings: 'Who is this knobhead?', 'What did he expect?', 'This is embarrassing'.

'Tell us, Richard, what happened out there today? We have seen the pictures and it looked completely out of control.'

'It were mental! As soon as we got into the ground they were chucking all sorts at us. The police and their stewards just let 'em get on with it. Some of our stewards were pointing out Cardiff fans to the police but they said they couldn't do owt.'

'From the pictures we could see the match officials and Leeds players being showered with missiles. Disgraceful scenes.'

'Alan, there were women and kids with blood all over 'em. We were having to pass little kids over our heads to get 'em out of there. I tell you there were a lot of Leeds fans very scared today.'

'Someone shut this knobhead up.'

'It's a dark day for football, Richard. It seems as though we have taken a giant step backwards.'

'I just want to make one last point, Alan.'

'Go ahead, Richard.'

'During the game all the Cardiff fans were chanting this Istanbul song.'

'Disgraceful. Absolutely sickening. Where do these morons come from?'

'Well, the point I want to make is: are Leeds fans expected to take this kind of treatment every time they visit a third world country?'

It takes a second to sink in and then everybody is laughing: 'Top fella', 'Nice one', 'Welsh bastards'. Some distorted sense of pride is restored.

With half an ear still on the radio the 'old boys' are busy formulating a common position on the day's events. Certain agreed 'truths' emerge:

- Leeds 'turned out' a 'very impressive firm';
- it was the Cardiff City Soul Crew's responsibility to 'get to us' before the game;
- the Cardiff fans who were seen throwing missiles at us and those who were seen on the pitch 'were all little kids';
- the Cardiff fans all 'sang songs' and 'wore Burberry baseball caps', so they could not be 'proper lads';
- the Cardiff fans were not truly intent on 'getting to' the Leeds fans since, if they had been, they could easily have 'steamed' the police lines;
- Leeds fans 'were up for it in the car-park afterwards', but the Cardiff City Soul Crew 'bottled it' and 'didn't show'; and
- on the balance of probabilities, the Leeds 'old boys', even though they were vastly outnumbered, would probably 'have done' the Cardiff

City Soul Crew, who had proved themselves to be 'cowardly', 'young singers', 'bottle-throwers' and 'dog-kickers'.

These 'truths' became more firmly established each time one 'old boy' suggests their plausibility to another 'old boy'. The rate at which these 'truths' are exchanged on the coach can only be described as frantic.

We arrive back at Kings Cross just before closing time. The coach driver says that he has enjoyed himself. Dave lets it be known that the driver will be happy to carry us on future excursions: 'We won't want it all time but could do it for big 'uns.' Everybody seems enthusiastic at the prospect of the London 'old boys' travelling together again: 'Yeah, Man U, Cup games an' that.' As the group disperses a dozen or so of us go to the bar on the concourse of the station for a final drink. The day's 'truths' are affirmed once more. The alcoholic who grabs George around the waist and asks in a slurred voice for the price of a drink has seemingly drunk away his sense of balance for the night. George pushes him backwards. The drunk is trying to tell George what a nice guy he is. All of a sudden the drunk collapses in a noisy heap and everybody in the bar is staring in our direction. Roaring slurred threats of retribution, the old man tries to find his feet. Our group becomes self-consciously uneasy at the attention now being paid to us by the other drinkers in the bar. I think about what has just happened. For the first time today an 'old boy' has struck out, albeit gently, in anger.

Tolerating the 'old boys'

> Tolerance suggests respect for others, a recognition of individual rights, as well as an acceptance of individual difference and social diversity. It is, however, not an expression of benevolence, but rather it embodies a sense of disapproval and implies a degree of suffering or sufferance.
>
> (Hancock and Matthews 2001: 99)

Throughout the 1980s a tiresome ritual was played out at Leeds United's Elland Road ground on match days. Just after the second half kicked off the two girls who worked in the refreshments bar behind the away fans' paddock would be led by stewards to the side of the pitch. From there they would make their way around the perimeter of the pitch to deposit their takings in the office located between the Kop and the West Stand in the northwestern corner of the ground. As they neared the home fans in the Lowfields Road stand the chant would start up: 'Get your tits out for the lads!' All along the stand the singing would get louder. As they reached the northeastern corner of the ground the chant would be taken up by the Boys Pen, as 13-year-old virgins screeched: 'Get your tits out for the lads!' In the final strait the noise reached a peak as the Koppites joined in.

The Lowfields Road stand made way for the 17,000-seat East Stand at the beginning of the 1990s. After spending eight years in the old Second Division Leeds United had been promoted to the old First Division, going on to win it in its final year, and then found itself in the exciting new world of the Premier League. The construction of the imposing new stand seemed in many ways to underscore the club's determination to establish itself firmly in the new elite. The demolition of the Lowfields Road stand was, in hindsight, richly symbolic. It was as if the club was chasing away the ghosts of the 1980s, the hooligan spirits crushed under the weight of the new 'family-friendly' stand. The Lowfields was often a chaotic and lawless place. The away fans and the Leeds fans, separated by metal fences, would engage in a constant exchange of missiles and chanted threats. Occasionally one side or the other would rush the police lines and attempt to 'steam' the opposition. Often, thin crocodile lines of police would attempt to breach the heart of the mayhem. These lines would often dislocate and momentarily disappear as they fell under the pressure of the crowd's surge. The Lowfields Road was where 'Mad Eddie' and a dozen other Leeds fans infiltrated the Millwall supporters and began a refrain of 'He's only a poor little Cockney . . .' The 'old boys' look back fondly on those times and never tire of telling stories about them.

The proliferation in the past ten years of those whom I have characterised as 'old boys' needs to be understood in the context of changes in the regulation of the game itself and also the wider social processes at play. Talk of 'social exclusion' has a particular political currency at present. In invoking the terminology of exclusion, politicians denounce its debilitating effect upon society and promise policies designed to reverse the trend. Within the rhetoric of political debate we are urged to embrace the politics of 'inclusion'. The political project of inclusion filters down into most spheres of social activity. Commentators concerned with football matters have begun to talk about the need to facilitate the greater inclusion of minority groups who have hitherto been excluded from the game. Those who may once have felt uncomfortable attending a football match are encouraged to believe that they are welcome and that the game is now 'safe'. By adopting an intolerant stance, resonating with a wider societal shift towards being more punitive and less forgiving (see Young 1999), the authorities make it clear that violent modes of 'fandom' will be excluded from the modern game. The drive towards greater inclusion, with its implicit threat of exclusion, is most keenly felt in the upper echelons of the game, where the economic rationale for such a cultural shift, in the form of increased attendances at games, corporate sponsorship and so on, is most apparent.

The process of inclusion/exclusion effectively reduces instances of disorder and 'inappropriate' behaviour in and around high-profile and lucrative football fixtures. The 'hooligan' becomes an increasingly exotic bird: he is rarely spotted and speculation as to his near-extinction is rife. However, in the rush to proclaim the death of hooliganism commentators often develop and propagate misunderstandings about the social processes at work. Many conceive the reduction in hooliganism as being affected by the physical weeding-out of 'hooligans'. This perception is facilitated by society's tendency to adopt a criminalising abstraction (see Lea 2002), so that nothing beyond the master-status of the criminal label, in this instance 'hooligan', is considered. There is no space within the abstraction to consider other human qualities and roles, such as 'lover', 'caring', 'bank manager', 'frugal'. By abstracting in such a way lazy and false assumptions are compounded.

The 'old boys' shape their identities as football fans around nostalgic and distorted memories of the 'firm' and the 1980s. They clothe themselves in the uniforms of yesterday's 'heroes', making themselves conspicuous by their choice of fashion labels, in particular their love of all things Stone Island. They 'talk the talk' of battles imminent and past. They bemoan the middle class's appropriation of the modern game. In an inversion of mainstream histories of the game, they perceive the 1980s as a 'golden age'. Yet, for all their posturing, what they do not do is fight. They do not throw bricks, attack policemen or carry knives. All of that would be too 'risky'. Paradoxically, the 'new' regulation of the game allows a comfortable 'space' within which the 'old boys' can gather. The new geography of 'acceptable' and 'unacceptable' behaviour requires cartographers to re-draw the borders of inclusion and exclusion. To emphasise the more punitive and resolute politics of 'inclusion', the borders of toleration and non-toleration are marked with ever darker ink to illustrate 'the closing of the pass' – the thick line between 'in' and 'out'. Somewhat unexpectedly, this 'thick line' draws many to it who once inhabited zones of 'fandom' much further away from the 'battlefield'.

When borders are less easily crossed, when the fears of invasion and confrontation wither, bravado burgeons and memories become hazy: 'I was there and I would do it again . . . if only I had the chance.' The poses adopted by the 'old boys' are unlikely to suffer the rigours of serious interrogation. The Leeds 'old boys' who travelled to Cardiff discovered that even such a seemingly dangerous mission was rendered safe by the exclusionary mechanisms now in place. Prerequisites for the day out included having the 'right' names listed on one's mobile phone; wearing the correct designer labels; and an ability to reproduce the history of 'the good old days'. An ability to engage in physical confrontation was surplus to requirements. The 'safety fence' that keeps the 'old boys' within the tolerated zone of football support can be seen to be bolstered by two processes. First, it is structured by the workings of exclusionary mechanisms: a large physical police presence; the presence of a dedicated intelligence officer ('black Stan'); the use of cameras to record 'faces' and incidents. The second process at work is the calculation of risk by the 'old boys' themselves. To the extent that the 'old boys' believe that the exclusionary mechanisms have been specifically designed to fetter their enjoyment of match days, and that they may ultimately be employed to exclude them from further attendance, the 'old boys' engage in risk calculation. Violent confrontation becomes increasingly unlikely because the exclusionary mechanisms in place reduce substantially the possibility of two groups of opposing fans meeting 'toe to toe'; and the 'old boys' are mindful that to be seen, or filmed, or reported as being involved in violence will almost certainly result in exclusion.

David Lacey, writing in the aftermath of the match day described above (*Guardian*, 12 January 2002), declared that: 'A beast once thought extinct is again on the loose. Hooliganism, the curse of the 70s and 80s, is back.' Lacey's sentiments were typical of many expressed that week. The 'trouble' at Cardiff seemed to take many by surprise. The fact that Manchester United fans had also gone on to the pitch at Villa Park on the same day and that, later in the week, missiles were thrown onto the pitch at the Den and Stamford Bridge, seemed to confirm for many that hooligans had wormed their way back into the game. Lacey's comments were more subtle than most, however. He went on to suggest:

> Not that crowd violence is news in Cardiff, even now. Ninian Park is a land that time forgot, a place where raptors still rule. The low figure of arrests suggested a battle-weary police presence . . . So long as Cardiff City rattled around in the dungeons of the Nationwide League their hooligans were a little local difficulty. It took a high-profile FA Cup tie against a Premiership side to catch the nation's attention.

The behaviour of Cardiff fans is 'tolerated' in a way that is quite distinct from the way in which the behaviour of the Leeds supporters is handled. As Lacey suggests, a culture has been allowed to develop that suffers the excesses of the Cardiff support, however disapprovingly. Very little excessive behaviour is tolerated in the upper reaches of the game. The Cardiff fans who invaded the Ninian Park pitch in their thousands did so with a confidence that startled the Leeds supporters. It seemed incredible to the Leeds fans that so many would engage in behaviour that ultimately risked exclusion from the football domain. However, the fact that only six men were charged with public order offences in connection with the trouble supports the contention that the mechanisms of exclusion at play in the lower divisions are much less severe than in the Premiership.

The Leeds 'old boys' organise themselves in a way that responds to what will and what will not be tolerated. They take a certain amount of pleasure in inverting the rules of officially sanctioned modes of support. They prefer to travel independently and poke fun at official supporters' groups. Large numbers of 'old boys' congregating together in defiant pose often give the impression of mischievous intent. The 'old boys' go through the motions of defying authority, but they go only so far. In embracing the seductions of deviance (see Katz 1988) they never go further than 'safe sex'. Protected by the 'rubber' of careful calculation they perversely enjoy the disapproval of the 'straight fans' and the authorities, but feel confident that their activities fall short of warranting exclusion. Many make the mistake of equating the 'old boys' with the individuals who previously fought in the ranks of the hooligan 'firms'. In some cases they are the same people, but the majority of 'old boys' have little substantive claim to hooligan pasts.

In a late modern society characterised by a decline in tolerance, where old certainties are giving way to widespread feelings of uncertainty, risk and vulnerability (see Giddens 1991; Beck 1992; Young 1999) the 'old boys' adopt what Giddens has termed the 'calculative' attitude. In negotiating the new risks of exclusion they situate themselves in 'safe spaces', close to the gaze of those who might exclude them, and go through tolerated rituals that celebrate a nostalgic affinity to the golden age of hooliganism. They resent the new 'inclusive' world of football because they instinctively sense the disapproval of those now in charge of the game. They make sense of the new threats of exclusion, calculate how best to avoid them and remain determined to enjoy themselves as best they can. Their impotent poses betray a sullen acceptance that things will never be the same as they once were, and that old friends, mobile phones and a repertoire of stories relating to 'the good old days' offer only temporary relief.

5

'With his money, *I* could afford to be depressed': markets, masculinity and mental distress in the English football press[1]

STEPHEN WAGG

In mid-September of 2002, Nigel Miller, a custody sergeant in the Durham Constabulary in the northeast of England, was off work, suffering from stress. He was nevertheless given permission to act as assistant referee in a Premiership football match between Leeds United and Manchester United. The British popular press reacted with some indignation. 'He's not fit to patrol the streets', scoffed an editorial in the *Sun*, ' – but he's perfectly well enough to run the line at the Leeds v Manchester United match. *How much more stress can you get than making split-second judgments on whether Beckham and Co are offside or not?*' (18 September 2002, 8).

This incident defines what seems to be a growing trend: the tendency for the English football press to debate invocations of stress on the part of football people; and that tendency is the central concern of this essay. I am not concerned with mental distress itself, so much as its use as a political motif. My broad argument will be that, as English football has become more governed by free market values and arrangements, its public chroniclers have become impatient with claims to stress on the part of football people. They've preferred to speak the language of competence: in the modern game, men must either shape up or ship out. Mental distress, in this rhetoric, signifies either inefficiency, as with Sgt Miller, or the self-indulgence of a feckless, but highly remunerated, public entertainer. This media scepticism is, I suggest, part of a wider tendency to challenge the notion of mitigating circumstance in an increasingly competitive, 'risk' society. It is not therefore merely the concept of stress that's being challenged, but more fundamental ideas of community which help to underpin Britain's post-Second World War political consensus.

The chapter is organised around two case studies: those of First Division player Kevin Beattie in 1974, and Stan Collymore, a footballer in the English Premiership, during the season of 1999–2000. Once again, it is concerned, first and foremost, to comment on the way contemporary football discourse handles the notion of mental distress – a condition from which both Beattie and Collymore were held to be suffering. These case studies, however, inevitably, raise further questions – about masculinity in relation to football and the media and, in the matter of Collymore, about the accumulated social and political impact of the Premiership itself. The Premiership, I argue here, while generating huge revenue and public interest, has nevertheless failed to establish full legitimacy in the eyes of its public. The market reforms, of which it is a product, have hugely enriched many of the people who run, or play for, Premiership clubs. This, as with similar market reforms in other spheres – the British railways, for example, and other public services – has caused considerable public indignation, but on the whole it has been this indignation, and not the reforms themselves, that has been addressed by the English sports press. Collymore became the unwitting focus of this form of address in February 2000, in what amounted to a minor moral panic about footballers' behaviour. Moreover, during this episode, in a particularly piquant conjunction of events, Stanley Matthews, the symbol *par excellence* of a kinder, gentler, more dignified and humbly rewarded English footballer, died – inviting inescapable comparisons between his time and the present one (see Whannel, 2003). The discourse of the English sports media on these events, I contend, relates directly to the recent market reforms in English football and, indeed, shows something of the impact of market changes on the sports media themselves. These market reforms are, of course, part of a widely acknowledged pattern of economic liberalisation around the world during the last twenty years. This liberalisation, in the opinion of many, has wrought a transition in many societies from 'managed capitalism' to 'disorganised capitalism' (e.g. Dicken, 1986; Hall and Jacques, 1989; Lash and Urry, 1991). I begin by detailing some of the important material changes that English football has undergone and some of their likely social consequences, before moving to discuss contemporary media discussion of footballers and notions of 'stress'.

New times? Football, fame and wealth

English football, it can safely be said, entered on a new era in the 1990s. This era, symbolised of course by the inauguration of the FA Premiership in 1992, has a number of important defining features. Stewardship of many clubs has passed to representatives of national or international, rather than local, capital. Through the involvement of satellite television, TV spectators now hugely outnumber those paying to watch a game 'live', and most of the latter category part with between £20 and £30 per game to see Premiership teams play in all-seater stadia. Football, in England and elsewhere, has been consecrated as a commodity, giving rise to a commercial sub-sector of specialist advice on football finance, and in March 2000, England's most prosperous club, Manchester United, was valued at £1 billion (Cassy, 2000). Most importantly in the present context, the higher echelons of the English football world over the final two decades of the twentieth century actively relinquished the notion that 'the strong must help the weak'. This ethos, which had inscribed much of the English League's history until the last quarter of the twentieth century (Taylor, 1999: 248–77) and, indeed, the history of other leading English sports (Vamplew, 1988: 112–53), was progressively dismantled in the 1980s. Moreover it was a threat by leading clubs to break away from the Football League that helped bring the Premiership into being (Goldberg and Wagg, 1991). The massive commercialisation of the game worldwide has led to a crop of books variously concerned to ponder what happened to 'the people's game' (see for example Horton, 1995; Sugden and Tomlinson, 1998; 1999; Yallop, 1999) and how some vestige of it might be salvaged (Brown and Walsh, 1999). As I noted in Chapter 1, the leading member of the country's growing cadre of football academics recently pronounced: 'Finishing positions in the F.A. Premier League now largely reflect who is paying what and to whom. High payers finish first; low salary bills usually mean relegation' (Williams, 1999: 66). These salaries, when measured against the national average and against British football's own not too distant past, are very high indeed. The weekly income from playing alone of Manchester United captain Roy Keane is widely accepted to be around £52,000 per week, double and probably treble what most of the club's followers might earn in a year – or, in some cases, given United's global 'fan base', a lifetime. Keane is currently the highest paid player in the Premiership, but most clubs in this division now have a cluster of million-aires among their playing staff. Top footballers are celebrities of some long standing, but their celebrity rests increasingly not only on their expertise, but on their public visibility and their wealth. As celebrities, they are now often to be found in gossip columns and in journals dedicated to exploring 'lifestyles of the rich and famous', and thus have become part of a discourse and a pattern of consumption that historically has mixed rever-ence and resentment in equal parts. There are, in principle, equal markets for news of the pleasures of celebrities (parties, cars, soft furnishings) and of their pain or inadequacy (drugs, divorce). For instance, awe-struck media commentary on the skill, wealth and domesticity of England foot-baller David Beckham goes hand in hand with a proliferation of jokes about his, and his wife's, supposed intellectual shortcomings. The *Daily Mail*'s 'Night and day' supplement, for instance, recently offered a collec-tion of these. Sample: 'Q. How do you make Posh and Becks laugh on

Friday? A. Tell them a joke on Tuesday' ('Night and day', supplement to *Daily Mail*, 13 February 2000: 43).

Free markets and mental distress

The principal point I want to make here is that the proliferation of economic liberalism has helped to generate a new political framing of mental distress. In 'managed' capitalist societies, where certain levels of state responsibility for the mentally ill were taken for granted, radical challenges to the consensually agreed medical provision were often made from a libertarian position. R. D. Laing, Thomas Szasz, Erving Goffman and others variously opposed the prescriptions of mainstream psychiatry and called for the emancipation of distressed individuals. In more recent times, amid rhetorical invocations of greater 'individual responsibility' and political policies to promote 'care in the community' for the mentally ill, the field of mental health has become more exposed to market philosophies and disciplines. In practice social class has become a greater factor in the addressing of mental distress, with better off patients often seeking help from among a growing diversity of treatments and receiving it on a private, fee-for-service basis. For the poorer sections of society, professional and institutional help has become sparse, with neo-liberal administrations borrowing freely from the radical precepts of the 1960s in justification (see Sedgwick, 1982 for a full account). In public commentary, meanwhile, the very notion of mental distress itself has often been on trial. One of the most notable instances here was the trial of Peter Sutcliffe, the so-called 'Yorkshire Ripper', in 1981. That Sutcliffe had committed the killings of which he was accused was not in doubt. Contention in court was wholly concerned with whether he was 'mad or bad'. The prosecution, led by the Conservative government's Attorney General, successfully established, against unanimous medical judgement, that he was bad (Ward Jouve, 1988: 34; see also Burn, 1984). Such a verdict, delivered on an apparently deranged lorry driver in defiance of the copious testimony of mental health professionals, illustrated the difficulty now in showing that a working-class wrongdoer was mentally ill. Moreover, if there was diminishing recognition for *psych*osis – in effect, living in another world – even less sympathy could now be expected for those claimed to be suffering from *neur*osis – that is, difficulties living in this one. In contemporary societies, steeped increasingly in free-market doctrines, the idea of neurotic mental illness can be easily waved away, along with any other purportedly extenuating circumstance. In May 2000 a US county prosecutor reflected on the recent execution of a young woman:

She claims she was horribly depressed, she was overweight and she was a single mom, and she didn't have enough money. My response to that is 'Welcome to America'. Plenty of folks are in far worse situations than she was.

(Borger, 2000: 14)

In the public discourse of contemporary industrial societies – discourse that is increasingly influenced by the popular, and the not so popular, press – two important and linked assumptions can now be discerned. First, that mental illness, of dubious validity in any event, is 'no excuse' when someone does wrong and, second, that mental distress, given its sharpened class dimension, is often no more than the self-preoccupation of the rich. This distorted rendering of a class reality invites the angry cry: '*We* could afford to be depressed with *his* money'.

Football, mental distress and the English sports pages

Mental anguish, while not the most recurrent theme in the discourse of the English football press, has nevertheless become part of the taken-for-granted culture which national football reporters have trawled for stories. In the great majority of cases, however, reportage in this area has concerned footballers who grappled unsuccessfully with the problems of wealth, celebrity and excess. Since the mid-1960s prominent British footballers including George Best, Jimmy Greaves, Paul Gascoigne, Tony Adams and Paul Merson have all made public their addictions – in particular, to alcohol. Mental distress here then, has been linked to a specific problem – addictions – and, in general, it's worth noting, these addictions – be they to drink, drugs or gambling – have drawn more sympathy than reproof from the press corps. Moreover, both Adams and Merson produced redemptive memoirs in collaboration with *Observer* football writer Ian Ridley (Adams and Ridley, 1998; Merson and Ridley, 1999). However, if a footballer has been diagnosed as suffering from depression – to the lay person an altogether more ephemeral condition – press response is likely to be more mistrustful.

This, I suggest, is at least partly because problems of addiction can be seen, regardless of the their psychological complexity, essentially as matters of *consumption*. They belong therefore to the realm of the personal, and the personal difficulties of the rich and famous, as any journalist knows, offer vicarious pleasures to a variety of readers. But, ironically, the less definable condition of depression may have greater implications for the public world of employment. If, as a result of depression, someone is falling out with colleagues, questioning managerial

for the second half. His motive – that, among other things, he has been upset by barracking from sections of the crowd – strays into the same territory as that occupied for the previous four days by Kevin Beattie. The football world – managers and press alike – will tolerate no further talk of 'stress'. In the *Daily Mail* (21 December) Weller's manager Jimmy Bloomfield states: 'There is no excuse for this as far as I'm concerned. I think it's a disgrace'. (Elsewhere in the same issue there is a further re-evaluation of the Beattie affair: 'Well, just how much does a new baby affect a star footballer's form?'.) In the *Sun* on the same day Bob Wilson asks gravely whether Beattie might not 'crack again' in a World Cup or European Championship game, while the *Daily Mail* on Christmas Eve has Norwich City manager John Bond calling for Weller to be blacklisted by Football League clubs.

On 23 December the *Daily Express* has what appears to be the final feature on Beattie's troubles. Out walking his dog after dark, Beattie has been stopped by a man who, Beattie assumes, wants to wish him a happy Christmas. Instead the man says bluntly: 'Beattie, you're chicken'.

From the Beattie incident we can note the following. To a football world still attuning to the wealth and celebrity that the abolition of the maximum wage (in 1961) and increased television coverage have brought, signs of mental distress in a leading footballer receive, initially, a tentative response. But, quite rapidly, the definers of the event cease talking about a distressed individual and begin to describe a weak one. The duties of the 'model professional' in the modern football market are reasserted and this reassertion draws on notions of a masculinity unpolluted by emotion. Real men absorb the pressures, turn up for training on time and do as they are told. They do not 'crack'. No official medical label has been attached to Beattie, the club doctor having passed him as fit, so the question of treatment does not arise. When he (and Weller) have been reproved, the incident is forgotten – it merits only two short paragraphs in Beattie's autobiography, published in 1998 (Beattie, 1998).

Mad, bad or sad? The Stan Collymore affair

By 1999 Stan Collymore, who turned twenty-nine in that year, had a long established reputation in the English football world both as a gifted footballer (three games for England, the first in 1995) and as a troublemaker. A native of England's Black Country in the northwest Midlands, he was rejected as a teenager by local League clubs Walsall and Wolverhampton before making his name with non-League Stafford Rangers. Success there brought him into the League at Crystal Palace and subsequently Southend before Nottingham Forest paid £2 million for him in 1994. After two seasons at Forest he moved to Liverpool for a further £8.5 million. In 1997, having, among other things, refused to play for the club's reserve team or to move to the Liverpool area, he transferred, for another large fee (£7.5m) to the Birmingham club Aston Villa, the club he had followed as a boy. His performances for Villa were generally accepted to be disappointing.

The apparently mild-mannered Collymore, defined by many coaches as 'difficult' since his youth, had often been at the centre of controversy. During the early 1990s he had variously fallen out with team-mates, defied managers and been involved in scuffles in nightclubs. Some of the incidents in which he had been involved were said to have had a racial dimension: Collymore, who is black, had been said to have reacted to racial insults. Little, however, was ever made of this. Now, in February 1998, he accused his former teammate, the Liverpool player Steve Harkness, of racially abusing him. Twice in the spring and summer of that year he was publicly accused of physically assaulting girlfriends. In July the sportswear firm Diadora withdrew £1.2 million sponsorship of the player when he was seen, tactlessly, to be wearing Nike trainers. In November he was sent off during a match against Liverpool after a violent tackle on Harkness. In January 1999 he failed to show up for a Villa game and was admitted to the Priory clinic in southwest London. I want now to detail the press coverage of Collymore's difficulties and related matters during 1999. To do so I will draw on the sports pages of the *Guardian* and the *Observer*. The *Guardian* is one of four major 'quality' daily newspapers in England and, along with the *Independent*, the most liberal on social questions. The *Observer* is its broad equivalent in the Sunday press. The *Guardian*, it should be remembered, had given the Beattie incident minimal and exclusively factual reportage back in 1974.

On 25 January 1999, *Guardian* football columnist Martin Thorpe reports a forthcoming showdown between Collymore and Villa manager John Gregory, following Collymore's refusal to accept a place on the substitute's bench. The player's agent has suggested that the 'decision not to play was prompted by illness but Gregory has discounted this and is treating the case as one of insubordination'. The basis for this judgement is not made clear, but Gregory nevertheless asserts: 'I've supported Stan since he joined this club. I wanted to find out myself about him as opposed to listening to all the stories.'

Two days later, with the definition of Collymore as 'ill' now introduced into the discourse, Paul Weaver in the same paper mockingly confronts the notion of footballers in mental distress:

> With the weary hope that the players concerned are not otherwise engaged with their shrinks or wriggling in strait-jackets in the local giggle house, with the wistful dream that the 22 footballers might keep hold of their marbles for at least 90 minutes, I plan to attend a Premiership football match on Saturday.

Weaver then lists a number of leading sportsmen who have been diagnosed recently as suffering from stress-related illness, but insists that 'sometimes it is difficult to muster any sympathy' and alludes to 'a general feeling that such players need a hefty kick up the backside'. Despite then quoting a sport psychologist and a stress counsellor, both of whom are more willing than he is to acknowledge the existence of stress (and who 'make much sense'), Weaver prefers to invoke the memory of autocratic club manager Brian Clough, retired since the mid-1990s. What Collymore needs, insists Weaver, is some of Clough's 'brutal and sometimes witty pragmatism'.

On 29 January, again in the *Guardian*, Niall Quinn, himself a Premiership footballer, addresses the issue:

> Two weeks ago in this space I gave what some people described as a robust defence of professional footballers. I stand by what I said then concerning players, their environment and their wages. ... [but] a tiny fraction of footballers can make it difficult for the vast majority and this week Stan Collymore has been making things very difficult indeed.

Quinn remembers Collymore's last game for Crystal Palace, in which, he acknowledges, Stan took some 'serious abuse from Palace fans and reacted with an ugly gesture'. Here, Quinn had thought, 'was a boy with problems'. But these problems, Quinn made clear, lay not with the abusers, but with Collymore himself, who 'has a major chip on his shoulder'.

By the end of January, then, on the sport pages of the English broadsheet press, a perceptible bandwagon about arrogant and self-indulgent footballers seeking to dignify their bad behaviour with medical labels has begun to roll. Collymore's club manager, John Gregory (a primary definer of the player's situation throughout) has given the affair an explicit social class dimension: 'Stressed out? Try telling that to a 29-year old at somewhere like Rochdale with three months left on his contract, a wife, three kids and a mortgage' (Ridley, 1999). In the *Observer*, football writer Ian Ridley, collaborator on the autobiographies of two recovering-addict footballers, now leads for the defence. Collymore, he says, though wealthy and gifted, is a loner prone to surfing the internet and weeping when he tries to discuss his problems: he suffers from low self-esteem. Maybe, suggests Ridley, clubs should think of appointing counsellors and relinquish their 'old-fashioned macho ideas about trick cyclists' (Ridley, 1999). In an adjacent column, Wimbledon player Robbie Earle is of the same view:

> As it is, Villa may have to sell Stan at a knockdown price and then spend millions replacing him – all money which might have been saved by employing a stress counsellor, as other big companies do.

This, of course, is a market rationale for recognising mental distress, but Earle, significantly one of the few black voices heard in the Collymore furore, also contests the dominant depiction of Stan as a man:

> I have met him a few times off the field and he has always struck me as quiet and deep-thinking. ... Perhaps coming into the professional game later in life makes a difference, too. If you have grown up in a football environment it makes it easier to deal with the dressing room banter and realise that when others make fun of you they mean no harm. It is not unlike the army.
>
> (Earle, 1999)

On 6 February the *Guardian* reports further reflections by Gregory on Collymore, now receiving treatment in a clinic: 'I do not know if he is coming back and in all honesty I do not care. How many more chances do I have to give Stan?'

The following day, on the correspondence page of the *Observer*, a week on from the articles by Ridley and Earle, there is little endorsement of their view that someone in Collymore's predicament needs counselling. 'In the crowd at Villa', writes Mike Turner from Stockton-on-Tees, 'there will be those with bigger personal problems than him and no £20,000 a week to pay for private treatment. Surely your article should have told Collymore to get out on the pitch and use his extraordinary talent to bring a shining light to the lives of less fortunate individuals'. Similarly, Graham Rea of the Birmingham district of Yardley, argues that it's 'difficult enough for some to put together the price of admission for themselves and their family without being lectured on the difficulties of existing on £20,000 per week' (*Observer*, 7 February 1999, 13).

Toward the end of March, Gregory seems to confirm privately to reporters that Collymore is finished at Aston Villa: 'there are suggestions that Gregory has totally run out of patience with Collymore and that the former England striker's contract will be cancelled in the summer'. On the record, however, Gregory states that the player 'needs full-time treatment to overcome a difficult problem' (*Guardian*, 25 March 1999, 28). (It might be noted that much of the, often populist, discourse to which both the Beattie and Collymore incidents gave rise, are ambiguous in this crucial respect: the problem of stress is simultaneously recognised and denied.)

In July the *Guardian* returns to the general issue of public mental distress with a feature on private clinics. The article is jaunty in tone and focuses on Roehampton Priory, styled here as 'an exclusive bolt-hole' for celebrities. 'In return for £3,000 a week, usually for several weeks, the Priory has chased their demons for them'. Here the staff outnumber the patients and the car park is full of 'jeeps and BMWs' (Beckett, 1999).

On 20 July the *Guardian* reports that Gregory has despatched Collymore on loan to the First Division club Fulham, sending him on his way with more angry words:

> I know he was suffering from clinical depression last season but the day after the season finished he checked out of the clinic where he was receiving treatment and went on holiday. I understand he has fully recovered but, if he hasn't, then he should pack the game in.

Fulham, football reporters Peter White and Jon Brodkin remind readers, is in southwest London – 'Helpfully the Priory clinic is nearby'.

In early November, Peter White writes in the *Observer* that, improbably, 'Aston Villa outcast Stan Collymore has declared that he is prepared to withstand the barrage of criticism he has been subjected to by his manager John Gregory and will fight to re-establish himself at the club'. 'The bottom line', insists Collymore, 'is I want to play for this club more than I have ever done' (White, 1999). By the end of the year, however, Gregory, despite a serious injury to his main striker Dion Dublin, has shown no sign of relenting. In the *Guardian*, White quotes Collymore thus: 'I feel physically and mentally fit to play in the top flight, and I know I could make a difference. ... The manager has decided not to take up this option and I find that very baffling' (24 December).

In early February 2000, Stan Collymore signs for the Premiership club Leicester City. Leicester agree to part with what is, by the standards of the contemporary transfer market, a minimal sum: £500,000, payable only after Collymore has played fifty games for Leicester. On 12 February he plays his first, away to Watford. Next day, Alan Smith, formerly assistant manager at Crystal Palace when Collymore played there, observes that mental distress makes for a precarious investment:

> Stan Collymore's state of mind has been the subject of great debate over the past year or so, and it amazes me that more clubs do not ...

check out a player's mental as well as physical health before they sign him.

As for the player himself, views

> about him tend to be polarised, that he is either an ultra-sensitive soul who needs love and affection, or that he is simply mad. I would suggest that the truth is somewhere in between, and part of the problem is that he is insecure and none too bright.
>
> (Smith, 2000)

On Monday 14 February, in the *Guardian*, Jeremy Alexander's match report of Collymore's Leicester debut maintains his newspaper's tone of mockery and unelaborated scepticism. Most of his eleven column inches are devoted to Collymore, on the ground that 'as a main attraction the game could have driven strong men into clinics'. Although Collymore has played quite well, he is dismissed as 'a charmer who can strike with either foot and both personalities' and he 'remains a conundrum wrapped in contradiction and stuffed with scrambled ego'.

After the Watford game, the Leicester first team squad fly to the Spanish resort of La Manga for a brief training holiday.

Stan Collymore: folk devil and moral panic

On the evening of 16 February, prime-time news bulletins of all the major television channels in England carry an item about the expulsion of the Leicester City party from their Spanish hotel. Players and coaching staff have been accused by the hotel management of misbehaviour and have flown back to Leicester. They are shown, half illuminated by press lights, driving solemnly past a contingent of reporters and into the night.

On the morning of 17 February all the sports pages of the major English daily newspapers lead with stories of this incident. The coverage of the episode is extensive, especially in the tabloid press: the *Sun*, the *Mirror* and the *Daily Star* devote six pages to it, the *Daily Express* four and the *Daily Mail* three.

Three – the *Daily Star*, the *Mirror* and the *Sun* – lead with it on their front pages. Across the papers, while there are predictable differences of presentation and the use of language, there is nevertheless a degree of unanimity. All the papers carry quite detailed accounts of the Leicester players' behaviour, based on the testimony of the managing director of the complex from which the Leicester party have been evicted, and of disgruntled hotel guests, but also of Collymore himself. There is an acknowledgement that Leicester players have been drinking, become rowdy and annoyed other guests. The hotel's managing director told the *Guardian*:

> They were insulting and rude to people, asking ladies to dance who didn't want to and being obnoxious. Around a dozen of them were drinking for several hours and they became increasingly loud and drunk. They were jumping on chairs and tables and being generally unruly, upsetting a lot of our other clients.
>
> (p. 34)

At the end of these disturbances, a fire extinguisher has been let off, on his own admission, by Collymore.

Three things are important to note about the press treatment here.

First, in spite of the acceptance, common to all press accounts of the matter, that up to a dozen Leicester players were involved in the disturbances, Collymore's name is the organising focus of every story. He features, for example, in virtually every headline: *The Times* refers to 'Collymore and team sent home in disgrace'; the *Sun* has 'COLLY RUNS RIOT'; the *Daily Star* says 'Colly's a wally on new team's jolly'; the *Mirror* tells of 'COLLY'S SHAME'; the *Daily Express* laboriously parodies a song from *Mary Poppins*: 'SUPER COLLY'S FRANTIC ANTIC, ISN'T HE ATROCIOUS?'; while the *Guardian* speculates on the player's possible dismissal with 'Collymore's career in the balance'.

In all papers likewise the bulk of the narrative and quoted testimony concerns Collymore. Here the managing director of the hotel complex, Tony Coles, is primary definer. In regard to the fire extinguisher, Mr Coles assures the *Independent* that there is 'absolutely no doubt' that Collymore let it off. To the *Daily Express* he insists 'Collymore set off the fire extinguisher. He was at the centre of the disturbance', and to the *Sun* Mr Coles states: 'Collymore lived up to his controversial reputation by grabbing a fire extinguisher and letting it off'. (The same paper prints the headline 'YOU MORON, COLLY' paradoxically above a large picture of another Leicester player, Gerry Taggart, apparently drunk with three £20 notes stuck to his face – pp. 4–5.) In the *Mirror*, Richard Pillow, a businessman staying at the La Manga hotel, testifies: 'I always thought Stan Collymore was misunderstood. After what I saw last night, I realise he obviously is not. He behaved like an animal'. An unidentified female guest told the *Sun*: 'Collymore and some of the younger players were chatting up some girls. The atmosphere was all very friendly until Collymore went mental'. The following day (18 February) the *Daily Star* on its front page accuses the Leicester players of drinking more in a night than the players of

Norwegian club Rosenborg (also staying at the hotel) drink in a year. Again, no other individual players are accused; instead they are styled collectively as 'Collymorons'. And so on.

Second, the affair is widely depicted as an affray: 'Drunk yob [Collymore] trashes bar' in the *Sun*; the *Daily Star* reports a 'booze brawl'; the *Guardian* and the *Daily Telegraph* quote Coles – 'It was a shameful spectacle, a bunch of well paid professionals having too much to drink and behaving like hooligans'; the *Mirror* and the *Daily Express* both write of a 'drunken rampage'; and the *Daily Mail* tells of a 'drunken fracas'. In the *Guardian*, Daniel Taylor suggests that the discharged fire extinguisher covered forty guests with foam. On the 18th, as other papers are beginning to relax their extravagant use of imagery, and elsewhere in their pages Collymore claims to have squirted only one person (the Leicester City physiotherapist), the *Daily Star* is still compounding the indictment: 'Leicester's sick soccer louts joked about the drunken rampage that got them kicked out of a top Spanish hotel, it was revealed last night'.

Third, in virtually all the press commentary on this event an explicit link is drawn between the class position of top footballers and what is held to be a crisis in public confidence about their behaviour. Collymore, suggests James Lawton, chief sports writer on the *Daily Express*, 'has come to represent all the weaknesses, the betrayals and the self-indulgences of today's superstar football'. In the *Sun*, John Sadler describes Leicester supporters queuing 'in bitter cold – some in blankets' to buy tickets for the club's forthcoming Worthington Cup Final. 'The shameful outcome' continues Sadler,

> of an epidemic of indiscipline in the English game – this time reaching its dreaded height when a certain Stan Collymore let off a fire extinguisher that had hotel guests running for the exit. It is fast becoming apparent that there are high-profile and handsomely-paid players who are unworthy of the people who idolise them.

The *Daily Mail*, is, ironically, the only paper to try to understand Collymore's behaviour, but this is nevertheless in the context of four pages, the theme of which is 'THE SHAME GAME'. Thus, on page 94 Ian Ladyman writes of an 'insecure Collymore' acting out of 'a childlike desire to ingratiate himself with one of the most close-knit dressing rooms in Premiership football' – making the player briefly a social actor rather than a folk devil. And on page 95 John Greechan gives further context by citing a number of similar escapades from post-war British football history. But this is within a contrary paradigm of disgrace, brought by the 'antics of the Premiership's millionaire stars' (p. 93). Moreover, while the *Mail*, historically hostile to such explanations, treats briefly with the possibility of extenuating social circumstance, the *Guardian*, the favoured paper of the liberal professions, sternly repudiates such notions. Here Jim White writes:

> Condoned, excuses made, blame apportioned elsewhere: it is the daily diet of the modern footballer. Football has been overrun by a bastardised form of Californian regression therapy. There is no need to take responsibility for your own actions because it is always someone else's fault: referees, opponents, the media.

Later on the 17th of February, in the *Leicester Mercury*, the local evening paper, it is said that Leicester City have 'pledged action'. A press conference is held at which Collymore apologises, and it is announced that he has been fined £35,000 and warned as to his future conduct. Expenses and hotel repair bills have been met by the players. Some Leicester folk, however, remain unimpressed by the furore. 'They should just leave the guy alone and let him talk with his feet. I hope they enjoyed their night', says thirty-five year old Pat James, a black man living in the city. 'Everyone does it, it's just lads when they're together', suggests Jenny Blackwell (eighteen), also of Leicester (*Leicester Mercury*, 17 February 2000, 58).

On Sunday 5 March, the tabloid *News of the World* on its front page accuses Collymore of a further bar brawl, this time at a hotel in Buckinghamshire. For Collymore, who has been warned by Leicester about his future conduct, this seems to imply dismissal. However, there is no response from the rest of the press and no more is said of this latter incident.

Collymore himself appears on BBC television's *Football Focus* programme on 18 March, where he is interviewed sympathetically by black ex-professional footballer Mark Bright. In the programme Collymore strives to explain depression: 'I think that we confuse depression with feeling down ... but this was an illness that got me to the brink'. If he hadn't sought help, 'there's a good chance I wouldn't have been here now'. The studio discussion which follows the interview, however, maintains a discourse in which the idea of mental distress ultimately cannot be accommodated. BBC pundit Mark Lawrenson, while appearing to acknowledge his own ignorance in the matter ('Only he knows what he's been through') nevertheless counter-defines Collymore as faint-hearted: 'There are that many footballers out in the country that haven't half his ability, but have got more than his application. And it's the application, now, that he has to show'. Ultimately, for Lawrenson, as in virtually the entire press commentary on the affair, Collymore is simply an inefficient performer in the football market: 'I don't think he was ill at Liverpool and, for me, he didn't produce there'.

Another fine mess: the symbolic destruction of Stan Collymore

The 'Collymore Affair' was instructive, in a number of ways. In this conclusion, I want briefly to outline the issues that it raises.

First, the episode represents a show of strength by the English football press. This press – and the sports press generally – operate in a growing and increasingly competitive market. By early 2000 several national daily newspapers were producing stand-alone sports supplements and the English press was collectively disgorging 400,000 words in a single weekend on sport (Buckley, 2000). Football will account for a consider-able portion of these words, but, in football discourse, competition is especially fierce. By the middle of any week in the football season, Premiership matches have been shown and/or described by broadcasters and the reflections of many of the protagonists made public. Further infor-mation about the Premiership clubs is provided, and renewed daily via teletext, club-call telephone lines and websites, both official and indepen-dent, and messages to mobile phones. Then there are the fanzines, specialist football periodicals and television magazine programmes. The press, therefore, as in other areas, falls back increasingly on *comment*. This comment is designed, at least in part, to provoke a reaction from the read-ership, via correspondence pages and telephone lines. The *Mirror*, for instance, invited readers to 'VOTE NOW FOR BRITAIN'S MOST STUPID FOOTBALLER', offering two phone lines – one for Collymore and one for England player Paul Gascoigne. Moreover, the press enjoys far greater scope for extravagant denunciation than broadcasters, who are ordinarily required to observe balance in their reporting. This means the press may often lead the way in defining an event or an individual, with other media, governing bodies and the like agreeing to be bound by their definition. For example, in January 1999 the then England team manager Glenn Hoddle was widely condemned in the football press for apparently suggesting that disabled people might be paying, through their disable-ment, for mistakes in a past life. His comments had first been made in a radio programme some months earlier and had provoked no response. However, when they were effectively re-stated in *The Times* (30 January) Hoddle was immediately denounced by the football press. Mainstream broadcasters reported the furore and Margaret Hodge, Minister for the Disabled, was among those calling for Hoddle to resign. In the *Guardian* (1 February) Jim White dismissed Hoddle's claims that he'd been misinterpreted. This, argued White, was merely a symptom of the 'Don't Blame Me' syndrome' – a syndrome he would later invoke in the Collymore episode. Hoddle quit his job the next day.

These minor moral panics – or 'feeding frenzies' as they are colloquially known – reassert the power of the press as crucial definers of football matters; football people and their affairs, it is implied, are essentially *texts*, ready to be skewed, this way or that. This acts as a discipline on football institutions, reminding them of the ever-present need for 'good publicity'.

Second, once the press campaign has been transacted, Collymore's principal offence becomes defined: it is to have brought bad publicity to his football club, allowing him, and them, to become negative texts. Specifically, he has allowed the press to remind the public how wealthy footballers are, and a recurrent press image of the reckless rich of the Premiership betraying their noble, self-denying supporters has been enhanced. In the wake of a press conference in which apologies and tough punishments are proffered, Leicester City place a press statement on their official website:

> Our players wish to make it clear that they fully recognise and appreciate the commitment and magnificent support from our fans through the season, particularly in recent days when many fans have had to make sacrifices to obtain Wembley tickets. The players realise they have let down supporters and the club and wish to make a full and unreserved apology.
>
> (http://www.lcfc.co.uk)

The following week the club arranges for Collymore to meet Chris Wheeler, a teenage Leicester supporter who has a brain tumour. 'Stan is a really nice bloke', Chris tells the *Leicester Mercury*, 'He is very down-to-earth, and I could talk to him like he is one of my friends' (23 February 2000). Thus a paradigm for discussing the Premiership is reinforced. In this paradigm the issue of the structure of individual reward and the issue of the personal behaviour of those individuals become merged. The (perfectly tenable) argument that these are *separate* issues is implicitly denied. Class relations here are taken as given; the sole issue is how they should be managed.

Third, taking the press treatment of Collymore over a period of a year or so, he becomes trapped in a formidable double bind, half acknowledged in a couple of the newspapers. Initially condemned when he does not accept the boisterous, masculine mores of the dressing room, he is later condemned, with added vehemence, when he does. The discourse of both the Beattie incident and the Collymore saga shows a football world increasingly impatient with talk of mental distress and the medicalisation of social difficulty. The men of the modern professionalised and highly remunerated football world have got to do what they have got to do. Talk of stress threatens the efficiency and the legitimacy of the whole enterprise. When Collymore claims to be suffering from clinical depression, his manager, while agreeing to treatment for the player, ultimately rebuts this definition. Collymore cannot be depressed, he says, because he has talent, fame and wealth; men with fewer advantages – who play for Rochdale, perhaps – *they* might be depressed. To claim depression, in this context, is to deny individual responsibility, and this in part explains the strength of the subsequent condemnation of Collymore. When Collymore is defined as mentally distressed, the sports press collude in the general scepticism of the football world. There are jokes about 'scrambled ego' and the smart motors in the clinic car park. Later, when Collymore suggests that the fire extinguisher incident, though regrettable, has been exaggerated and, thus, makes a second plea for sympathy, the sports press, in general, remain unfeminised and unforgiving. We told you so, they insist; we said he was bad, not mad.

Finally, this market-driven populism, it should be noted, now appears increasingly to characterise the English sports press as a whole. While, as a recent article in the *Observer* noted, to 'dole out "SHAME" and "DISGRACE" in 124-point block capital letters is the lot of tabloid editors' (Arlidge, 2000), the sports pages of the contemporary broadsheet press are now no less dismissive of socially contextualised explanations. On the contrary, the *Guardian*, an historically liberal paper, whose football reporters showed little interest in the Beattie affair of 1974, maintained a scepticism about Collymore's depression throughout and, after the hotel incident, led the condemnation of 'spoiled brats' (White, 2000).

English football has become, via modern mass communications, one of the most visible forms of work in the world. The terms under which people work in the English football industry, and the vocabulary with which their work is described domestically, are increasingly those of the free market. This vocabulary finds no place for mental distress, the symptoms of which are instead generally seen as signifying self-indulgence and lack of moral fibre. A sports press visibly dubious in the 1970s has, in the late 1990s, become openly derisive of those who can't cope. Thus, through football discourse, mental illness itself is called into question and other workers are taught the disciplines of the market – for example a *Guardian* editorial told the teachers' unions that 'Performance pay has not hurt Manchester United' (22 April 2000).

To adapt Euripides, those whom the modern sports press wish to destroy, they first insist are perfectly sane.

Note

1 For help in collecting material for this essay I'd like to thank Ian Bent, Galfrid Congreve, Adrian Goldberg, Peter Golding, Alec McAulay, Anne Wagg, Cassie Wagg and Roy Williams. Thanks to Paul Norcross, Steven Groarke and Paul Daniel for commenting on drafts of this chapter. An earlier version appeared in *Football Studies*, 3/2, 2000, 67–87.

6

Still a man's game? Women footballers, personal experience and tabloid myth

JOHN HARRIS

Introduction

The following chapter explores two dimensions of the relationship between women and football. First, drawing upon extensive ethnographic research, I examine the experiences of a women's collegiate team in the south of England. In relation to social exclusion I address a number of issues relating to equity and equality within the sport and highlight how the women have had to battle hard in order to be recognised as footballers. I then focus on the image of the game and the perceived link between lesbianism and women's football, as this was by far the strongest theme to emerge in the primary research, and was the most important issue to the women themselves.

The second part of the chapter looks at the relationship between women and football as portrayed in the English tabloid press. Here, the highly sexualised and subordinate role of females in relation to sport is critically assessed. Sport, and particularly football, is delineated as an exclusively male domain where idealised conceptualisations of hegemonic masculinity are promoted and celebrated. This study moves beyond the sports pages and also examines the wider picture through an analysis of the portrayal of women and football in the main body of the newspaper text.

Sport within many cultures is a strictly male affair where women are largely marginalised and/or excluded. Organised sport, as we know it, emerged, to a large extent, as a masculinist response to a crisis in the gender order of the late nineteenth and early twentieth century. Sports such as football became significant for a number of males as a retreat from what was perceived as a 'feminised' modern culture, and served to bolster a sagging ideology of male supremacy (Messner 1992). Sport is arguably civilised society's most prominent masculinity rite, and is viewed as an arena chracterised by conformity and control, deference to male authority, pain and social isolation (Sabo and Panepinto 1990)

The paucity of coverage afforded to women's sport stems from the widely held belief that sport is just for men (see Hall 1996; Hargreaves 1994; Lenskyj 1986; Messner 1992; Messner and Sabo 1990). Centuries of discrimination, shaped by the cultures and beliefs of a number of societies, have deemed it 'unladylike' for women to partake in numerous physical activities. Sport is a microcosm of society, and sporting success is still largely equated with masculinity. Whilst sporting success for men reinforces and promotes masculinity, women who achieve in sport are perceived to have failed as women because in certain profound symbolic ways they are deemed to have 'become' men (Willis 1982: 123). Few other sports are as protected and 'valued' as football, with its exalted position within English culture.

Football is, without doubt, the national game for most parts of Britain. Hopcraft (1968: 9) suggested that 'it is inherent in the people', and that it should be viewed not as a phenomenon but an everyday matter. The football world is viewed as a place where boys become men, and is characterised by its almost exclusive maleness (see Hornby 1992; Mason 1980; Morris 1981; Tomlinson 1995). Given its global appeal, it is also something verging on a universal language (see Horton 1995; Sugden and Tomlinson 1998; Wagg 1995). Recent years have seen an increase in the number of girls and women playing football (Cox and Thompson 2000; Lopez 1997; Sports Council for Wales 1995). It has also been suggested that there has been an increase in women spectators at professional football matches in England (Coddington 1997). Women's football, like many other sports played by females, receives very little media attention and continues to be a marginalised activity within the media. In spite of continued opposition, and the suggestion that women's football is a game suitable only for lesbians or 'butch' females (see Caudwell 1999), the game has made sound progress over the past decade. This is most vividly highlighted by the words often quoted in connection with FIFA's (Federation Internationale de Football Association) promotion of women's football, that 'the future is feminine'. The popularity of the game today is evidenced by the fact that an estimated 30 million females world-wide now play the sport (Cox and Thompson 2000).

The work presented in the first part of this chapter forms part of a doctoral study undertaken to provide an insight into the world of female, collegiate football players (Harris 1998). The data for the doctoral study was collected over a period of two years and involved extensive field observations coupled with in-depth semi-structured interviews. An interpretive approach was adopted, as it was thought that this provided the opportunity for the women to best articulate their own points of view. Such an approach promotes the uniqueness of human enquiry, celebrating the permanence and priority of the real world of subjective first-person experience. In attempting to see the world from the participant's point of view, the aim is to try to understand how individuals construct social reality in relation to these interests (Sparkes 1992: 34).

Field observations took place at a range of venues in and around the football world of these women, including matches, the bar, and various sites around the college campus. Interviews were conducted on the campus where the majority of the women studied. Each of the women was given a pseudonym to ensure anonymity and confidentiality of responses.

Getting started

As women's football had only started at the college one year prior to the commencement of this research, I was interested to find out how and why it had begun. Some of the players identified the 'cliquey-ness' of the hockey team as being a major factor in their playing football, as the following comments highlight:

> Em, well I was playing hockey in my first year here, and em I really enjoyed it, but the players were really cliquey as well. I dunno, like a lot of the second year players, but it was really cliquey, and I met Lorna there, cos Lorna plays hockey as well. And I dunno what happened because we got to hear about someone starting a women's team so that because like I'd got interested in football, I thought yeah, I'd like to have a go at that.
>
> (Donna)

> Well, when we first came to college in the first year there wasn't a ladies football team, and, um, there was a group of us who wanted to play football. We didn't want to play hockey as it was already really cliquey, so um there was this bloke Shawn who had his football prelim, and he wanted to start it up, and he did it, and I went along, it was just like he encouraged everyone.
>
> (Hannah)

Patricia's words demonstrate the initial problems the students encountered in getting a team started at the college:

> Well basically when we started no one took us seriously ... it was OK, we set up a friendly match, but there was no ... we had to use the boys kit, no special treatment and when we went up to the astroturf we had to pay for it and the boys would get it free, they would have particular times. Maybe because it was a new sport at the time and they could not fit it in, but at the time it was frustrating when you are trying to get something off the ground.

The reasons for the initial struggles, and their attempts to gain acceptance and recognition, are based on both the fact that it is women's sport, and moreover, that they are women playing a man's sport. Studies of other sports including body-building (Miller and Penz 1991); boxing (Halbert 1997); and golf (Crosset 1995) highlight similar struggles for female participants.

This first game I attended was my introduction to a part of the college otherwise unknown to me. The pitch on which this game took place was located over the far side of the building, cordoned off by large hedges. After a few more matches it became obvious that this was the 'girls pitch'. In addition to being hidden out of the way, the pitch was also one of the most uneven fields I had ever come across, having a tendency to become very sticky, and was on the whole, a most difficult surface on which to play. To me, the fact that the women always had to play there was a sign of their 'ranking' within the structure of sport at the college. However, when it came to the interviews, I was aware that, given the focus of my research, my view may have been a little clouded. Therefore, I decided not to mention the pitch, but would ask the players themselves about where they thought they were 'ranked', in terms of importance, of the five (four male, one female) football teams the college had.

Opinions as to where the women saw themselves ranked within the football infrastructure of the college demonstrated that they are all aware of the fact that they are not on an equal footing with the male teams. The feeling amongst many of the women, that they were not treated as well as they should be, is visibly shown in the following statements:

> Being the top team, the first team in soccer, we're supposed to be sort of the first to get first aid kits, um minibuses etc. Um, sort of, in the late days we didn't have a first aid kit, and you know there has been injuries at that point, and we feel that we've come second place to the men.
>
> (Lorna)

> From getting transport, to getting first aid kit, to getting recognised – I mean it is getting better, but it's getting over that little edge, it is like 'Why can't we have the first aid kit?', 'Oh, the men's football team has got it.'
>
> (Patricia)

> It's not taken seriously ... transport, we only had a bus 'cos one of the other teams weren't going where they were supposed to.
>
> (Mary)

It would have been easy for the students to have simply given up in their quest to develop women's football at the college given the resistance that they undoubtedly faced. The developments made during the time that this research took place highlight a real determination to implement change even though the football players' stance was not overtly political and most of the women strongly resisted the feminist label (see Harris 1998).

The comments above are representative of the general consensus amongst the women, that they 'come second place to the men', and that they have had to battle hard for *any* recognition and assistance. Other studies of women's football in England (Davies 1996; Lopez 1997) endorse the views presented by the collegiate players and demonstrate that such struggles are commonplace at all levels of the women's game.

Images of women's football

In adopting an inductive, emergent research framework, I wanted to know what the women who played the game thought that its image was, and for them to give me their own 'insider' views of the sport. One of the questions that I asked in all of the interviews was 'What do you think is the image of women's football?' All of the women were quick to point out that the game suffered from a poor image and that their own participation was normally associated with lesbianism. This is highly significant, and constituted the most visible and consistent theme to emerge in the whole of the research. Surprisingly, this area is often ignored in works on women and football (e.g. Coddington 1997; Davies 1996; Lopez 1997; Williams and Woodhouse 1991). Yet, as has been made clear in other work (e.g. Blinde and Taub 1992; Crosset 1995; Halbert 1997; Young 1997), this conjectured conflict between athletic participation (particularly in supposed 'male' sports such as football) and femininity, is a most significant area and one that warrants further academic analysis. From being a neglected area of research, more recent studies of women's football have begun to explore the areas of sexuality and identity within the game (Caudwell 1999; Cox and Thompson 2000).

In the first interview that I conducted, I discovered that one of the most talented players on the team had actually given up football for a while at school, having been 'accused' of being a lesbian. In her view, the game had a 'butch' and lesbian image, and she recalls that:

> They'd sort of accuse you of being a lesbian and that sort of thing, and I was like, at that point I didn't quite know what it is. I went home and said what's a lesbian [laughs] and you know, I've never really understood what it was. Its only been in the last couple of, three years I've really understood what it is.
>
> (Lorna)

Although as Lorna makes clear, she was not really sure at the time of what it (being a lesbian) meant, its mere usage (in a derogatory way) was strong enough to stop her playing the sport for a time. The strength of this association between women who play football and lesbianism, manifests itself most visibly in *all* of the interviews. The woman who stopped playing for a while could perhaps be one of a very large number of girls, who at an impressionable and sensitive age, move away from sport (particularly supposedly 'male' ones), because of the presumed association between participation in that activity and homosexuality. Furthermore, from this interview and other conversations with this individual, I suggest that she may never have played the game again, were it not for this perceived 'safer' environment of the college.

In addition to the upset and confusion that this incident brought, Lorna also noted that 'in the team that I played for (previously) there were a couple [laughs] er who sort of had their preferences'. This was not, it would appear, merely an isolated example, for other women also had similar tales to tell. Tracey described her football coach at her previous college as someone who reminded her of the secondary school PE teacher whom they believed to be a lesbian:

Tracey: Well everyone said she was, well we know for a fact she was.
JH: How do you know?
Tracey: Because one of the girls on the team went out with her.

This seemingly 'fits' the general (stereotypical) perception of a female football player, which in the eyes of a number of the women on the college team, was delineated as follows:

> Um, I think … that a lot of people think that it is lesbians that play football.
>
> (Rebecca)

> Most ladies that play football are gay, like a lot of people think that this team at the college is lesbian.
>
> (Patricia)

Research undertaken in New Zealand presents a similar picture where many football players reported having their sexual identity questioned after saying that they played the game (Cox and Thompson 2000: 11). Caudwell's (1999) study also demonstrated that respondents frequently referred to lesbianism as a criterion when asked to convey the perceived image of women who played football.

'The look'

In attempting to learn more about the meanings constructed here, it became apparent that these views were based on myriad factors, ranging from the fact that football was (and is?) perceived as a man's game to the 'look' of a number of female football players. As Miller and Penz (1991: 150) note in their work on body-building, 'the norm that depicts women as experts in the management of appearance is embedded in the larger Western conception of femininity'. Maguire and Mansfield's (1998) study of aerobics clearly highlights how women can be persuaded to manipulate their bodies for the expression of patriarchal notions of femininity (see also Cole 1993; Markula 1995; Tomlinson 1995). Within the sports world it is suggested that 'feminine' is often used a code word for 'heterosexuality' (Griffin 1992; Hall 1996).

What is particularly salient here, is the way in which many women who are athletic or 'get stuck in' during a game are labelled lesbian. Further comments from the students as to the perception of a woman football player further demonstrate this point:

> You think like 'hello' [laughs], I mean some are gay, and some are really butch, and some of the girls on our team look a bit dodgy.
>
> (Patricia)

A lot of women that play it are quite big. You can't have a team full of skinny girls.

(Rebecca)

Mary offered a most interesting insight into the college team, and suggested that its members were in fact made up of two distinct groups:

There's the rowdy ones – me, Donna – and then there are the girlie ones [laughs] who have to make sure their make-up is perfect, like Tracey, Hannah and Lucy – they tend to avoid being associated with us if they can help it.

Mary described the group she pictured herself as belonging to, as the ' 'ard uns', those who 'got stuck in during a game'. As to why she referred to the other group as being 'the girlie ones', she replied:

Cos they have to look wonderful, I mean you can't look wonderful after a game, but they are like 'oh my mascara has run' [laughs], it's like 'get a life', there are more important things.

Rebecca, one of the ' 'ard uns', equating of the 'skinny girls' as having a low level of competence in sport, highlights the way in which athletic prowess and a 'desirable femininity' are often seen to be incompatible (see Halbert 1997; Miller and Penz 1991; Willis 1982; Young 1997). Comments from other women as regards the surprise of some people on hearing that they play football, would seem to support this view. A common theme that ran through a number of interviews was the conceptualisation that certain women were too pretty to play football. Crosset (1995) uncovered a similar situation in the world of women's golf, where sporting competence was often positioned as oppositional to desirable femininity.

Sonia construed the fact that 'as the sport is seen as a masculine game', and that 'people who are lesbian are considered to be more macho than the heterosexual woman', then this perpetuates the belief that female football players are gay. The image of female football players was delineated as:

Like boys' haircuts, or stocky. Like when we went to Luton we thought 'Oh my god, is that a girl?'

(Patricia)

Cos it's a man's sport, and cos, you know, some girls who play football are really like rough, have got really short haircuts and stuff [laughs], and some people think 'Oh no, they must be gay.'

(Donna)

I would say that they are really big, muscly girls, most of them gay with short-cut hair, and just like one of the lads drink pints of beer.

(Jane)

Kolnes's (1995) study highlights how female footballers in Norway viewed short hair as unfeminine and that long hair was important in emphasising femininity. Cox and Thompson's (2000) research also uncovered a similar picture, where long or medium-length hair was used by the football players to 'create an impression of conventional femininity that differentiated them, not only from men, but also from the stereotypical short-haired lesbian'.

Sexuality

Although the students cited the example of the heterosexual environment of women's football at the college, the fact that the females who made up this group were 'all different shapes and sizes' (Lorna), and that they had 'a cross section of different looks here' (Patricia), concern was mainly expressed when they had to defend their involvement in the sport, as to their own individual sexuality. This is shown most vividly by the words of Donna:

> Well there was something I heard last year that I wasn't too happy about. I think that it was Imogen actually, you know Imogen [I nod], she was saying something to one of the lads that oh, I think she was pretty drunk at the time, something about oh girls playing football must be gay. When I heard that I was like, oh you know, I couldn't believe it but I suppose some people do think that.

As a woman who plays what is perceived as a more 'feminine' sport (hockey), Imogen's views are demonstrative of an attitude that equates females who play 'masculine' sports with sexual deviance. Following Halbert (1997), and her study of female boxers, it appears as if the same rationale is employed here in people's perceptions of the women who participate in this sport. Like the boxers, the football players are viewed as challenging the social construction of femininity. This, according to Halbert (1997: 17), is construed as a rejection of heterosexuality as if to say 'women who are real boxers are mannish and thus aren't real women, so they must be gay'.

Comments from the women about to their own positioning within the football hierarchy of the college, demonstrated their acceptance of male football as being more important. Elsewhere I have argued that they therefore play an active part in the sustaining of male hegemony in football (Harris 2001). The student players view their sport as different to the male game and, in many ways, seemingly do not endeavour to copy their male counterparts. Yet the women were determined to be different to those clubs, like Wanderers, whom they felt were 'too man-like' in their approach to the game:

> Wanderers, they wanted me to play for them, and apparently the whole team are lesbians, so I said 'no'. I said 'yeah', then my mate said 'Do you know they are all lesbians?' – so that did put a thing on it.
>
> (Hannah)

> Oh yeah I know they are [lesbians], cos Mary plays for them, and
> Mary's gay. She used to go out with one of the secretaries there, and
> they split up and now they're not letting Mary play in the first team
> because of that [laughs].
>
> (Donna)

Of all the players who made up the college team, it was soon apparent that
there was only one (out) lesbian on the team. Mary's own introduction to this
team outside of the college (Wanderers) initially came about through the fact
that she was dating one of the players. Such an occurrence, she said, was
commonplace, and a number of women were introduced to the club in similar
circumstances. Yet it is also important to note that the team referred to here is
not a team solely for lesbians, although, as is evident from earlier comments
from one or two of the college players, such an image is easily cultivated.

Early on in the interview, Mary mentioned that her 'social circles were a
little different'. Later on, approximately half way through this ninety-minute
session, she talked about dating one of the other players. She then talked
quite openly about the environment, and how playing for the club was so
markedly different to playing for the college. Conscious of the opinions
expressed by Hannah and others, I then asked 'How many lesbians are there
in the team?'

> There are two teams. In the first team there was only five, and in the
> reserves there were more ... it is probably easier if I tell you the straight
> people [laughs] – Vicky – ten out of eleven.

However, she also noted without any prompting on my behalf that the
number of women who trained with the team had dropped. This 'started
easing off after Christmas ... about 60 per cent lesbian, and people leave
because of it'. This draws attention to the barriers faced by heterosexual
women within a predominantly lesbian environment, and highlights how
social exclusion operates at a number of levels.

Within the college, the majority of women players dismissed an individual's sexuality as relatively unimportant. This stands in stark contrast to
the homophobic attitude of the majority of male sporting teams (see Sabo
and Panepinto 1990; Schacht 1996), where even today, talk of anyone
'coming out' would most probably be greeted by a fierce condemnation, and
almost certain violent reaction. The views of the football team at the college
showed a more accepting attitude, although the terminology employed may
also be taken to indicate that they were far from comfortable with this:

> There's only this particular one [lesbian], but nobody in the team has
> got a grudge against it.
>
> (Lorna)

> Last year someone confessed to it.
>
> (Hannah)

The words employed here by Hannah are disapproving. 'Confessed' usually means to admit to doing something wrong. Lorna, in suggesting that nobody has got a grudge against it, is also indicating that perhaps they could reasonably be expected to be offended. It is interesting to note how different the words used by these two players are to the discourse employed by Mary, whereby she states that *'only* five' are lesbians.

Although it certainly appears that the issue of sexuality, and having gay people on the team, is not resisted to the extent that it is in male football, there is also evidence to suggest that a certain amount of resistance is displayed. As one of Mary's friends noted:

> I don't know whether some of the new girls know that. I mean last year when it first came out a lot of footballers started making jokes about it, you know behind her back as well like [laughs] [...] and I didn't know what to do cos I didn't want to laugh or anything.

Caution must be expressed here, for within many sporting cultures there is often a very fine line between what may perhaps be perceived as homophobic, and what is accepted as banter. Hargreaves (1994: 261) notes how heterosexist jokes and innuendoes are part of the (innocent and humorous) everyday language of sport.

There is also a level of humour expressed here within the discourse as relates to sexuality. As Mary herself recalled:

> Yeah on the college team, there is always one of us [lesbians] – me [laughs] – and on other college teams, everyone is always quick to point her out to me. What am I supposed to do – go and talk to her – excellent [laughs].

Yet it is also sometimes the case that when an individual does 'come out', then this can cause concern to other members of the team. One of the women said: 'I certainly don't shower with them anymore.' It is because of this physical exposure, and the fact that participating in team sport necessitates sharing a locker room and showers with each other, that conflict around sexuality emerges. Griffin (1998) has suggested that there are 'three climates' for lesbians in sport, which are hostile; conditionally tolerant; and open and inclusive. This social environment here is probably best described as conditionally tolerant. Only occasionally did any of the students refer to situations within the college team. As one of the women commented:

Woman: We shared a shower for about two years, and then you find out its weird.

JH: Why is that weird?

Woman: Because you remember the times when you were drunk and cuddling up to each other.

Such a view could be borne out of the woman's own contempt for homo-sexuality, but could also be a result of the desire to avoid being labelled a lesbian herself. As stated previously, it was when their own individual sexuality was questioned that the women displayed the most resistance and condemnation of the lesbian label.

Mary was also able to recognise the disapproving reaction from some of her team-mates:

> That is another locker room thing, like you get the ones that aren't too impressed with me, they try to avoid being anywhere near me.

Conscious of the presumed link between being a feminist and being an athlete, particularly in a perceived 'male' sport, many of the students were keen to state their femininity and heterosexuality. Other commentaries on women in sport have noted how various strategies are employed by female athletes to emphasise their heterosexuality, and disassociate themselves from the lesbian label (e.g. Crosset 1995; Halbert 1997; Hargreaves 1994). Halbert (1997) describes how a number of the women in her study embark upon a process of 'identity management' to avoid the lesbian label. In deploying Mary's descriptor of the 'girlie ones', it would seem that many members of this particular group appeared to be doing the same.

There is a complex relationship between participating in a perceived male sport and constructing an appropriately feminine, heterosexual identity. This is seemingly accentuated, and further problematised, by the media representation of both women and sport. As Cox and Thompson (2000: 18) have noted, women often experience contradictions, ambiguities and conflicts through their participation in the sport. Football culture is not a fixed, static arena but a dynamic social space where traditional images can be challenged and new identities are constructed.

Another theme that emerged throughout the interviews concerned the media and its (non) representation of female athletes. In order to further examine the link between women and football, a tabloid newspaper's coverage of Euro 96 was analysed with a specific focus on the portrayal of women, and the part that they played in the championships. Although much research has pointed to the under-representation and sexualisation of female athletes I was interested in learning more about the relationship between women and football as portrayed outside of the sports pages.

The media

The mass media have long been recognised for the role that they play in shaping opinion and framing attitudes. As I suggested, past research has pointed to the under-representation of women in the media, and the fact that when females are represented, it is usually on the basis of stereotypes (Davis 1990; Luebke 1989; Vande Berg and Streckfuss 1992). A number of studies focusing on women's sport have supported this view (e.g. Duncan

1990; Hilliard 1984; Rinalta and Birrel 1984). When women's sport is covered, in addition to the focus on perceived 'feminine' activities, reporting often trivialises the achievements of female athletes and focuses on the bizarre and the unusual (Hilliard 1984; Rowe 1995; Willis 1982). Research has suggested that only between 0.5 per cent and 5 per cent of all sports coverage in British national newspapers is devoted to women (Sports Council 1994).

The women, who shared with me their life stories, talked of how there were no visible role models for them to aspire to. Lorna's views are representative of the general picture:

> I just didn't see any women playing sport properly. You know, not on telly or anything. I only saw men play proper sport.

By 'proper sport', Lorna was referring to the top-level activity to which she was exposed through the print and electronic media. Studies of women participating in other sports such as golf (Crosset 1995) and boxing (Halbert 1997) paint a similar picture, in which media exposure is minimal.

I examined every copy of the *Sun* newspaper over the course of the tournament, analysing any article that had both women and football in the text, and/or any photographic image of women where football paraphernalia was evident. The aim of this chapter is to articulate the message being disseminated by the newspaper, using its own words wherever possible. Hereby, the analysis includes a great deal of 'Sun-speak', characterised by numerous 'puns', sexualised language and fiercely nationalistic overtones. It is also worth noting that the 'tabloid-talk' identified here has many similarities to the everyday football discourse employed within the game (see for example Dunphy 1976; Parker 2001).

A place in the *Sun*

The *Sun* newspaper was selected as it was by far the most popular selling daily newspaper in the country. Born out of the 'swinging sixties' (in November 1969), the newspaper has been described as 'ruthlessly downmarket' in its never-ending search for controversy and indignation (Haynes 1995: 34), and has established a significant 'reputation' for its sensationalised coverage of events. The three things that encompass the paper's position and popularity within British popular culture, are its sensational headlines, such as 'Freddie Starr Ate My Hamster', Page 3 Girls (topless models), and its football coverage. The importance of sport to the newspaper is shown by the fact that large numbers of its readers start the paper at the back, hence the familiar red *Sun* logo on the back page also (Grose 1989: 80). The centrality of the national sport to the newspaper's popularity should not be underestimated, and in an era of an ever increasing distance between football players and fans, the *Sun* has embarked on a never ending quest to provide its readers with stories from the 'private' world of football stars. Very often though, within British popular culture, this is primarily characterised by the search for 'scandal', and is demonstrative of the way in which 'heroes' are moulded before the press eagerly awaits their fall. The newspaper has also been used before as a focus for academic study about football (Tomkins 1993; Wagg 1991).

Wagg's (1991) research looked at the newspaper's portrayal of the England football manager. Bobby Robson was referred to as a 'plonker' (a colloquialism for penis), whilst his successor Graham Taylor was infamously depicted as a turnip. Headlines such as 'Turnip in Graham' and 'Swedes 2 Turnips 1' (after England had lost to Sweden) formed part of a vitriolic campaign against Taylor and are indicative of what Wagg (1991: 225) describes as 'impatient, reactionary saloon-bar masculinity'. Tomkins (1993) questioned whether football was a game that requires masculine qualities. His research found that generally, the texts on the game did not promote a traditional type of masculinity. In the *Sun* newspaper however, attempts were made to present footballers as men with exceptionally powerful physiques (Tomkins 1993: 290), even though the average football player does not fit this description. With the sole exception of war, it is through their coverage of football that the unashamed patriotism of the newspaper is at its strongest. It draws heavily on the claim that the English 'invented' football, and articulates a sense of profound hurt when foreign teams are the victors. The staging of the European Championships, and the countries that England were drawn against, saw this jingoism come to the fore in the popular press, and was even a topic for debate in Parliament.

By presenting an analysis of one publication, this does not mean that I am ignoring the various stylistic, ideological and political differences within the English print media. Moreover, it recognises that in addition to the many differences between various publications in the English press, there are also a number of similarities. One of the most important of these, is the way in which the popular press covers sport. Therefore, an analysis of any of the other tabloid publications would have shown a very similar picture. Clayton's (2001) study of both the *Sun* and the *Daily Mirror* newspaper's coverage of the Euro 2000 tournament highlights many commonalties.

'Football's coming home'

The first day of the tournament (8 June), and football is front page news with a picture of midfielder Paul Ince, draped in the England flag under the headline 'We're Ince This Together' (a play on words of the song to be performed at the opening ceremony). This is demonstrative of the way in which the tabloid press has developed a form of language which 'enables various oral cultures to find resonances between it (vernacular speech) and their own speech patterns' (Fiske 1992: 106). On page 5 of the issue there are two topless models, who are described as the first 'fantasy footballers' of the championships. The fact that football is front-page news in this and a number of other newspapers shows just how big an event the tournament is.

Further on in the newspaper we are told that 'England expects every *man* to do *his* duty' (my emphasis), and cheer the boys on. Such discourse implies that supporting the national team is an activity reserved exclusively for males, and it appears as though the newspaper is directing the country's men towards an aggregated, unified force protecting all that is masculine within the game. Following England's 1–1 draw, Monday's edition of the newspaper notes how 'Fans Give Tel Hell over Flop' (10 June). The team are branded a national disgrace, and one fan writes that 'we couldn't win an egg-cup, let alone a trophy'. The cartoon of the day states quite clearly 'Plonkers'. These extracts are demonstrative of the fickle nature of the football fan, and also the level of expectancy that is placed on the back of the national sporting teams (see also Wagg 1991).

'Kits out for the lads'

Tuesday's edition of the newspaper features a front page exclusive that some of the England footballers were 'out on the booze' just hours after the 'dismal performance against the Swiss' (11 June). Teddy Sheringham, the England striker, 'stood by the dance floor chatting and laughing with a group of *admiring* blondes' (my emphasis). At this point we have now seen the two principal roles that women are to serve within the tabloid press during the course of the competition. First we have the scantily clad model, and second the admiring woman (a function that would be more readily fulfilled by various wives and girlfriends as the tournament unfolds). Morris (1981: 182), in his unique and insightful work on 'the soccer tribe', suggested that the type of girl selected by the football player 'fits the pattern one would predict'. Here Morris (1981) powerfully articulates the fact that a football player's partner is often the antithesis of her 'tribal warrior', and is expected to fulfil a quiet, passive and glamorous role. The link between beauty and passivity is visibly demonstrated within the reaction to collegiate players deemed too attractive to play the game. There is also an implied link between unattractiveness and sporting competence (see Crosset 1995; Harris 1998).

The front page of Thursday's edition has a model dressed in an England kit with the slogans, 'Bang the Drum for England' and 'Get Yer Kits out for the Lads' (13 June). This is the first play on words on the misogynistic chant often heard on football terraces. Research by Woodhouse (1991) found that such chants and other intimidation/abuse was one of the main reasons that put women off going to football matches. This play on words is a common occurrence in the tabloid press. The pleasure lies in spotting the pun, which then 'matures into greater pleasure of making one's own pertinent meaning from the collision of discourses within it' (Fiske 1992: 107). The following day's edition tells a story of a woman who sold her television as she was fed up with how much football her boyfriend was watching (14 June). This confirms the roles that women and men are (traditionally) expected to fill within English culture. The powerful everyday images that are portrayed as relates to this must not be underestimated. Some of the collegiate footballers noted how as young girls they were socialised into 'hating football'.

An analysis of the total sports coverage during the period of this research found that over the course of the championships, there were 252 pages of sports news in total. Disturbingly, a sum total of only four pages (1.6 per cent) was devoted to women's sport. This though, I believe, only tells part of the story, for this total comprised news on just two sports – athletics and tennis. Alarmingly, when we consider the seasonal nature of the two sports featured, this may actually signify an over-representation of the average coverage. Clayton's (2001) exploration of the *Mirror* and *Sun* newspapers uncovered a higher proportion of coverage than this, but little change in the sexualisation and subordination of females.

On the day of the Scotland match, former Page 3 Girl Samantha Fox is pictured on the front page, dressed in an England strip, under the caption 'England Expects every Man to Do His Beauty' (15 June). There is also a story of the 'man bites dog' variety with an article about a man who is being driven mad by his three female flat-mates who are all 'soccer mad'. This is another image often portrayed in the popular press, whereby a story is given prominence because of the uniqueness or supposed bizarreness of it. Prior to the Holland game, for the first and only time in the tournament there is a woman on the back page, although the Dutch journalist in question is there for no other reason than the figure-hugging shorts she is wearing (18 June). Whilst attractive women, often wearing very little, frequently appear on the front page of such publications, the back page is very much a traditionally male space. It is almost inconceivable that a female would be pictured upon the back page of the newspaper. There is, perhaps, only one female athlete who has been 'accepted' on the back page and that is Anna Kournikova. Kournikova was by far the most photographed female athlete in the world. Yet the attention she receives is related more to physical attractiveness than athletic competence. She epitomises hegemonic femininity whereby 'feminine' female athletes are afforded a disproportionate amount of media coverage (see Choi 2000; Harris and Clayton 2002).

Strike the pose

An analysis of the photographic images of female athletes featured in this period highlights a similar story. Of the very few photographs that are featured over the course of the championships, the largest and most prominent of these is of the tennis player Mary Pierce (19 June). However, this has more to do with the revealing dress that she is wearing as opposed to any on-court performance. Non-task relevant commentary is prevalent within articles focussing upon what are perceived as attractive athletes due to their sensual, feminine bodies. By exalting an athlete such as Anna Kournikova as the idiosyncratic sportswoman the tabloid press are maintaining masculinity through ideological representations of femininity. Needless to say, it is apparent that women playing football do not link with such conceptualisations within British culture, and we rarely see photographs of female football players within the national press.

Photographs are so much a part of our daily lives, that we very rarely consider how they may influence us. We view photographs as accurate and real, – as something that appears to be a completely truthful source of information (Barthes 1977; Berger 1972; Kuhn 1985) – and because a camera operates mechanically, seemingly with little human intervention, it appears to be a completely objective rendering of reality (Barthes 1977). The use of pictures of bare-breasted women to promote sport is neither new nor unique to football. During the period under study, there was in addition to what has already been cited, Page 3 Girls adorned with a jockey cap (on the day of Ascot), and a tennis racket (to mark the start of Wimbledon fortnight). Hargreaves (1994: 167) has noted how the use of women holding such objects suggests a provocative sexual statement, that 'real' sports are for men, and that women are there to provide excitement and arousal.

Photographs of the male sports stars fulfil an altogether different function, and the England players received an expedient amount of coverage as they progressed in the tournament. One of the 'tribal heroes' (Morris 1981) when England defeat Spain is defender Stuart Pearce, whose wife talks of her 'lionheart' (24 June). In spite of all of the coverage that has gone before, the amount of attention given to football on the morning of the Germany match has undoubtedly reached a crescendo. The extent to which the national side have aroused the interest of the country is shown by a feature in the 'Sun Woman' section entitled 'En-Girl-And'. The editor states how 'now even I've stopped hating footie and gone Euro 96 loopy'. This feature vividly shows the far-reaching effect of the tournament. In many ways 'Sun Woman' represents an escape from the dominant narrative within the newspaper, and its preoccupation with sport and sexualised images of women. The very fact that football has now reached this particular part of the publication is, I believe, highly significant. But, it is Euro 96 the event, and not the sport itself that has captured the imagination of this particular woman.

The success of the men's national team in 1966 and 1990 had on each occasion resulted in an upsurge of interest in the game amongst women (see for example Lopez 1997; Williams and Woodhouse 1991). It was predicted before the tournament had begun that Euro 96 would have a similar effect. Such major events, perhaps, afforded the opportunity for a wider number of people to be exposed to the national sport. The Football Association made a concerted effort to attract more women to the Euro 96 games through a poster campaign using slogans such as 'How Can I Lie Back and Think of England ... when Venables Hasn't Finalised His Squad' (see Harris 1999). Some of the football players that I spoke to talked about the tournament on their return to college, but none of them had attended any of the games.

In spite of the effect on adult behaviour and self-image that the media has, it is believed that its impact is even greater on children, who do not possess the more refined capacity of adults to judge the validity of media content (Chafetz 1978: 95). It has been noted that in the children's weeklies football is treated as a way of 'being macho' and 'one of the boys' (Hargreaves 1994: 149). Tomlinson (1995: 137) has also observed how the representation of sport in boys' comics is an 'idealised fantasy' in which masculinity is conceived as being an unproblematic, natural and crucially non-feminine state of affairs. The implication of this to girls who desire to play sport, and particularly football, is apparent. The aim of the second part of this chapter has been to highlight the message that is being portrayed to women and young girls, which is that sport is still an essentially male activity, where females are afforded only subordinate and/or highly sexualised roles. Such representations undoubtedly have an effect. The use of more 'glamorous' athletes may also be rendered problematic, and it is suggested that this can actually put young females off sport (Choi 2000).

Concluding remarks

This chapter has highlighted both the resistance facing female football players and the representation of women, in relation to sport, presented within the tabloid press. The two are invariably linked as the media have such an influence upon our lives today. Claims that 'the future is feminine' may have some substance within a global sense, but on closer reflection this does not seem to be the case in England. The creation and promotion of a hegemonic masculine ideal through the game of football means that the sport is more resistant to change than most other areas of culture. The further development of women's football is more problematic than many writers suggest and, as I have argued elsewhere, the claim that 'the future is feminine' may be a little quixotic (Harris 1998). The cultural barriers and the continued stereotypical observations related to 'image', in women's football, warrants further investigation and analysis. Women within football may continue to be marginalised and socially excluded, particularly in an age where stated idealisations and promoted conceptualisations of masculinity prove increasingly problematic for many men. The limited number of studies undertaken on the game (e.g. Davies 1996; Harris 1998; Lopez 1997) highlight the fact that discrimination and exclusion occur at all levels of the sport. The notion of Walvin (1975) and others that football is 'the people's game' will continue to be challenged at the beginning of the twenty-first century.

7

Out on the field: women's experiences of gender and sexuality in football

JAYNE CAUDWELL

In this chapter I offer a particular analysis of women's active involvement in football. I make use of, and rely on, findings from my PhD research, which involved postal questionnaires and in-depth interviews. Eight hundred and seventy questionnaires were sent out between October 1997 and March 1998. The sample was selected via the regional league system in place at the time, which consisted of ten regional leagues in England and Wales. Four hundred and seventy-three questionnaires were returned. This preliminary research was followed by 14 semi-structured in-depth interviews with women football players aged between 21 and 42. The analysis of this research material reflects an engagement with feminist poststructuralism (a theoretical position that is explained briefly below). The discussions that follow are influenced by my location within the social relations network and from a feminist perspective it is important that this position is made transparent. In this vein I provide a brief autobiography. This is followed by a brief overview of the history and contemporary form of women's participation in football.

Using women's testimonies, the account focuses on gender, sexuality and the local operation of power relations in football contexts. In this way it seeks to show how power affected the women taking part in the research on a microsocial level. Finally, I explore the bodily sites/sights where gender and sexuality are conflated, and illustrate how corporeality is central to both the reproduction and contestation of 'compulsory' heterosexual femininity.

The account that follows represents a particular football epistemology. It supports the notion, developed by Donna Haraway (1988), of 'situated knowledges', through an engagement with the local. It therefore cannot support universal or 'grand' theories about women's active involvement in football. Nevertheless, it provides valuable insights into these women's different and dynamic experiences of gender and sexuality, and explores the relationship between playing football, gender and sexuality.

Autobiography

As a girl I loved playing out of doors. I was defined by others as a tomboy because of my constant involvement in physical activity and, more importantly, because of my appearance. This passion for physical activity was later formalised by way of participation in sports. I lived not far from the River Severn and took up sculling when I was 14 years old. By then I had already become a member of the local hockey club. I spent weekends sculling in the mornings and playing hockey in the afternoons.

During my years at home and later at university I learned about sport, and, implicitly, about gender and sexuality. I understood heterosexual femininity as compulsory. I struggled to conform to hegemonic femininity, and it was only some years later that I decided not to struggle and not to conform. I moved to East London to teach and in this setting became aware of football. I started to play when I was 26. Some ten years on I have played in the Greater London League, in the National League for a team in the West Midlands and more recently in the Northern Division of the National League for a Yorkshire side.

My involvement in football is significant, since it was while playing the game that I became aware of 'out' lesbian sexuality. Unlike hockey or rowing, the cultural arena of football seemed to provide a safe social space for players who also chose not, or were unable, to conform to 'compulsory' heterosexuality and heterosexual femininity. Until this sporting moment I understood lesbianism as belonging in the 'closet', or the 'glass closet' as Pat Griffin (1998) describes the environment facing those who have come out but must not flaunt their sexuality.

It is my journey from the monolith of 'compulsory' heterosexual femininity to the celebration of the diversity of gender and sexuality that informs the arguments presented in this chapter. In addition, it is my lived experiences of sport, specifically of football, that have underpinned my engagement with gender theory. Locating the self in the production of knowledge is axiomatic to feminist politics and theory, which is why I make my social position as a white, middle-class, lesbian/queer academic and footballer visible.

Feminist poststructuralism in brief

Poststructuralists work from the premise that power is 'an invisible web of interrelated effects, a persistent and all-pervading circulation of effects' (Braidotti 1992: 188). Power relations are viewed as local, unstable, unfixed, fluid and reversible (Kenway and Willis 1998). References to networks of power relations and power as a dynamic effect appear eminently in the work of Michel Foucault. In *Discipline and Punish*

Foucault (1975) describes what he considers to be the intricate and local operation of power, and argues that networks of power, or power matrices, can produce regimes of power, and that these function to regulate and discipline individual action. In particular, his work considers how sexuality is regulated. According to Foucault, power is exercised and not possessed; therefore individuals are invested with, and transmitters of, power. In short, we are both objects and subjects of power, and power can be viewed 'as a productive and positive force, rather than as a purely negative, repressive entity' (McNay 1992: 38).

Judith Butler (1993) supports Foucault's claim that individuals can exercise power. However, in her work on gender she remains mindful of the limits of freedom, arguing that individuals can act in their own interests but this choice usually occurs within the limits of intelligibility. In other words, we behave in ways that are recognisable according to gender 'norms' and gender 'ideals'.

The poststructuralist and more specifically feminist poststructuralist analysis of the operation of power within social relations is relevant to the discussions that follow, for three reasons. First, such an approach allows for an exploration of the impact of power regimes and disciplinary power on women who play. Second, it attends to women's experiential diversity. That is, through an emphasis on the micro-functioning of power it is possible to focus on women's different everyday lived experiences. Finally, the feminist poststructuralist view that power is exercised and not possessed provides the opportunity to consider the contestation and transformation of power regimes.

The state of play: past and present

Women's active involvement in football in Britain has been traced back to the second half of the nineteenth century (Fletcher 1993; McCrone 1988 and 1991; Parratt 1989) and speculatively plotted to the early eighteenth century (Williamson 1991). Sheila Fletcher (1993) documents records of girls playing football in private schools in Brighton and Nottingham in 1870, and one newspaper, the *Sketch*, provides photographic evidence of women playing in 1895. Writers have also mapped a more recent history focusing on the twentieth century (Duke and Crolley 1996; Lopez 1997; Newsham 1997; Pfister, Scraton and Fatings 1999; Williams and Woodhouse 1991). Of these, Gail Newsham (1997) offers an account that illustrates the place of football in the lives of women who played for Dick, Kerr's Ladies between the 1920s and the 1950s, and Sue Lopez (1997) concentrates on women playing around Britain and abroad between the 1960s and the 1990s.

'Women's football' is often cited as the fastest-growing sport in England (Lee 2001; Chaudhary 2001). In 1990 there were 9,000 players and 314 clubs (Gibbs 1995); in 1998 there were 14,000 women players, 15,000 girl players and a total of 1,700 clubs (Crinnion 1998); and more recently it has been claimed that 'there are now 55,000 playing the game' (Chaudhary 2001). The Football Association (FA) even has a hotline number for a service telling girls how and where to get involved in the game. These increases in participation rates reflect improved opportunities to play. Teams are now organised within a league structure, which includes ten regional leagues, four combination leagues, three national leagues and two national reserves leagues. At the international level there is a senior squad, an under-16 squad and an under-18 squad. As a way to encourage elite performance the FA Talent Development Plan was launched in March 1998. The results of this strategy have included the development of centres of excellence. The first centre was opened in Southampton for girls under 12, under 14 and under 16, and an academy of excellence was opened in Durham in September 1998.

Nevertheless, in sports texts football has been marked as male. Male sports historians and sociologists have effectively positioned the game as an integral part of men's lives and of male working-class culture (Finn and Giulianotti 2000; Fishwick 1989; Giulianotti and Williams 1994; Granville 1969; Mason 1996; Moorhouse 1996; Sugden and Tomlinson 1994; Tomlinson 1983; Walvin 1975 and 1994; Young 1968). This extensive documentation has largely ignored and/or omitted women's involvement in, and experiences of, playing football. Omitting women from the analysis arguably allows football, sport and culture alike to be defined and marked as male.

The arguments of Elizabeth Grosz (in Alcoff and Potter 1993) are pertinent here. Through a critique of knowledge as sexist and 'phallocentric' (male-centred), she describes what she regards as male hegemony in the production of knowledge and argues for a positioning of the female in epistemological debates, in order to dislocate and transform traditional epistemologies. Taking such a critical feminist approach to the academic literature on football helps to expose how some writers have constructed football as a male phenomenon. This has resulted in the visibility of particular footballing epistemologies within academic discourse. That said, more recent analyses (Caudwell 1999; Cox and Thompson 2000; Henry and Comeaux 1999; Scraton *et al.* 1999) seek to explore women's experiences of playing and go some way to producing 'new' football knowledges.

Football and the research participants

There is a substantial literature within sports sociology that considers the functioning of gender relations in sport (see, for example, Dworkin and

Messner 1999; Hargreaves 1994; Lenskyj 1990; McKay, Messner and Sabo 2000; Messner and Sabo 1990; Scraton and Flintoff 2002). Here I offer a further contribution via an analysis of the accounts of the women, and through a focus on their girlhoods and early experiences of playing. The existing literature evidences the many sites and practices that produce gender relations within sporting arenas, and the following discussions further explore gender relations within the formal processes of schooling and informal play spaces. Such a focus draws attention to the operation of disciplinary power in the regulation of women's active involvement and illuminates challenges to existing regimes of gender relations. This brief analysis considers the local, particular and shifting configurations of gender relations that make an impact on the women.

For the women taking part in the questionnaire research the most common length of time they had been playing for was between five and ten years. A significant proportion had been playing for between ten and 15 years, and some for more than 15 years. Nearly two thirds of the respondents had been playing for at least five years. When asked how they had been introduced to football, just over one fifth of the respondents answered 'in the playground'; the second most common answer was 'by a female friend' and the third was 'by Dad'. The influence of the informal setting of the playground and the experience of playing football for more than five years were themes that also emerged in the 14 interviews. Eleven of the interviewees had started playing football before the age of 14. Nine of these 11 women described playing on a regular basis. The reasons that all 11 gave for playing football were diverse: they included the influence of female friends, fathers and brothers, as well as informal playground experiences and/or informal play on the housing estates where they had lived. For the three women who started playing as adults, the influence of a local or university team was cited as the main reason for starting to play.

For the 11 women who described their experiences of school it was evident that being a girl within the education system was a central issue. One respondent, aged between 30 and 32, used strong language to describe her experience: 'in school forced to play traditional female sports. Banned from playing football'. Another interviewee, Tracy, aged 23, mentioned and emphasised the response that she got when she tried to play football at school: 'girls can't do that'. These remarks illustrate how gender and sport are socially constructed on the premise of sex difference. The idea of 'female sports' and the notion that sex forecloses certain sporting opportunities demonstrates the functioning of discursive practice. These experiences were shared by many of the women and the following comments further illustrate this point:

> When I was at school none of the girls were allowed to play even if they wanted to.
>
> (respondent aged between 21 and 23)

I wanted to play football as a child in the school team and was not allowed. Same with boxing.

(respondent aged between 36 and 38)

In school and college the teachers wouldn't let us play football during PE [physical education] or with the boys.

(respondent aged between 18 and 20)

The evidence suggests that when these women were girls the relations between girls and boys were based on the knowledge that boys could play certain sports and girls could not. In this way modes of knowledge were produced. Practice within PE classes and school sport defined the difference between girls and boys, and functioned to regulate girls' active involvement, as is indicated in this comment: 'when I was at school I was never allowed to play football with the boys because they said, and the teacher said, it's a boy's game' (respondent aged between 18 and 20).

Clearly, social and discursive practices produce and reproduce what is 'normal' and 'natural' sporting behaviour for children. In these cases, girls' active involvement in the game was regulated but boys' participation was not. The findings refer to gender relations at the microsocial level and indicate that school sport and physical education were, and probably still are, sites for the social construction of football and gender. That said, it is important to remain mindful of power as exercised and not possessed, and how this contributes to the instability of power regimes. The research findings indicate that the situation in some schools was different. Two of the women interviewed were physical education teachers: both reported that the girls in their schools were given opportunities to play football. For example, Collette, aged 32 and teaching at a school in east London, talked about her approach when she introduced girls to football in PE lessons:

Often the girls think they are not any good. They listen to the stereotypes – they believe girls aren't good at football. I try to tell them [that] it is all to do with experience – 'When [you were] playing with little dolls at three, what was your little brother doing?' – he was out playing football with whoever.

Helen, aged 23 and teaching in the east Midlands, also talked about the future of football in schools for girls: 'Now, because of more people like myself coming through from sports colleges and coming into teaching, we're setting up more girl's teams.' Collette and Helen reported their provision of frequent opportunities for girls to play football at school. Their experiences of teaching girls to play reflected individual efforts on a micro-level to challenge the naturalised relationship between boys and football. Their particular situations demonstrate that power relations exist in a number of ways and their actions contest practices within schools that position football as a 'boys' game'. In conjunction with the comments that report girls not being allowed to play, the testimonies of the teachers demonstrate the micro-operation of power and resistance within the education system.

To demonstrate further the complexity of gender relations within the education system, it is worth considering not only the social and discursive practices that make an impact on girls' relationships to football, but also the material practices. The success of Shrewsbury girl players aged under 16 and under 13 (reported in the *Guardian*, Education section, 22 June 1999), offers an example of the importance of material sites in the social construction of the game. The Shrewsbury girls were provided with the opportunity to play as a result of the Shropshire schools development plan. The development plan had been initiated with £138,000, a portion of '£10 million of funding, provided jointly by the [National] Lottery and the [FA] Premier League' (Revell 1999). The funds were distributed with the intention of providing opportunities for girls within schools. The effects of this material practice were localised, of course, but the Shrewsbury girls' experiences of increased participation once again challenged the construction of football as a 'boys' game'.

Staying with material practices but moving on to the women's experiences of further and higher education, the findings also illustrate how young women who have experience of universities in England and Wales are further schooled in relation to gendered notions of footballers. For example, the findings suggest that certain practices within universities have an impact on women's participation:

> Our team has recently had problems regarding sponsorship and grants from [the] AU [Athletic Union]. Our team has been awarded only £150 this year, while the men's team has been awarded £1,200. While we understand that there is obviously a degree of difference in skill between our teams, essentially the running costs of both teams are similar.
>
> (respondent aged between 18 and 20)

> Men's football and rugby also seem to have more priority when it comes to new kit, etc. . . . Our uni[versity] athletic union is supposed to replace our kit every three years, we've had the present one for about four or five years. Why?
>
> (another respondent aged between 18 and 20)

The material differences in provision for students, in the form of financial support and playing kit, seem to reflect and reproduce wider gender relations. Rosi Braidotti (1992) calls for a re-visiting of the material sites where women are excluded and disqualified. Clearly these comments, albeit limited in scope and from a small number of women, suggest that universities' sports policy and the distribution of funds to student sport may well be sites where women are disqualified. In addition, women students in the sample found that their participation was trivialised in other ways, for example: 'Playing football for my university team in the final of SESSA tournament. We only played 40 minutes each way as the ref[eree] (man) decided the pitch was too big for women to play 45 minutes and plus they didn't want to delay the all-important men's finals' (respondent aged between 30 and 32).

Such regulation has been challenged elsewhere. It has been argued that football in the United States, for example, has been 'constructed as a sport suitable for women' (Henry and Comeaux 1999: 278). Through legislation, notably Title IX of the Education Act, adopted by Congress in 1972 and made mandatory in 1978, practices that exclude and disqualify women from football are deemed illegal. The effect of this change in policy and provision has been an increase in the numbers of girls and women taking part in sport. At the high school level the figure rose from 294,015 taking part in 1971 to 2,240,000 in 1996. More specifically it has been suggested that 'soccer emerged as a primary beneficiary' of Title IX (Henry and Comeaux 1999: 278) and it has been estimated that half of the 18 million soccer players in the United States are female (Lopez 1997).

Nine of the 14 women I interviewed talked about playing football frequently during their girlhoods. They shared continuities of experience based on informal play, either out of doors near their homes or in a playground at school. From their accounts four themes emerge as significant, namely: where the women lived when they were girls; the influence of brothers; the space available to play in; and playtime opportunities at primary school. Some of these findings support recent research with 'top-level European women footballers' that found, for example, that on average players started playing between the ages of four and six, and that their early experiences 'were generally in informal spaces within local neighbourhoods' (Scraton, Fasting, Pfister and Bunuel 1999: 102).

As feminist geographers have pointed out (see, for example, Duncan, 1996; Massey, 1994; Valentine, 1993), the use of public space by girls and women disturbs the gendering of space. In particular, Doreen Massey (1994) has illustrated how public space used for physical activity and sport has been, and remains, dominated by men. She describes a familiar scene when she recounts her girlhood memories of the 'dank, muddy fields' of the Mersey flood plain being 'divided up into football pitches and rugby pitches'. She recollects that on Saturdays 'the whole vast area would be covered with hundreds of little people', likening it to a painting by L.S. Lowry. Her lasting impression is bewilderment that 'all of these acres of Manchester . . . had been entirely given over to boys' (Massey 1994: 185). Such accounts offer poignant reminders that public spaces are 'gendered' and largely male-dominated. The following discussion, supported by the women's narratives, may be considered against this backdrop. It is significant that the research participants 'played out' and 'played on' in public spaces. Their presence as girls positions them as 'space invaders' (Massey 1994), literally of gendered public spaces and metaphorically of gendered social relations.

Where the women lived when they were girls appears to have been relevant to the reasons why they started to play football. For instance, Shirley, aged 33 explained: 'I lived on an estate, a council estate, and every Sunday there was a massive game, everyone just used to come out and play, and I just used to join in.' Donna, aged 30, also talked about the significance of living on a council estate when she was asked when and why she started playing football: 'Just because purely I lived on a council estate where there was loads of . . . well, more boys than girls really and so we all used to play, just play in the street . . . you just put your jumpers down for your posts and off you went.'

The greater visibility of boys than of girls became more apparent when some of the women started to talk about the influence of their brothers. Rachel, aged 34, described her interest in playing as having been greater than that of her brother, who was two years older, but, as she acknowledged: 'I wouldn't have been able to play if I hadn't have had him – I wouldn't have been able to play with his friends.' Kaz, aged 31, also returned to the relevance for her of living on a council estate. She also registered the impact that her brothers had on her early experiences of playing: 'I had four brothers at home so I did things with them . . . I was brought up on an estate – council estate – and we had the perfect square outside . . . It wasn't one particular day, I was just brought up on it [football].' Similarly, Tracy, aged 23, positioned the influence of her brother and the space they used to play on as central to her reasons for starting to play: 'I started playing football when I was about five because my big brother done it. We used to have a little green just up the road to my Mum's. There used to be these two trees . . . we used to go up there and play.'

Three of the women talked about similar experiences at about the same age within the school setting. Bev, aged 43, admitted that she 'loved the game from the age of six or seven' and started to play regularly when she went to school. Collette, aged 32, also remembered liking football and playing it in the school playground. She specifically recollected the informal process of team selection among her male peers: 'You know the terrible situation where you used to get picked at primary school – captains picking teams – I used to get picked by the boys, which was a major feat.' Nadia, aged 26, explained: 'Why? I think the boys wanted to play the girls at football, so I just joined in . . . I kept playing with the boys and I started wearing trousers to suit playing football at break time.'

Class is significant here. As Shirley, Donna and Kaz all mentioned, growing up on a council estate influenced their participation in football.

Shirley acknowledged the ease with which she was able to join in mass games on Sundays and also referred to the low costs involved: 'I mean, football is one of those sports where you just need a ball.' Kaz referred not only to the accessibility of the game but also to where she lived in London as being relevant: 'I think living on a council estate made it quite easy. You had a football and a football's cheap. We had the square . . . Living in the East End and that, I think, just gave me the opportunity – it's, like, accepted.'

This acknowledgement of the significance of working-class culture in the East End of London reinforces the idea that football has a stronghold in working-class urban areas (Horne, Tomlinson and Whannel 1999). Clearly, it is not only male players who affiliate with football's working-class culture. Players completing the questionnaires were asked their view on whether 'more working-class women play football than middle-class women'. Nearly one third of the respondents 'agreed' with this statement, a quarter were 'neutral' and almost half 'disagreed'. Clearly there is no definitive answer, since both working-class and middle-class women participate. There is no indication of class exclusivity, unlike in the appropriation of soccer in the United States by the middle classes (Henry and Comeaux 1999).

From the findings it appears that the effects of class are not entirely oppressive. In other words, since football has a working-class inflection working-class women appear to have the cultural and social capital that can enable them to participate. That said, it is still the case that class is a social factor that emerges as significant in relation to the ways in which women experience access to football.

In relation to the importance of class, the economic profiles of those completing the questionnaires were varied. Sixty-five per cent of the respondents were in paid employment; of this group 80 per cent were in full-time employment. Of those in paid employment, 55 per cent were taking home less than £200 a week, 32 per cent were taking home between £200 and £300 a week, and 12 per cent were taking home more than £300 a week. Income becomes significant when considering the financing of participation in football. During one of the interviews Bev mentioned that 'what's made it easy for me is I've always earned a good living – so I can afford to play when and where I want'. Helen also talked about how financing the playing of football was an issue:

> The club is in financial difficulty because the girls can't afford to pay the subs that we need to keep going . . . Because we're in the National League now, you have to take a minibus, you have to go as far as Blyth, then all the way down to Brighton, so we end up paying probably about a fiver every time we travel . . . There has been a couple of people drop out of the team because they can't afford it.

From this account it is evident that money is a constraining factor. However, most of the women who did talk about class positioned it as being conducive to participation. Most of the women identified football as a relatively cheap sport. The research suggests that, despite being on low wages, working-class women represent a large proportion of those women who play football.

The research material also indicates that the women normalised football in their lives. That said, the women reported various practices that worked to regulate their involvement. As with the process of schooling, the women told of how officials, providers, spectators, peers and the media 'policed' their participation. It is apparent that at these sites, and through social, discursive and material practices, power operates to 'gender' the game. There is evidence that the women challenged the gendering of the game on the local level and in doing so reconfigured football's gender relations. Such contesting of hegemonic notions of football and gender is also evident in the research material that exposes relations to power based on sexuality.

'Compulsory' heterosexuality – football's sexual imperative?

It is difficult to separate gender and sexuality, and it is important to keep this in mind when reading the following discussion of the women's experiences of relations to power based on sexuality. Through an analysis of the stereotypes of women players I point to the ways in which lesbian sexuality has currency in football contexts. Moving on from the stereotypes, I make use of the research material that indicates that there is a lesbian presence in football. Sport can provide safe sporting and social spaces for lesbians, and some players have challenged and transgressed the heterosexual norm by risking being 'out'. I make use of the term 'out' as a way to indicate players' disclosure and display of their lesbian sexuality. In the same way I make use of the notion of being 'in the closet'. However, I recognise the complexities of being 'out' or being 'in the closet' and I question why lesbian subjects are so often positioned as being responsible for the disclosing of their own sexuality while heterosexual subjects are not. I consider the extent to which players can disclose and display their sexuality, and illustrate how some players 'queer the pitch' by creating 'dykescapes'. The discussion focuses on both heterosexual dominance and 'non-heterosexual' or lesbian subversion.

Both the responses to the questionnaire and the interview material provide evidence that women who play football are subjected to sexual stereotyping. Some of the questionnaire responses highlighted the strong connections made between football and lesbianism: 'You are kind of typecast as being a dyke for playing men's sport'; 'Women footballers have stereotypes attached to them, e.g., "butch", "gay", and it seems to roller-coaster, tarnishing all players'; 'Playing a traditional male sport, people stereotype and assume you are a butch lesbian, which clearly I am not'; 'Many people often assume that you are gay if you play a traditional male sport'; 'People assume I can't play and am crap, but others assume that there is a contingent of lesbians.' Some of the interview participants reported comments being shouted while they were playing, for example: 'When you're training up the park, wherever you are training, the lads will come along [and shout] "dykes"' (Bev, aged 43). Tracy, aged 23, believed that the main stereotype was 'dykes basically, innit'. Sam, aged 28, had a similar view – 'they think they're all bloody dykes' – as did Shirley, aged 33: 'You feel that people probably just assume you're gay as soon as you say you play women's football.' Kaz, aged 31, acknowledged this stereotype and referred to another misconception: 'big, butch, lesbians basically playing football and running around . . . also girls screaming when the ball hits them'.

These comments indicate that the lesbian stereotype has currency and may work to displace notions of hegemonic heterosexuality. It may seem that there is some form of lesbian dominance. However, further analysis indicates that the sexual imperative in football is not absolute, but shifting and dynamic.

While I accept that the stereotypes are used as a way to control women's sporting bodies, it is evident from the research and from my own involvement in the game that there is a lesbian presence in football. In the next section I discuss lesbian presence as it relates to the notion of the 'closet' and I explore the women's experiences of 'out' lesbian sexuality. The women's testimonies provide evidence of an actual lesbian presence, but the 'closet' and being 'out' exist as major features of these narratives. The terms 'closet' and 'coming out' indicate the position of heterosexuality as dominant. Being in the 'closet' and being 'out' must be understood in relation to heterosexuality as the 'norm'. In this way visibility reflects sexual relations to power. Although the stereotypes appear to illuminate the ubiquity of lesbianism in football, the extent to which players disclose their sexuality varies. That is, individuals act in ways that are affected by dominant sexual and gender structures of power, namely heterosexuality. To be recognisable as a 'woman' can often mean staying in the closet.

Lesbian presence/absence and visibility/invisibility

During the interviews with the 14 women in the sample there was frequent acknowledgement of the lesbian presence in football. The 12 women who were able and willing to offer personal narratives talked about the situation in the teams they played for. Of the six women who identified themselves as heterosexual, five were playing for teams that were predominantly lesbian. For example, Laura, aged 33, described her experience: 'Well, there are a lot of gay women in women's football. I mean, there's no doubt about that . . . There are gay women in all the teams that I've played in.' Similarly, Shirley, aged 33, had a long playing history although, unlike Laura, she had played in only one team. She explained: 'A lot of my friends who play were gay, and their friends who then came into the team were gay, because it was a lot of friends . . . and they come along and play.'

I am not suggesting that all women's teams are made up of lesbian players. However, the material supports the argument that there is a lesbian presence in football. The issue here is not to establish how many lesbians play football; instead it is to offer a starting point from which to discuss lesbian visibility in football. In other words, how easy is it for lesbian players to disclose and display their sexuality?

The 'closet' and 'coming out' position heterosexuality as the dominant form, since nonconformity to heterosexuality is implicitly expected to be hidden and silent. In addition, the process of 'coming out' places the responsibility for challenging the dominant sexuality on 'non-heterosexual' individuals. Many of the women interviewed talked about situations particular to their teams and/or clubs. These testimonies provide evidence of the extent to which lesbianism is overt and normalised. Helen, a self-defined heterosexual aged 23, offered her understanding of sexuality as it relates to football:

> There are quite a high percentage of lesbians that I know of in football. I mean there's me and about two other straight people in our team, everybody else is gay . . . a lot more women who play football are a lot more open with their feelings, and quite sort of happy in the way they are, so they come out more. I think football enables them to come out, rather than football attracting . . . do you know what I'm saying?

Here the suggestion is that dominant heterosexuality is challenged simply because there are fewer heterosexual players. Although majority status erodes notions of the 'closet' and reduces lesbian silence, the accounts do not refer to the intricacies of lesbian visibility. The women who identified themselves as lesbian, gay and/or dyke offered differing accounts of the extent to which other people were aware of their sexuality. For instance, Sam, aged 28, commented that she was 'gay and out, and not going back', and that other people 'don't have much choice really . . . If they don't know, then they soon do.' These comments suggest that Sam was very overt about her sexuality and intended to remain visible as a lesbian. Some of the women favoured a less conspicuous approach. Di, aged 29, appeared to be 'decentring' her sexuality (to use a term from Seidman, Meeks and Taschen 1999): 'I'm me . . . If somebody asks me, yes, I'll say I'm gay. I don't cover my sexuality, but I don't promote it either.'

Some of the women talked about being 'out' in certain situations and not in others. This suggests that they were stepping in and out of the 'closet'. For example:

JC: Does the rest of your team know about your sexuality?
Kaz: Er, I should think so. I don't know. We don't really speak about it . . . all the ones who are gay know . . . The new girls, now I don't usually make it quite obvious to new people who are there, because I don't really want to scare them away . . . They'll think we're all a bunch of butch lesbians, you know, out to get them or something.

Kaz was talking about deliberately staying in the 'closet': she censored her sexuality so as not to intimidate new players. This is interesting, as it is their safety she positioned as important, not her own safety, which is often the case when individuals conceal their sexuality. Kaz was prepared to be 'out' to other lesbians in the team, although this was somewhat assumed rather than made explicit, since they 'don't really speak about it'. However, her fear of being read as a butch lesbian demonstrated her own anxieties surrounding lesbian sexuality. She seemed to me to be taking on the tensions that 'butch' appears to invoke. This strategy depends on the seemingly ubiquitous butch figure as she appears within stereotypes and points to the complex functioning of homophobia: lesbians can be seen to be homophobic. By practising self-surveillance in relation to her sexuality Kaz was placing herself in the 'glass closet' (Griffin 1998).

Sam, Di and Kaz offered three different accounts of their sexuality. Their experiences demonstrate the power of 'heteronormativity', the normalising of heterosexuality. These women felt that they were forced to negotiate various strategies in dealing with the positioning of their lesbianism in relation to hegemonic heterosexuality.

'Dykescapes'

In addition to the feminist geography on space as 'gendered' there is some critical analysis of space as 'sexualised' (see Bell and Valentine 1995; Ingram, Bouthillette and Retter 1997; for specific work on lesbian space see, for example, Johnston and Valentine 1995; Moyer 1997; Munt 1995; Nestle 1997; Rothenberg 1995; and Taylor 1998). The discussion on lesbian visibility provides evidence that some of the women subverted and resisted the construction of heterosexual space. Here I refer to 'dykescapes' as a way to focus on lesbian 'space invaders' (Massey 1994: 185).

The interview material provides some evidence that lesbian players challenge the conspicuous 'heterosexing' of the spaces they use. The two women who played for different 'out' lesbian teams in the Greater London

League provide the most coherent examples. The two teams, Hackney and Phoenix, have been particularly active in their campaign to become more visible. For example, Hackney appeared in the national press: 'Hackney Women's Football Club has blown the whistle on the whole game by coming out *en masse*' (Davies 1991: 34). The team's use of signs and signifiers of lesbian sexuality supports this public coming out. The players openly adorn symbols of lesbianism with the labris and triangle as part of the club logo, and use the freedom rainbow colours as part of the summer tournament kit. Freedom flags, blankets and towels are also displayed to mark the communal social space that the team use at venues. In addition, Tamsin referred to other ways in which the team's members establish themselves and their space:

> We sing gay songs and get funny looks from some people, but most of them are sort of like, it's an excuse, it's actually because everyone knows we are an out team. All the other lesbians in other teams will go past and smile at us . . . They know we are gay so they can join in a bit, it's a really positive feeling. . . . It's the whole thing about safety in numbers, I mean, there's usually about 30 of us.

Here Tamsin described achieving recognition from lesbian players in other teams. This is significant: as Carrie Moyer (1997) argues, one of the important aspects of subverting heterosexual space is the pleasure of recognition. In many ways playing for an out team promotes the pleasure of recognition: lesbian visibility is inherent. Sam, aged 28, mentioned how women in her publicly 'out' team manifested lesbian desire: 'we talk about sexuality, like, who were we shagging at the weekend, who did you pick up . . .?'

The creation of lesbian space by teams such as Hackney and Phoenix involves a variety of strategies that serve to 'brand' sporting space. Bev Skeggs (2000) identifies such a process as 'symbolic presence and recognition politics'. Her work on the visibility of 'gayness' in Manchester's 'gay village' shows how lesbians and gays, through entitlement and ownership, occupy territory within commercial city space. However, Skeggs also argues that the commodification and capitalist exploitation of gay and lesbian culture regulate this branding. Unlike this city space, the 'dykescapes' constructed by out players and out teams tend to be transient: they exist when the team plays and are more prevalent at one-day or two-day tournaments. Although footballing 'dykescapes' tend to be transitory, the overt displays of lesbian sexuality dislocate the heterosexing of sporting space. The commercial market and the process of consumption do not regulate these moments of lesbian occupation of space. Instead, I argue, they represent 'authentic presence and recognition politics' within footballing space.

The footballing body – sites/sights for the conflation of gender and sexuality

So far in this chapter I have considered the various ways in which power relations affected women's experiences of football. Here I begin to argue that it is 'compulsory' heterosexual femininity that steers this regulation. This argument is developed through a focus on corporeality: that is, how women who do not cite or are unable to cite the hegemonic heterosexual feminine body ideal are effectively excluded because they are not recognisable as 'women'. I also begin to highlight how lesbian subjects can transform gender/sexual boundaries.

The conflation of gender and sexuality can be traced back to the early nineteenth century. It has been claimed that sexologists such as Richard von Krafft-Ebbing, Havelock Ellis and, later, Sigmund Freud relied almost exclusively on gender cues to assess and describe sexual identity (Bland 1995; Gibson 1997; Somerville 1998). They developed a medical discourse that, it has been argued, omitted multiple expressions of gender variance and sexual variance (Halberstam 1998), and squashed sexuality into a narrow range of identifiable categories. Foucault argues that such an approach transformed sexual acts 'through complex discursive practices into stable notions of identity' (cited in Halberstam 1998: 75). The corollary of sexology is a paucity of sexual and gender identities for women (and for men).

Susan Bordo (1993) has suggested that it is the body that functions as a site for the reproduction of femininity and Sandra Bartky (1988) has identified three disciplinary practices that produce the body as recognisably feminine. In brief, these are body size; the use of the body as an ornamental surface; and the bodily display of a repertoire of appropriate gestures and postures. In this way femininity is an artifice that is regulated via social and discursive practices. In addition, Moira Gatens (1992) has argued that these mechanisms through which the female body is invested result in indicators of sexual difference. When women fail, or are unable, to cite corporeal femininity the body is read differently. In other words, they are excluded from the category 'woman'.

The interview material provides detailed accounts of how players were recognised as not looking like 'real' or 'proper' women. In relation to femininity, their bodies were not intelligible (Butler 1993). For instance, Laura, aged 33, cited remarks made by male spectators: '"Well, we don't think that number 9 on the other side's female" . . . "Have you had a sex test, are you sure that she's female?"'. Some of the research material (not specified here) suggests that certain indicators of femaleness and maleness are positioned as exclusive to either women or men, despite being apparent in both. Here I focus on the construction of femininity in relation to body size and body hair. The interview material indicates that it is impossible to disentangle 'femininity' (gender) and sexuality.

During the interviews many of the women talked about football's prevailing stereotype. Body size appeared as significant. Donna, aged 30, made explicit and implicit references to players' physical size as big and hulking. Her view was that women who play football are understood by others to be 'gay'. This was further defined in relation to being 'big': 'I think you immediately get labelled just because you play football ... just because you play you are gay ... and you've got to be ... and you are this big butch hulking around.' What this also suggests is that 'proper'/'real' women, that is, heterosexual and non-'big' women, do not play football. In addition to 'bigness', the body is also read in relation to body posture and gesture (Bartky 1988) as 'hulking'.

Athletes who train to develop their muscles for a specific activity change and adjust the surfaces of their bodies. By doing so they often go beyond the boundaries of 'femininity'. Displaying body hair also positions women as outside the limits of 'femininity', as is demonstrated here:

> The women I first knew as a 14-year-old were very strong physically. These were big tough women. At one point when I walked into the changing room, I thought I'd walked into a man's football team, because everyone had hair, everyone didn't shave their armpits, everyone didn't shave their legs.
>
> (Sam, aged 28)

Clearly body hair is a critical signifier of femininity. Bartky (1988, as quoted in Conboy *et al.* 1997) argues that 'a woman's skin must be soft, supple, hairless, and smooth ... Hair must be removed not only from the face but from large surfaces of the body as well, from legs and thighs' (Conboy *et al.* 1997: 136). The visible presence of leg and underarm hair disturbs the citation of corporeal femininity. In addition, hegemonic heterosexuality ensures that body hair is read in relation to (lesbian) sexuality. Tamsin provided an example of this: 'I know for a fact that when I was thinking of joining Hackney someone said "oh my God, you don't want to join them, they're all big butch hairy lesbians".' This positioning of having hair within the simultaneous equation of 'butch' equals lesbianism is common.

Having hair in the right places, that is, providing a hairless 'body text' (Bordo 1993), appears crucial to the intelligibility of 'femininity'. If the author of the 'body text' fails to provide the feminine hair aesthetic she risks being read as non-feminine and non-heterosexual, that is, as butch and lesbian. To be big and muscular, and with hair, disturbs the re-production of gender. This is because, as Bordo (1993) argues, femininity and masculinity have been 'constructed through a process of mutual exclusion' (as quoted in Conboy *et al.* 1997: 97).

Female masculinity – tomboys

The word 'tom' has been used historically to depict 'deviant' women. For example, prostitutes have often been referred to as 'toms' (as they still are, for example, in the television police drama series *The Bill*). This relates to the arguments presented by Esther Newton (1991) that sexually active women are in effect marked as male. In relation to football participation many of the women talked about being 'tomboys' when they were younger. Collette, aged 32, remembered being told that 'I was a tomboy because I started to play'; and Shirley, aged 33, described her experience of being boyish:

> When I was younger, as a teenager, I looked very boyish and whatever, and I think that not only did they assume sometimes that I was a boy . . . I would often get called 'sonny' . . . When they realised you was a woman, they assumed that you might be gay, because you look boyish . . . I think in the end my boyfriend was more embarrassed by that, you know we'd go somewhere and they'd say 'Come in lads'.

Rita Laporte (1971) argues that tomboyism tends to be consigned to girlhood, which presents less of a threat to patriarchal power, and Barbara Creed (1995) posits that it is the narrative of the tomboy that functions as a 'liminal journey of discovery in which feminine sexuality is put into crisis and finally recuperated' (Creed 1995: 88). The research demonstrates this point:

> Didn't get to play for a while as a teenager because I felt it wasn't right – I had to be a girl (respondent aged between 33 and 35).
>   Was not allowed to play at school and when I hit my teens I did not want to play because I wanted to be a 'woman'!
>
>   (respondent aged between 27 and 29)
>
>   When I was younger I stopped playing because I was called a tomboy, but now I don't care.
>
>   (respondent aged between 24 and 26)

As Halberstam (1998) suggests, 'tomboyism for girls is generally tolerated until it threatens to interfere with the onset of adolescent femininity' (Halberstam 1998: 268). Sportswomen's references to *having been* a tomboy and the later rejection of this form of masculinity beg the question whether some sportswomen conform to gender 'logic' through fear of not being recognised as 'woman' and force themselves uncomfortably into prescribed femininity.

The research provides evidence that some of the women did challenge hegemonic femininity. However, not looking like a woman/girl equates to looking like a boy or man. Some of the women actively appropriated a corporeality that could be read as masculine. However, this was largely contained within the relatively safe boundaries of tomboyism. For example, Di, aged 29, stated: 'Been a tomboy, always have been, always will be . . . I'm a working class tomboy'; and Tamsin, aged 29, described herself as a dyke: 'quite boyish, short hair, "sorted", likes a laugh'. The juvenile style receives less 'policing' compared to the butch. In the domain of sport the butch body is largely pathologised and abhorred, and read wholly in relation to aberrant sexuality. She is effectively excluded as a legitimate footballing body and this might go some way to explaining why none of the women came out as butch.

Conclusions

Through a feminist poststructuralist analysis of power relations I have highlighted the different experiences of football of the women questioned or interviewed in the course of my research. I have shown how disciplinary power operates within both gender and sexual relations, and through various practices. The effects of the operation of power are dynamic and shifting, and at times serve to regulate women's experience of playing, and this can often lead to the exclusion of some players.

I have identified three sites where exclusion was experienced. First, the women experienced the social construction of the game as a 'boys' game' through schooling and in relation to gender. Second, in relation to sexuality and as a result of homophobic practices, lesbian players were positioned as an anathema. Finally, and this time in relation to 'compulsory' heterosexual femininity, players who displayed 'female masculinity' were viewed as unrecognisable footballing bodies. This last example of social exclusion is significant because it has been declared that the 'future of football is feminine', notably by João Havelange of the Fédération Internationale de Football Association (FIFA). Such a statement can function to foreclose footballing opportunities for both players and the game.

Despite evidence of exclusion, I have also indicated how women's participation in football has affected existing regimes of power relations. For example, the women I questioned and interviewed normalised and routinised football in their lives, reflecting their girlhood experiences of informal play in local neighbourhoods and/or playgrounds. Some lesbian players have risked being 'out', and 'dykescapes' represent social and sporting spaces where lesbians feel that it is safe to display their sexuality. In this way gender and sexual relations to power have been reconfigured. However, the research findings indicate that as yet there has been no such celebration of female masculinity in football contexts. To conclude, the footballing butch remains socially excluded from acceptance as a viable player.

Acknowledgements

I would like to thank my colleagues at Leeds Metropolitan University, especially John Spink, for reading, and providing useful comments on, drafts of this chapter, and Sheila Scraton, for her advice and continuing support.

8

Talking to me?
Televised football and masculine style

EILEEN KENNEDY

In 1997 Finlay and Johnson published an analysis of *Saint and Greavsie*, a football discussion programme broadcast on the ITV network at Saturday lunchtimes during football seasons in the early 1990s. These scholars claimed that the role of television programmes based on football talk was to establish a discourse space 'in which men can interact without women and begin to perform masculinity' (Finlay and Johnson 1997: 140–41). Elsewhere (Kennedy 2000) I have argued that it is possible to identify markers of masculine style in televised football that constitute an address to a specific type of viewer – a 'masculine address' that excludes those viewers who do not identify with it. The evidence of such an address may explain the traditional lack of popularity of football with female viewers. Contemporary football discussion programmes, however, are no longer exclusively presented by men. At the beginning of the twenty-first century, can we find evidence to support the view that football discussion programmes still exclude women from their address? Does the presence of women on television football shows change the address to the viewers?

Of course, it can be argued that, historically, an attempted address to women has been built into all televised sport. Whannel (1992) presents evidence that there were some concerns even in the 1950s to broaden the appeal of sport on television beyond experts to the less committed majority. Whannel's research led him to conclude that one distinctive feature of the assumed model of viewers during the 1950s was that 'two oppositions – expert/novice and male/female – became condensed together' so that 'the implicit assumption becomes one of male expertise and female ignorance' (Whannel 1992: 30–31). The conventions that were adopted during that decade and that have remained in television sport – the magazine format, patterns of long shots and close shots, styles of commentary – were apparently intended to liven up broadcasts and thus to woo a floating audience of novices or occasional viewers. However, they could also be seen as elements in an attempted address to female viewers. Thus, according to BBC Television's guidelines for broadcasts of cricket matches, issued in 1952: 'During the day, particularly on a weekday, our audience must, generally speaking, be predominantly of the female sex, and I feel that they would prefer more commentary than the average male viewer' (cited in Whannel 1992: 31).

Whannel maintains that the 'characterisation of the target audience was a fundamental principle of television sport and its particular mode of address' (Whannel 1992: 38). Arguably, people's self-identification as targeted consumers has become a defining feature of contemporary consumer society. However, far from suggesting that the targeting of female viewers by the producers of television sport represented gender equality in the resulting mode of address, Whannel considers that wider cultural inequalities are coded into the text of televised sport:

> The cultures of sport in Britain have been distinctively male, rooted in masculine values and patriarchal exclusiveness. The knowledge of sport is differentially acquired by men and women. Television is identifying this, and reproducing it, not simply in the assumptions of the woman, drying the dishes, who likes to be told 'little tit-bits', but also in its very desire to inform women, which thus marks them as the subordinate onlooker, observing the culture from outside.
>
> (Whannel 1992: 31)

This chapter offers an analysis of one day's episodes of two Saturday lunchtime football discussion programmes broadcast almost simultaneously (one started a little earlier than the other) on competing television stations. Both programmes were broadcast on 8 December 2001, *Football Focus* on BBC1 and *On the Ball* on ITV1. *Football Focus* had an all-male presentation team and was broadcast on a public-service television channel, while *On the Ball* featured a female presenter and was broadcast on a commercial channel.

The similarities and differences that can be observed between the analysis of these shows and previous analyses of football on television may lead us to conclude that there has been a change in the address of football, in particular that contemporary football is less exclusively masculine in style than before. However, these changes might better be understood by alluding to the concept of 'pastiche', a style said to be characteristic of 'postmodern' culture, in which 'disparate styles and contents from what would normally be presented as quite different artistic eras and messages' are combined together in one work (Real 1998: 21). While the analysis below may be considered to reveal a difference in the style and address of contemporary football programmes, vestiges of the past are reproduced in the present. Contemporary viewers of televised football programmes require an increasing amount of 'cultural capital' to recognise that it is they who are being addressed. The address of these programmes remains imbued with discourses of gender, race and nation. The inclusion of some necessitates the exclusion of others: just as a host of social interests are written into televised football, others are systematically written out.

The gendered address of televised sport

Analysis of the gendered address of types of television programme has largely been limited to those programmes, such as soap operas, that are assumed to be popular with female viewers. This is hardly surprising, since television has been thought of as a feminine medium, due to its domestic location and a dominant style of presentation that allows for the interrupted viewing that is compatible with home-based working. Throughout the world more women than men watch television programmes, including programmes in all those television genres that are thought to be more popular with men, such as national news and current affairs (Stoessl 1987). Yet there is one exception to this pattern – sport:

> Worldwide, more men than women watch televised sports. In Norway, for example, 64 per cent of men and 49 per cent of women watch televised sports. In Germany, 75 per cent of men and 52 per cent of women regularly watch televised sports. Sports is the only TV program[me] type that attracts more men than women.
>
> (Cooper-Chen 1994: 266)

Even if these figures do not look dramatic, it is to be remembered that research on television-watching has indicated that female viewers allow men to dominate the choosing of programmes when they are at home (Morley 1986 and Gray 1987). If 75 per cent of men are watching a programme, it seems likely that a roughly equivalent number of women would be watching it too. If not, there appears to be a significant element of rejection of that type of programme by women. Yet there has been little analysis either of what keeps men watching televised sport or of what, seemingly, dissuades women from doing so.

This analysis is intended, therefore, to consider how viewers of televised football are addressed and how gender might be an important aspect of that address. The chapter draws on the work of the late Anthony Easthope (1990), who sought to identify those features repeatedly found in television programmes and films popular with male viewers. Easthope suggested that a set of three characteristics amount to what can be thought of as 'masculine style' in popular culture: clarity, banter and obscenity. To consider televised football according to this schema requires a wider array of signification to be taken into account, but it remains a fruitful exercise and it is illuminating to take each of these three elements in turn.

By way of a brief comparison, Modleski (1984), in her analysis of soap opera, found that the close-up was a defining characteristic of the genre. There, she says, it is easy to forget 'that characters even have bodies, so insistently are close-ups of faces employed' (Modleski 1984: 99), and their presence activates the 'gaze of the mother', providing 'the spectator with training in "reading" other people, in being sensitive to their unspoken feelings at any given moment' (Modleski 1984: 100). Just as Finlay and Johnson argued that football talk programmes enable men to begin to perform masculinity, Modleski's observations might lead us to think of soap opera as a space where women can begin to perform femininity. The following analysis of episodes of *Football Focus* and *On the Ball* explores to what extent, if at all, any of these features can be discerned in contemporary football discussion programmes.

Clarity

For Easthope, 'a style of apparently plain statement of truth without obvious personal bias is a masculine style', because 'It goes along with the masculine ego and its desire for mastery. Truth in this style is presented as something to be fully known, seen in complete detail . . . the idea of vision is supposedly as "clear" as water, as "transparent" as glass' (Easthope 1990: 81). The transparent style fetishises truth by treating itself as invisible and 'not really a style at all', thereby avoiding the problematics of what consitutes 'truth' or 'reality'. Meaning is presented as 'fixed, free-standing, closed round on itself', and truth as 'objective and impersonal, something revealed once and for all, and so there to be mastered and known' (Easthope 1990: 82).

In 1975 Buscombe edited what has become a classic study of televised football, called, rather appropriately, *Football on Television*. There are interesting things to be learned from this study, which become all the more interesting when compared to more contemporary representations of football on television. The articles in *Football on Television* focused on the televising of the World Cup in 1974, specifically on the match between Scotland and (former) Yugoslavia. Buscombe compared two title sequences from ITV and BBC broadcasts of the game. He focused on the use of graphics to distinguish between the two, since the camera shots within both sequences were derived from the same German television coverage. He observed that ITV included more graphics and studio shots than the BBC did, which could be related to ITV's conception of itself as a more 'popular' channel, with viewers who were more responsive to vicarious patriotism (transposed to interest in Scotland's fate) and whom it was trying harder to mobilise: 'Their titles employed a tartan motif in the graphics (which was replaced by orange, the colour of Holland [*sic*], with rather indecent haste once Scotland were removed from the competition). And in the programmes themselves ITV were franker in their chauvinism, the panel coming out in a rash of tartan jackets and rosettes' (Buscombe 1975: 23).

Buscombe remarked on the lack of non-naturalistic colour in televising football action, meaning that colour at all times approximated the natural: the grass was shown as green and the sky as blue, for example, suggesting a claim to 'reality'. He noted different subcodes at work in the title sequences, however, where non-naturalistic colours were used, leading him to suspect that the World Cup programmes constituted a mixed genre. Similarly, the neglect of the technical possibilities of television in its broadcasting of football, adding further to the effect of realism, was reversed within the title sequences. This, for Buscombe, betrayed the producers' view of the programmes as more than football – as football plus show business, designed to appeal to those who liked light entertainment as well as to those who liked football. In terms of framing, long shots showed play between individuals as well as goals, while closer shots showed individual effort, in almost every case focusing on a star player. This, Buscombe believed, reflected the emphasis in the programme on stars and goals, which 'is not necessarily the whole of what football is about' (Buscombe 1975: 30).

Buscombe observed that the camera positions – on one side of the pitch, approximately on the halfway line – were in accord with the 180 rule of classic realist cinema, which dictates that, if two people are placed opposite each other and the camera is showing them from one side, the director may not cut to a shot showing the characters from the opposite side. Such a position, Buscombe suggested, was a simulation of the view traditionally associated with an older, richer and more neutral football spectator seated in the stands at the halfway line, since standing spectators would go to either end of the stadium. As for editing style, rapid cuts between shots, again borrowed from Hollywood conventions, this time to signify excitement, characterised the title sequences, while editing was restricted to simple cuts during the match, further promoting the effect of realism.

More than 20 years later my own analysis of the televising of the Euro '96 match between England and the Netherlands on ITV revealed how little things had changed. Despite extensive developments in the techniques and technology of television, the same codes used in the broadcasting of Scotland v Yugoslavia in 1974 were still in use in 1996.

ITV's title and introductory sequences for Euro '96 abounded in non-naturalistic colour and extensive use of graphics, and, in an echo of the tartan motif noted by Buscombe in the coverage of the match in 1974, graphics, such as players' statistics, were projected in front of images comprising the theme: white clouds in a blue sky, above green tops of white cliffs or green fields and distant mountains. The BBC's coverage of Euro '96 appeared more sombre, with less use of graphics, which, when present, were overlaid on solid colour. A similar difference was observable in the two channels' use of theme tunes: there was a markedly patriotic and populist electronic version of 'Jerusalem' on ITV, in contrast to the controversial, because distinctly European (indeed, European Union), flavour of the fourth movement of Beethoven's ninth symphony, the 'Ode to Joy', on the BBC.

While non-naturalistic colours were ever present in the opening sequences, short pre-match recorded segments and graphics showing the players' statistics, the televising of the match itself conformed to the realist convention of naturalistic colour. When the match was shown skies remained blue and grass remained green, while other sequences made full use of the colour spectrum available to contemporary television technologies. The 'football plus show business' feel to the sequences preceding the match, which endured from 1975 to 1996, compounded the populism of ITV's address. In one segment graphics imitating cuttings from tabloid newspapers passed over the screen, indicating an address to the readers of the papers to which the featured headlines belonged.

What is most remarkable, then, in a comparison of the results of Buscombe's analysis and my own is, despite the time lapse, the absence of any major differences in televisual style. The conventions of realism, already grounded in televising football in 1975, remained fairly unchanged 21 years later. The number of cameras covering a match may have increased, but their positions – in the stands, behind the goals, or handheld on the touch line – were the same. For the most part the 180 rule still held: it was breached once in England v the Netherlands, when both teams were lined up immediately before the singing of the English (in fact, of course, British) national anthem, when the teams were shot first by a camera facing them and then by a camera behind them, positioned in the stand opposite. It is noteworthy that this exception occurred before the match began and was not repeated.

To return to Easthope, then, the techniques of realism in the broadcasting of football could be considered an aspect of the masculine style of clarity, as could the presence of on-screen graphics displaying group and team statistics, team lists, diagrams, and players' names and positions, appealing as they do to the discourses of science and knowledge.

While the episodes of *Football Focus* and *On the Ball* under discussion here did not feature live football broadcasts, a traditional feature of this kind of programme is discussion punctuated by football action highlights. However, apart from a live shot of players emerging onto the pitch, depicting the commencement of the second-round FA Cup match between Brighton and Rushden and Diamonds, early on in the programme, *Football Focus* featured no football action that was not used to illustrate the various items throughout the show. Since ITV had bought the right to show highlights of the Premier League, its programme, by contrast, was packed with action highlights. Yet, while the image remained in accord with Buscombe's analysis of the codes of realism in football broadcasts, this realism was undermined by fast-paced editing, jocular commentary, non-realist opening sequences and on-screen graphics.

For example, after an initial item on the England team's accommodation in Japan for the forthcoming World Cup, the anchor, Gaby Logan, announced 'some *action*'. There followed a fast-moving, blurred sequence as the camera travelled up to and into a football ground, and then emerged onto the terraces, to the sound of a tense drum beat. The title of the section, 'On the Road', was shown as if painted as a sign on a road. A series of highlights from Premiership matches was shown, each new match being indicated not just by the names of the teams but by a graphic in the top right-hand corner of the screen of the name of the football ground: Stamford Bridge, Upton Park, Craven Cottage. The commentary, like the music, was upbeat, interspersed with the tense drum beat to separate the matches. Intimacy with the viewers was signalled by the presumpton that they would have prior knowledge of the names of the grounds and the reputations of the players: 'A couple of Fowler moments, be honest, though, if it had been anyone else we wouldn't have shown you that one'; 'At the Cottage . . .'. There were also plenty of puns, such as 'The kid's done OK, Brian', referring to a commentary catch phrase and to the coach Brian Kidd.

There was, however, a great deal of discussion of league tables in both programmes, accompanied by illustrative graphics, which often remained on screen while the pundits' analyses could be heard. Other uses of graphics in the two programmes could also be considered to be elements of an appeal to science and clarity. The episode of *Football Focus*, for example, featured a series of graphics, 'Focus Facts', that appeared intermittently at the bottom of the screen in the style of a card index. The counterpart in the episode of *On the Ball* was a graphic strip at the bottom of the screen, showing 'Team News' from the Premier League. 'Focus Facts' gave information about the FA Cup, compared Manchester United to its competitors and gave odds on the next Manchester United manager. However, when 'Focus Facts' appeared during an item on Canvey Island FC, giving notable information relating to the club, this extended to no more than remarking that Canvey Island was the home of the R 'n' B band Dr Feelgood.

Aside from the action, both programmes regularly mixed genres and used plentiful non-realist camera techniques. A sequence in *Football Focus* featuring Vinnie Jones, the former Wimbledon player turned minor film actor specialising in 'hard man' roles befitting his footballing reputation, blurred sport and film, using black-and-white images intercut with colour. In the studio a quick discussion of the Division One table preceded an introduction to the next section – 'The Vinnie Jones guide to FA Cup giant-killing is coming up' – followed by a plug for *Sports Personality of the Year*, anther BBC programme. There was a link to Jones's new film, centred around a prison football team, and the monitor in the studio showed a still image of Jones in a typically aggressive pose, in extreme close shot, roaring. The image cut to the back of Jones's head at a football ground, with 'Mean Machine' visible on the back of his football shirt. He turned and looked down into the camera, with a menacing expression on his face. He then walked and talked into the camera, as the colour cut to black and white on key phrases. This film footage was interspersed with scenes from Jones's new film as well as shots of footballers training and playing to illustrate his points. Jones concluded the section with 'Remember fortune favours the brave' and a movie shot featuring him yelling 'Come On!' with fist clenched in close-up.

Drama and narrative were added to *Football Focus*'s representation of the FA Cup competition at every turn. An interesting example is its graphic table of FA Cup 'survivors', which combined drama with an appeal to clarity. An item on Hinckley United, a non-League team still in the competition, combined colour and black-and-white images, non-realist (because obvious) editing styles, and music to create characters from a team unknown to most viewers. Old black-and-white action footage was accompanied by classical music, which cut to fast house music and colour images of the contemporary team training. The players introduced themselves to the camera, interestingly without mentioning their names: 'I'm the guy whose goal got us through to the second round' and so on. The manager, the chairman and then the 'assistant physio' introduced themselves, the physio, shown on a ferris wheel, being described as 'Brian "Buster" Kendall', a former coal-miner and 'clearly one of the game's great undiscovered characters': 'I'm the man that's been doing this for 46 years.' The interview with Kendall, conducted on the ferris wheel in close shot – he was working at an amusement park – used nostalgia for the old days of football to create a dramatic storyline with a 'character'. A sequence about the town of Hinckley and the history of the club followed, with an interview with the manager in close shot against a backdrop of Bosworth field, the site of the historic battle in 1485. More shots of previous FA Cup matches were shown before the interviewer, who was never shown on screen during interviews, said 'Don't you just love the Cup?', as images of a fairground ride, involving the thrill of an enormous drop, were shown. *On the Ball* featured fewer dramatic sequences, having more action highlights to rely on than the BBC programme did.

Remembering that Buscombe (1975) had observed a 'franker chauvinism' in ITV's coverage of the World Cup in 1974, it is interesting to observe the 'orientalist' discourse of the item on the England football team's accommodation in Japan for the forthcoming World Cup. Foreshadowing the sequence on Japan, maps of Japan appeared, presuming a lack of acquaintance with the geography of the country on the part of the viewers. The distances between key cities were indicated. A sequence of images then appeared to the sound of traditional *taikô* drumming: a rising sun, young Japanese men playing beach football, their goal in the style of a thatched arch reminiscent of a Japanese garden feature, drummers and a crowded street scene. The music changed to a modern classical tune, an image of a bridge appeared and the voice-over talked about 'this luxurious Awaji island', asking 'Guess who's staying here?' Two women dressed in traditional Japanese costume were then shown moving in front of a hotel bar. The film was speeded up so that they appeared to bob up and down. One said 'Deibido', the other 'Bekkamu'. A shot of a white male reporter, dressed in jumper and jacket, appeared, then a sequence involving a tour of the hotel, using the same speeded-up camera technique as before, along with punning commentary, such as the remark 'They won't get bored if it's a lengthy stay' over scenes of a swimming pool. Various Japanese members of the hotel's staff announced the names of England players and of the manager – three chefs said in turn 'Suben', 'Yoran' and 'Erikuson'

– and the voice-over informed us that 'the staff were England fans before they qualified'. A concluding shot showed the staff lined up outside the hotel, bowing as the camera pulled away. Shots of a Coca-Cola flag outside the training ground, along with a Mickey Mouse statue and a pagoda, were then shown.

Scenes of fans, mainly female, beating drums and chanting, introduced an interview with Steve Perryman, a former Tottenham player and then manager of Kashiwa Reysol, saying that he had thought that 'the Japanese were very reserved, just sit and quietly watch, but it's not like that', before a shot of a female fan shrieking in dismay. Perryman's voice continued to be heard over images of more fans, again mostly female. He said: 'They need to have an idol, be it a pop star, be it a film star, or a football star.' The commentary announced that the Japanese are expert followers of fashion and that nine years before 'they gave football their own cultural twist', as a cameraman wearing a shirt imprinted with 'J League' was shown, before cutting to female fans eating with chopsticks, while the commentary stated that the J League had been successful up to a point, but that its trendy appeal was wearing thin. The classical music recommenced and the commentary contrasted the Football Association's deliberations over whether to renovate Wembley Stadium with Japan's decision to spend £4 billion on building new state-of-the art stadiums in time for the World Cup. A discussion of the potentially adverse weather conditions followed, before shots of the Japanese police practising anti-hooligan tactics against the threat of 'the mindless minority that follow England'. Upbeat classical music accompanied a fast-moving collage of images, including several of *geisha*, and a clip of the hotel manager suggesting that 'we'll be able to provide fish and chips' before laughing in what might have been embarrassment. A wide, establishing shot of the studio followed, showing a monitor running the previous sequence in the foreground. Logan joked: 'They haven't heard, Graham [Taylor], that we've now got a nutritionist, obviously, so that's one thing up our sleeves.'

Logan's concluding jokey remark, the visual gags in the sequence, and the use of image montages and music all indicated not only a distance from realistic football action coverage, but also the potential for banter in sound, image and graphics. The next section explores this further.

Banter

The phenomenon of football-related comedy, spearheaded by David Baddiel and Frank Skinner's *Fantasy Football* on British television, indicates the interrelationship between humour and football. Yet it can be seen as a particular type of humour, the specifics of which may be extracted to point to another aspect of masculine style in televised football. Easthope (1990) considered that banter, even if not exclusively masculine, was so often used as a form of masculine exchange that it could be seen as a second feature of masculine style. There are three aspects to banter according to Easthope, one relating to its mode of operation and the other two remaining to its content:

> As humour or comedy, banter makes use of every kind of irony, sarcasm, pun, clichéd reply, and so is an example of the joke . . . The content of banter has a double function. Outwardly, banter is aggressive, a form in which the masculine ego asserts itself. Inwardly, however, banter depends on a close, intimate and personal understanding of the person who is the butt of the attack. It thus works as a way of affirming the bond of love between men while appearing to deny it.
>
> (Easthope 1990: 87–88)

Finlay and Johnson (1997) claimed that football talk, as exemplified in *Saint and Greavsie*, was an instance of banter. They pointed to the 'playful antagonism between St John (the Scotsman) and Greaves (the Englishman), which is employed to legitimate racist and/or chauvinist remarks' (Finlay and Johnson 1997: 137). They went on to suggest that it was possible to observe within their dialogues, on the one hand, 'an outward assertion of the masculine ego underpinned by the aggressive emphasis on national difference. On the other hand, this aggression is often offset by the tacit expression of personal understanding between the interlocutors – illustrated by their physical closeness' (Finlay and Johnson 1997: 137).

Finlay and Johnson's wider concern was to demonstrate that the characteristics previously associated with women's gossip, as a uniquely feminine style of communication, are also applicable to televised football talk between men. The authors stressed the social function of football talk, which 'may initially appear to be about the exchange and supplementation of information (scores, league tables, players and teams), . . . [but] is actually much more. This is because this type of discourse also performs an important function where social relationships between men are concerned' (Finlay and Johnson 1997: 140).

These authors also suggested that, as existing research has indicated, the principal function of conversation is not always the exchange of information. The role of television programmes based on football talk is, then, to establish a discourse space 'in which men can interact without women and begin to perform masculinity': as with women's gossip, the function of the talk becomes a way of accruing 'a pool of common experiences' based on the dissection of the characters' lives, which can be 'commented upon, criticised and sanctioned', thereby creating a shared perspective on the world (Finlay and Johnson 1997: 140–41).

Finlay and Johnson, and Easthope before them, restricted themselves to a consideration of talk in their analysis of banter. However, television is more than just talk, as discussed above. We could consider all channels of communication observable in televised football to contribute to the effect of banter, including image, graphics, sound effects and music. It might also be observed that the surfeit of communication that their simultaneous use creates reduces the potential for effective information exchange – how is it possible to keep track of everything that goes on?

However, Finlay and Johnson did not conclude that football talk equates exactly to women's gossip. They suggested that the differences between the two forms are equally significant. The focus of women's gossip is the sphere of private and personal experience. Football talk revolves instead around infringements of rules and players' professional lives, and in so doing marginalises the personal. These authors went so far as to say that 'the appearance of concern for the lives of other people and a creation of intimacy' is 'ultimately revealed as a sham' (Finlay and Johnson 1997: 142). The effectiveness of banter in creating a sense of intimacy relies on its exclusivity, its operation within a shared realm of knowledge that is difficult to break into. In this sense, the traditional lack of address to women in football talk has been part of its address to men, which is ultimately related to its characteristic form of communication: approaching intimacy without engaging the personal.

The opening sequence of *Football Focus* provides an ideal illustration of the characteristics of banter that Easthope observed: it includes nicknames, slang and physical comedy, involving a classic outward expression of hostility resting on affection and intimacy. The episode of *Football Focus* that is the subject of this analysis opened with the male anchor, Ray Stubbs, located in the public space of a football stadium, holding the FA Cup. The image alternated from colour to black and white, perhaps signifying a combination of seriousness and nostalgia. Vinnie Jones appeared on screen, knocking into the presenter, whom he called 'Stubbsy' and taking the Cup from him, while saying: 'I've got some sound advice on how to get into the hat for the second round.'

Many of the features observed by Finlay and Johnson (1997) are in evidence in both programmes. The pundits in both shows were smartly but casually dressed and sat close together. In both programmes, however, the anchor sat separately and shots of all three together were rare. Nicknames, revealing intimacy with players, were used with regularity: 'Stubbsy' and 'Crooksy' on *Football Focus* for example, and 'The Governor' (for Paul Ince) on *On the Ball*. However, Graham Taylor, one of the two pundits on *On the Ball* (the other being John Barnes) mistook Gaby Logan's name towards the end of the programme, revealing, perhaps, an absence of intimacy, and while Logan engaged in jokes, examples of banter were more easily discernible within items such as 'On the Road' (mentioned above).

Finlay and Johnson (1997) contended that the intimacy within banter is ultimately revealed as a sham, since familiarity remains at a superficial level, with players' personal lives not being part of the discussion. This analysis might also characterise some of the items on *Football Focus* and *On the Ball*. The latter offered a piece on the financial problems of Nottingham Forest, for example, focused on a radio phone-in and featuring an interview with the team's captain.

Football Focus included an item on Manchester United, debating possible successors to Alex Ferguson as manager of the club. There was more to this sequence than objective debate. Ferguson was shown interviewed in close shot; then came a collage of newspaper headlines, documenting the club's troubles, bouncing around the screen, which was tinged red. The mixing of media gave an opportunity to evoke both the drama and the banter of the tabloid press: 'Gift of the Fab'; 'The Secret Battle for Manchester United'. The presenter for this sequence was the black former footballer Mark Bright, who wore a red scarf. A series of 'vox pops' with fans was then shown – a young man, an old man, another young man, a young woman – before a clip of Bobby Charlton in the stands and a close shot of Ferguson chewing in slow motion, allowing the viewer to ponder his facial expression. An excerpt from a radio interview with Ferguson in reflective mode followed, with the logo of BBC Radio 5 Live on screen alongside a still image of Ferguson in close shot. The discussion was intimate, about trust and disappointment with the press. A graphic sequence about possible successors to Ferguson followed in the style of a promotion for a Hollywood film. More 'vox pops' were shown, with fans pausing and shaking their heads in silence in response to being questioned as to who should replace Ferguson. Their silence drew attention to their facial expressions in this sequence. Then Peter Spencer, the sports editor of the *Manchester Evening News*, was interviewed in the paper's newsroom, with the sports page on the computer behind him. Spencer's suggestion of Eriksson was followed by a shot of Eriksson, then a graphic of Manchester United's December fixtures. An interview with Ruud Van Nistelrooy was shown, before returning to Spencer. The interviewer, who never appeared on screen, gave the statistics of the last games and asked whether Manchester United could make up its losses. In the studio the presenters continued to discuss statistics, while a graphic of Manchester United's central defenders appeared and the discussion turned to strategy. Individual players' injuries were mentioned and the 'Focus Facts' graphic reappeared, comparing Manchester United to its competitors and giving odds on the next Manchester United manager. The entire report had a serious, subdued feel.

A mixture of styles appeared in this sequence. It centred on the public domain while relating the issues to fans' emotional responses. The fans were shown within the public sphere, on the street, but were asked for their personal reactions. Statistics vied with the drama provided by newspaper coverage of the story and the Hollywood-style graphic sequence. The tenor of the interviews with Ferguson was particularly interesting. Modleski (1984) maintained that close shots were particularly evident in the 'feminine' genre of soap opera, allowing viewers to develop skills in reading people and their emotions. Such a possibility was presented here.

Similarly, on *On the Ball* an item on Paul Ince featured an interview in close shot, with Ince being asked penetrating questions. Ince, 'the golden oldie of the governors', was asked, to the sound of 'chill out' music, whether he had mellowed, while a black-and-white slow-motion image showed him walking during a match. An abrupt cut to a full-colour image and fast-paced, aggressive guitar music featured Ince performing an athletic tackle. As the commentary suggested that he was 'never going to grow old gracefully' Ince was seen being shown the red card. The interview with Ince that followed featured an array of camera angles, moving to extreme close shot as Ince described the closeness and camaraderie of 'the lads', and responded to questions about his future beyond playing.

There are other sequences from *Football Focus* that take the style of intimacy much further, to a point where it becomes difficult to suggest that it was a sham. The item on Canvey Island built up individual team 'characters' in a style reminiscent of soap opera, concluding with visual banter. Players were shown in the domestic realm and were asked questions that are intimate in nature – for example, how they had coped with retiring from professional football. After Stubbs introduced the item with the line 'Part-timers aren't going to give up their day job quite yet' the scene shown depicted a family home, where the wife was going out, presumably to work, kissing baby and husband goodbye. The commentary said that: 'Not so long ago, non-League clubs were full of postmen, builders and market traders. But times have changed. So here's a modern-day tale of the househusband, the golfer, the king of Canvey Island and a growing Cup reputation.' Sections focusing on various players matching these descriptions followed, beginning with the househusband, as the commentary told us that 'Neil swaps tactics for *Teletubbies*', the popular BBC programme for infants. Each player was asked to comment on the following one, so that 'the golfer' was described by 'Neil' as 'a bit of a character'. The golfer was Julian Dicks, a former West Ham player with a 'hard man' reputation, who had to retire due to injury. The presenter, Garth Crooks, another former footballer, greeted him on the golf course with 'Hell of a goal, Jul' and discussed his life after professional football: 'A lot of players when they move out of football find it difficult to find something they love doing.' Then came an interview with the manager, described by Dicks as 'larger than life'. A map of London and the Thames appeared, in bright yellow and blue, with a large bouncing arrow showing the location of Canvey Island in the style of *Dad's Army*, yet another BBC programme that viewers were expected to have seen. The groundsman was then shown shovelling mud from the pitch.

Another item on John Terry, an England Under-21 and Chelsea player, asked him to talk about his idol Eric Cantona, his ambitions and what kind of things he was learning. The emphasis on his youth was compounded by his being given a present to mark his 21st birthday, which he was then asked to unwrap on camera.

The item on Michael Ricketts illustrates the range of styles observable within *Football Focus*'s presentation. Ricketts, a black player, was featured against a black background, in close-up, while questions were fired at him in the style of a quiz show such as *Mastermind* (which was, predictably a BBC programme too). As he responded to the questions – 'Name? Age? Height? Weight? Position? Club? Number of goals this season? Career ambition?' – the answers appeared on the screen. Ricketts was shot from above, so that he was looking up at the camera, giving the impression of boyishness. He was discussed in terms of his financial worth – he cost Bolton only £250,000 – and his action on the pitch, with newspaper headlines and statistics describing his performance. No other English player had scored more goals in the Premiership that season. He was asked to describe himself as a player and to talk about his background; then shots of Bolton's club museum showed images of players from the past. The presenter, off screen, suggested that 'a visit to the club shop shows how hard it is for a new, young player to make an impression' as a shot of a book, *Bolton Wanderers: The Glory Years Remembered* was shown. The presenter explained that there was nothing in the shop that carried the name or face of Michael Ricketts, and the shop manager said that they might be bringing out a cartoon-style picture of Ricketts soon. Ricketts was asked to comment on his awareness of the club's history and old footage of Nat Lofthouse was shown. Describing Ricketts as 'Mr August in next year's Bolton calendar', the interviewer said that 'he knows where his heart lies'. Ricketts then said, in a Lancashire accent: 'Obviously I'm English, I was born here, . . . most of my family were born here.'

This sequence presented the player as a commodity and the questioning style was deliberately combative. Yet the intertextual references to quiz show formats undermined the apparent aggressiveness of the questioning, revealing the dual tension of banter as a form of interchange. Nostalgia for the past was combined with an exploration of Ricketts's personal relationship with celebrity, adding drama and intimacy to the profile. The emphasis on his youth infantilised the player. However, just as Ricketts was presented as a new face of football, he was situated within a discourse that referred to the 'glory years' of football's address to white, working-class male fans, as he was apparently asked to assert his identity as 'obviously' English.

Banter is not only identifiable within televised football broadcasts of all kinds, it also characterises a great deal of press reporting on football, in both tabloid and broadsheet newspapers. A question remains as to how the presence of banter modifies the often highly exclusionary nationalistic discourses of football – what exactly is the joke?

Obscenity

The player Paul 'Gazza' Gascoigne featured largely in my analysis of ITV's coverage of Euro '96. A sequence ostensibly detailing England's journey to its match against the Netherlands, shown before the match itself, was given over to relating the scandals, press condemnation and praise surrounding Gascoigne. Gascoigne was shown drinking before unflattering newspaper headlines, such as 'Drunken England stars in plane shame', appeared over images of bars and aeroplanes, referring to the scandal, shortly before Euro '96 began, of Gascoigne and other players causing damage while flying back to England. Imagery of knights on horseback from the opening ceremony was followed by an English goal, then a Swiss goal, from the championship's first match, England v Switzerland, which resulted in a draw, rather than the expected England win. Shots of Terry Venables, then shots of the goal-scorer Alan Shearer, were followed by an image of Gascoigne, while newspaper headlines attacking his performance, such as 'Collect your boots and get lost Gazza', passed over the screen, and his voice was heard condemning the press. Gascoigne was then shown again, this time outside his house confronting a reporter, who remained off camera. Gascoigne asked: 'Have you played football before?' The invisible reporter replied: 'I've played football, yeah.' Gascoigne then said: 'Do you want a game on the grass? One against one, me and you? Why not? You talk a good game.' Scenes from the England v Scotland match were then shown, accompanied by upbeat pop music and the commentator's voice animatedly describing Gacoigne scoring a goal. More favourable headlines then passed over the screen, such as 'Gazza rocks jocks to their socks', and a triumphant Gascoigne was seen being kissed by a team member in front of a cheering crowd waving England flags.

The figure of Gascoigne has been popular with academic critics of sport, such as Critcher (1991) or Horrocks (1995). Both of these authors point to contradictions in the media's construction of Gascoigne as a 'star', contradictions that this sequence preceding the England v Netherlands match illustrates. This sequence went so far as to make the fickleness of the press attention surrounding Gascoigne the subject of the story.

Both Critcher and Horrocks point to the lack of discipline in Gascoigne's play and his personality. Horrocks considers that the 'really interesting thing' about Gascoigne is that 'he has not moderated his behaviour for public consumption' (Horrocks 1995: 163): he has been seen belching into an interviewer's microphone, crying, drinking, being overweight. In media terms this may be his downfall, yet for Horrocks the simultaneous presence of obscenity and artistry within the body of Gascoigne exemplifies the way in which

> the body/spirit split is mapped on to dualities within class and gender. The working-class male is seen as corporeal, gross, eructating [belching], the middle class is more spiritual, more refined, but looks with envy and a certain excitement at the physical carnival enacted by men such as Gazza. Gazza's body and personality become a text, which is alienated from him, in fact becomes public property, upon which can be inscribed various messages.
>
> (Horrocks 1995: 163)

Easthope suggested obscenity as a third characteristic of masculine style, relying on a Freudian account of the sublimation of anal eroticism to be found in a fixation with tidiness and order, which can be indulged only by a recognition of the anal, the obscene. Horrocks's account of Gascoigne's gross 'proletarian male body' and its representation in the Euro '96 sequence both contain aspects of the obscene. Critcher's account of the star system suggests that Gascoigne's arguably obscene disregard for convention is in fact what qualifies him for stardom in the first place.

The inclusion of Vinnie Jones constituted arguably the only reference within the episodes of *Football Focus* and *On the Ball* being analysed here to the element of masculine style that Easthope referred to as obscenity. However, Jones's reputation for aggressiveness and lack of discipline has become a marketable commodity, in fact a persona that has led him into a career in films. The caricaturing of obscene behaviour undermines its power to transgress boundaries. *Football Focus* exploited Jones's persona, referring to it throughout the programme to build up to the concluding comedic sequence discussed above. The lack of obscenity in these programmes and the increasing presence of intimacy may be taken to signal a shift in the address of televised football, an address to a different kind of masculinity. However, one must also bear in mind that both programmes were broadcast in the daytime and were therefore subject to strict regulations banning obscenity of any kind, unlike, for example, the late-night football programmes presented by David Baddiel and Frank Skinner.

All-consuming football

Who was being addressed by these two episodes of *Football Focus* and *On the Ball*? The mixture of genre observable in both programmes indicates a resulting mixture of address. Live action, statistics and discussions of strategy contended with drama, narrative and intimate interviews in each programme. Commercial forces clearly motivated the difference in subject matter between the two shows. Both programmes were shown on the same day, at nearly the same time. Yet, little mention was made of the FA Cup on *On the Ball*, the content of which was mostly made up of recorded action highlights from the Premier League. Since the BBC does not have rights to air Premier League highlights, *Football Focus* responded with more banter and more drama than the ITV programme.

How can the address of the contemporary televised football magazine format, as characterised by these episodes of *On the Ball* and *Football Focus*, best be conceptualised? Does the mixture of genres indicate that all potential consumers of football are now included in the address of this type of programme? Characteristics associated with the 'masculine style' were observable in both programmes, notwithstanding the presence of a female presenter on *On the Ball*. Equally, aspects associated with more 'feminine' genres – drama, intimacy, close-ups – appeared with some regularity, and more so on *Football Focus*, with its traditional all-male presentation team.

Yet the range and variety of generic characteristics within these episodes of *On the Ball* and *Football Focus* resist easy identification of a singular address. Nostalgic black-and-white footage of the 'glory days' of traditional white working-class footballing masculinity vied with images of househusbands, and 'vox pops' with the contemporary 'fan on the street', mostly male, but some female, and including both young and old. *On the Ball*, although dominated by its presentation of football action, with its arguably clearer connotations of masculinity, featured plenty of representations of women: they appeared in the sponsor's opening sequence, in the presentation team and throughout the item on football in Japan, where most of the fans shown were female. Yet the images of women shown in this sequence bolstered the exoticisation of Japanese culture that characterised the piece, and through the intertextual mapping of sound and image they helped to delegitimise Japanese football supporters as 'expert followers of fashion' who confused pop idols and film stars with football players.

In his discussion of media sport Real (1998) refers to Fredric Jameson's use of the term 'postmodernism' to characterise what Jameson calls the 'cultural dominant' of the logic of late capitalism. Real is particularly interested in media sport's use of 'pastiche' as a style characteristic of 'postmodern' culture. Pastiche is perhaps the most appropriate way of considering the range of signifiers within the two football programmes analysed here. Optimistically, the mixing of genres in these episodes of *Football Focus* and *On the Ball* may well be thought to broaden the address of these programmes beyond traditional male viewers. Pessimistically, however, any change might be considered to be only a superficial one, retaining exclusive markers of masculine style and reproducing cultural divisions in their strategy of targeting viewers as consumers of football. Perhaps we should avoid adopting such polar positions on issues such as the effects of the increasing commercialisation of football. Gender and televised football have an increasingly complex relationship. Experience of football now unavoidably rests on consumption. Yet consumers respond to the discourses of age, gender, race and nation encoded into the commodity that reaches out to draw them in.

Critiques of contemporary culture suggest that people have become inculcated 'into the "system" of consumer society . . . immersed in its logic, its modes of address and manners' (Lee 2000: ix). The commodification of football has been seen to be part of this process. In recent years there has been a trend to characterise football as moving away from its traditional male, working-class fan base, to embrace both middle-class and female consumers. Whether in fact this is an accurate picture is debatable (see, for example, Brick 2001 for a critique of this characterisation). However, what appears to be enduring is the idea that nothing remains outside the system of contemporary consumer society, so that 'the taken-for-granted character, the very "ordinariness" of our consumer society . . . makes it forgivable that for most of us, most of the time, we are unable to reflect on what is in fact an "extra-ordinary" and quite remarkable form of social organisation' (Lee 2000: ix). The ordinariness or extraordinariness of consumer society hinges on people's ability to recognise themselves as consumers targeted by the media, willing to step into the address of advertisements, magazines, films, television programmes or radio broadcasts. People know when a particular type of media is talking to them and when it is not. How do they know this? By recognising, consciously or not, the complex array of textual markers that positions them as target consumers. Theorists of language and identity have argued for a long time that the process of identification is fundamentally relational: people know who they are only by recognising what they are not.

The pastiche of mixed genre characteristics might be said to offer inclusivity. Yet it can be argued that to step into the address of an item such as *On the Ball*'s guide to Japan, to appreciate its humour, to decode the signifiers, consumers would need to recognise themselves as white, male and English. The language of televised football is not shared by all.

9

'Play the white man': identifying institutional racism in professional football

COLIN KING

In this chapter I examine how white men understand the power they have within the institutions of coaching and management qualifications to force black footballers to integrate on their terms. I draw on my own experiences as a student on coaching courses in 1994 and 1996.

In my analysis I rely principally on the work of two theorists, Frantz Fanon (1967) and Erving Goffman (1956): first, on Fanon's notion of the 'white mask', which assists black players to survive inside football; and, second, on Goffman's notion of 'performance', with which I examine the different ways in which men act out processes of racism on both sides of the colour line. I then suggest that the idea of 'institutional racism', as influentially developed in the Macpherson Report (Macpherson 1999), must be broadened in order to identify the outcomes of both white and black men's actions, in an industry where formal qualifications are secondary to racialised forms of power and privilege.

More specifically, Macpherson's definition of institutional racism must be made flexible enough to explain how racism takes place inside the professional culture of football, so that black footballers are coerced into having to 'play the white man'. MacPherson defines institutional racism as:

> The collective failure of an organisation to provide an appropriate, professional service to people because of their culture, colour or ethnic origins. It may be detected in processes, attitudes or behaviours that amount to discrimination through unwitting prejudices, ignorance and thoughtlessness, and racist stereotyping that disadvantage racial and ethnic groups.
>
> (Macpherson 1999: 17)

I argue against 'unwitting prejudices' as an explanation for how racism operates. Through this notion white men are rendered incapable of taking responsibility for the consequences of their actions. In the institutional structures of English football, if white men are not aware of the impact of acting white, we must show how they normalise the privileges they have over black men, by analysing the unconscious ways they live their lives inside the world of football. The task is to then see how the patterns of social behaviour inherited and nurtured by white men lead to outcomes for black footballers that are not always simply 'inclusive' or 'exclusive'. In this chapter I aim to demonstrate that, despite white men's lack of insight, it is their way of 'doing things' that has 'institutionalised' implications for how cultures of whiteness operate. Unlike the macro notions of whiteness that Roediger (1991) refers to in his work on slavery, I am interested in exploring whiteness through the narratives and performances of white men inside the culture of professional football.

As mentioned above, I examine the 'white mask' used by black footballers and argue that this mask reflects how they feel pressurised to perform in order to gain positions in the institutions of professional football as managers and coaches. The concept of the 'white mask' is useful in looking at how these black players confront the emotional pressures placed on them by white men to dress, act and talk like them. The 'white mask' is an important tool in understanding the sacrifices made by black footballers who have tried to fit into the white man's social world in the postcolonial age and in the context of football. The 'white mask' reveals the complexities through which black footballers dealt with how they had to perform in the presence of white men while on the coaching course. I explore this relationship between 'mask' and performance more closely, to show how racism operates on two levels for black footballers. First, it operates through what Goffman (1956) refers to as the 'public front', which in terms of the institutions in football represents the formal face of the organisation. Second, and more crucially, racism operates, as Goffman's notion of the 'private front' – the hidden and back-door level – helps us to understand, in leading white men to dominate the unwritten rules of inclusion that black footballers do not see.

Consequently, using the notion of 'unwitting prejudices' as an approach to understanding institutional racism inside the institutions of football cannot reconcile the 'meritocratic', but in fact non-meritocratic, processes involved in getting a coaching qualification. It cannot explain how the notion of a 'level playing field' is undermined by the way in which white men operate closed networks when they retire from the brotherhood of masculine competition on the field of play. The colouring of opportunities afforded to white men can be disguised by the delusion that an FA coaching badge is the first important step towards getting a job as a coach or a manager in English football. What lies beneath this fantasy of equality is the set of prejudices that exist in the institutions of coaching and management qualifications, where the colour-blind institution of football suddenly becomes colour-specific through the ways in which jobs as coaches and managers are arranged. Black footballers do not always see the power that white men have to enforce the ways in which they should compromise themselves to achieve a position of dependency alongside them in this industry.

In this chapter I argue that white men see and use their power to discriminate against black men in different, invariably implicit, ways. They are implicit in the rules that govern the gaining of coaching and management qualifications in what Goffman (1956) refers to as 'settings': the playing field, the classroom and the bar area. The way that white men act in these settings reveals that whiteness is a set of performances that reflect the individuality of the ways in which they accept black footballers into 'their' institutions. Consequently, I shall use the metaphor of the 'white mask' to show how black footballers moving into coaching and management spaces use the 'mask' both as a public performance and as an internal mechanism to survive the pressures of being essentialised simply as a black coach or a black manager.

In analysing the challenges that black footballers face in integrating into a culture that white men have developed, I suggest the present ways of identifying institutional racism in football must be rethought. To see how racism takes place in the institutions of football I look at how men read, interpret and respond to new power dynamics in their roles as course tutors and course members. We can see how black men and white men have differential access to privileges in their approaches to obtaining coaching qualifications.

The metaphor of the 'canteen culture', cited in Macpherson 1999 as intrinsic to how institutional racism operates informally, is too simplistic to explain the contradictions of white male behaviour. I argue here that there must be more detailed reference to the forming of white networks, and to the social and political dilemmas that black footballers have to confront as they attempt to enter. By paying close attention to the difficulties that white men have in adjusting to the realities of sharing their power with men who are not white and do not act white, whiteness is revealed as an historical process and as a form of vulnerability.

Forms of whiteness and social exclusion on the coaching field

A coaching qualification sells a dream that black men can compete on equal terms with white men and that equity exists inside the institutions of football. To dispel this notion of equality, as part of my PhD research I took part in the full licence course (since replaced by the UEFA 'A' qualification) in 1994. I wanted to understand the cultural pressures placed on students by the location and the rules of the course.

Historically, white male control has evolved through the power given traditionally to the FA's Instructional Committee, made up of older white men from the army, the county FAs and universities, to impose the general structure of the course. As of 1994 they suggested that they could judge the competence of students, without regard to their own race or gender bias, by using an 'assessment sheet' to award marks from A to D on each of the following 14 criteria:

- general – appearance, enthusiasm and general manner, ability to inspire players, knowledge of content;
- organisation – skill in organising space and equipment, explanation/direction, realism in practices;
- observation – ability to diagnose key faults, ability to progress in relation to player's failure;
- communication – quality of voice, speech habits, effectiveness of instructions, effectiveness of demonstrations, skill in dealing with player's failure.

The format of the 'assessment sheet' has been changed since 1994, but the practical work, which comprises 60 per cent of the course, still shows how whiteness is a required performance. It is embedded in the structure of the course and enforced by white male personnel.

The legacy of colonialism was established by the instruction to engage in all the assigned pre-course tasks. The requirement to watch and read the English 'Winning Formula' videos and books by Charles Hughes, a white English gentleman in his 60s who was then the FA's Technical Director, set up a white male order. The pressure to reproduce a white, male, English order was reinforced further by the expectation that participants would perform in Umbro kit, Umbro being the makers of the national England kit. The unwritten command to follow this dress code formed part of the heritage in which one norm of whiteness becomes institutionalised.

Whiteness as a heritage could be seen to operate far more distinctly in the location of the full licence course, which was held at the National Sports Centre in Lilleshall, 30 miles from Birmingham in the leafy countryside of Shropshire. A regional and historical form of whiteness was evident in the 100 acres of rich green land, set in a white rural district and accessed through large iron gates leading to a mansion hung with portraits of famous white Englishmen. On entering the main building and walking on into the changing rooms, one was confronted by a notice board that read: 'This Building was donated to the Sports Council by the South African Government in 1939'. As in the work of Fanon (1967), buildings represent the colonialist past, in this case the large Victorian houses positioned some distance away from the playing field. The absence of black men from these houses reflected an echo of the apartheid era.

The tutors involved in the construction of the course were all white. They had had instilled into them patterns of language and behaviour that enabled them to stamp their personal style on the format of the course. Fanon (1967) showed in his work on Algerian society in the era of French colonisation that the black man must act white or disappear: in the context of football he faces a similar problem. On the course black men faced acts of social exclusion that could be detected in the way in which white men, predominantly middle-class former teachers, created routines. They had to follow these routines over 14 days, during which white men were placed in controlling positions as group tutors and group leaders. The power that white men have was enacted in the informal ways in which they responded to the course structure, while simultaneously conveying the illusion to the black participants that they had to abide by the rules in order to be successful on the course. White men, then, unconsciously failed to see the constraints placed on black participants who had not themselves been in structured rural environments under their own control:

> I don't think it matters where you come from. Everybody, once they come on this course, has as equal a chance as anybody. It does not matter what race or what sex you are, if you are a professional player or not, or if you were a teacher, everybody is judged on the same standards.
>
> (Steven Reid, course tutor, 1994)

What is reflected in this comment is the difficulty that white men have in understanding that their assumed place and way of being in this system may have unfair consequences – that their colour-blind position is the premise upon which they discriminate. It is therefore important to hold up a mirror to what white men do not see, to reflect back what seems unconscious to them. As a participant on the course, by observing how white men conducted themselves I was able to understand how forms of inclusion in the field of the coaching qualification function when white men cease being players and become the guardians of a system.

Performing in the field: performing to new, white, male figures

A new and unpredictable performance was demanded of the black participants in the setting of the coaching course. They used a 'white mask' to show that they could be no different from white men. The identities that they shared with white men, as players and as working-class men, changed when they had to compete against them for coaching qualifications. Black footballers now faced a group of players and tutors who shared an identity as white men, despite their different class backgrounds. A shared whiteness was then nurtured and a comfort zone was unconsciously created, in which white men could perform without having to name the privilege of being or acting white.

Black footballers, through their 'white masks', saw the privilege that white men had of entering the course through the canteen area without having to think about being a different colour. The 'white masks' then concealed the pressure of walking into a room and having to think whether one's colour was as important as the club tracksuit being worn, or the people that one knew. The 'white mask' is also a conceptual tool. It reveals that black men are entering spaces that have been colonised by white men before them, where a legacy of 'being at home' has been established.

The safety of being among other white men was reinforced by the presence of five white tutors, dressed in the same kit: Umbro hats, T-shirts, tracksuits, shorts and socks. This comfort zone of being around other white men in positions of power was enhanced further by the appointment of white sub-group leaders. In all four groups a paternal image of white male presence was promoted through the selection of older, well-known, white footballers. This gave authority to the manner in which the course coordinator outlined the expectations for the following 14 days. He stood in front of the group in a military pose, clipboard in hand, with his arms folded and his legs firmly apart. He spoke in a cold, harsh tone, without making eye contact, while he made explicit what would be expected of the participants in the course:

> It's important that all the sessions start on time. You must be out of your room, have your breakfast and be in the lecture room by 9 a.m., and then we come into this room for a group meeting. By the fourth day, when Football Association tutors have shown you all the practical demonstrations that may be given to you as a topic, you will be given your actual topic. It's important you study it, and I will be able to give some time in relation to your organisation. It is vitally important that we help each other out. All right, any questions? Good, see you in the morning.

> (course coordinator, 1994)

At this first stage of the course whiteness as a performance was enacted by the way in which the white men sit at the front of the group, unperturbed by the threatening tone of the announcement, while the three black participants positioned themselves at the back of the class. The black participants' smiles were the first examples of the use of 'white masks' as a coded response to demonstrate to white men that they could cope with the performance needed to acquire the coaching qualification. The smiles also concealed an internal fear that white tutors did not recognise the difficulties that they presented to black footballers, as illustrated in the following comment:

> There are definitely more black people on the course this year, but I am the only one in my group. The tutor and the other coaches, without even knowing it, have got a way of making you feel really isolated and for younger people it could really destroy them. If there are certain politics I think it depends what professional club you are with will influence your chance in getting the badge. It's certainly true the savages like me will need more help.
>
> (black course participant, 1994)

This comment reveals the power that white men had or were given to mystify black participants in the course, to make them feel inferior by invoking an uncertainty about how they should act. White men were now in the position of assessing whether black footballers were competent to be given coaching qualifications, on the basis of how they reacted to the course rules and their interactions with other white men. The black participants might also be accepted depending on the team they had played for and how they were seen as operating in relation to their racial identity.

For black footballers a new type of racism emerged that was different from the overt form that they had experienced on the playing field as players. Kovell (1988) describes two processes of racism under slavery in the United States: first, the 'dominant form', practised in the southern states, which abused the black male body, and which is similar to the abuse of black players on the playing field; and second, an 'aversive' form, practised in the northern states, where whites did not want black people to live among them. The aversive form of racism could be seen to operate in the way that white men denied black participants access to closed spaces, while creating a belief that a qualification was essential to the development of their careers. Black footballers were excluded from the networks that were deemed necessary to acquire the real qualification and that lay outside the formal settings of the course. They saw only the front of the stage, where the five white tutors demonstrated a coaching practice that was promoted as the only method of being awarded the qualification.

The influence of the five white tutors was evident in the 'command style' of coaching, which was similar to the method of control used in relation to black footballers who endeavoured to get coaching qualifications. This control was established in each of the sessions by the way in which the white tutor would stop the game, analyse a mistake and show the participants how to correct the mistake. The absence of black tutors from such presentations suggested that the performance would not be valued as authentic if it was not carried out by a white man. The 'command style' epitomises a quality of whiteness performed by white men that is actualised through a cold physical demeanour, a harsh tone and non-negotiable instructions. This was demonstrated in the following comment from a white course tutor, one example of how whiteness, as a performance and a narrative, was enacted on the course:

> Stop, stand still, let me take your place. This is what I want you to do. Do you understand? Good, now let me see you do it. Great, that's exactly what I want. That's good, you have done well. So have you. You could tuck in more, and what are you doing over there, half asleep?
>
> (white course tutor, 1994)

Although the five tutors adopted slightly different approaches to their coaching demonstrations, they shared a common body position, standing on the side, deliberately away from the students. They would stop the game with a loud shout and walk slowly onto the pitch. These are examples of how white tutors revealed the performance that all candidates would have to show they were comfortable in re-enacting. However, the possibility remains that it was the quality of the relationship with these white tutors that determined success or failure. Black footballers faced continual tests as to whether they could coach in a white setting, and command the respect of white participants and white tutors on the course.

The challenge to gain the respect of the white tutors was activated on the coaching field by the position of the head tutor, who sat in the top chair monitoring all the groups. He would then bring together the whole group for a question-and-answer session. Here he was able to assess the compliance of the students on the course, and also to assess how naturally the black participants were able to assimilate. This assimilation started with the participants being given four topics to coach, on which they would be assessed by one of the course tutors in front of their white male peer group. Here the black participants faced the unknown over whether white men were assessing them as candidates, without reference to their capacity to act in the same ways as white men. These moments, when the unpredictable responses of white men operated, can be analysed through two selected incidents. These show how social inclusion in the setting of the full licence course was determined by how black participants dealt with the pressures to be accepted as just footballers taking part in the course.

In the first example, Marlon Jenkins was being assessed on a coaching topic, 'finishing from crosses'. He set up his session and it began. The tutor placed himself on the opposite side of the pitch, tightly holding a clipboard with the assessment criteria. The crosses were poor and Marlon struggled to get the players to respond to his command style. The white tutor dropped his clipboard angrily, to show that the session was going badly, and that his codes and the ways of performing that he expected were not being followed successfully. He interrupted, without any apology, and walked deliberately into the middle of the session, while Marlon walked out of the session, his head bowed, looking ashamed.

For two minutes the white tutor shouted and screamed, demanding what he expected from the players. Immediately the crosses went in and, as if by magic, the session ran smoothly. Marlon took over. His voice croaked, his body shook. He was reluctant to go in and correct the mistakes made by the players. This powerful act by a white man arrogantly intervening left Marlon demoralised over his failure to match the tutor's ability to effect change in the performance of the players. He could not reproduce, through the 'white mask', the deference shown by others towards this white tutor in a setting where he has taught and performed before. When I talked to Marlon at lunch-time, he was still demoralised and unable to establish what role he should adopt. He reflected on his confusion as to how racism operates:

> I don't know what went wrong. In all my days as a professional player I've never been through anything like that before. Its nothing like the pro game, although they have taught me a lot and I have learnt a few new things. This tutor giving me bad marks and treating me just like a school kid, and he kept on coming in during my session. It just felt really intimidating.
>
> (Marlon Jenkins, 1994)

What lay behind Marlon's confusion was his mystification as to how white men could be so at ease and comfortable in a setting that was new and foreign to him. Despite Marlon's experiences of being around white men in professional football, he was adjusting to the power that white men have to conform more naturally to the rules that they had created in the context of the coaching qualification.

Later Marlon faced this same contradiction concerning the ways in which white men behaved and influenced his life when he experienced a change in tutor. During his second session the tutor who had given Marlon poor marks had to leave the course due to a family illness. His replacement, another white tutor, took over the responsibility for marking. He spent a great deal more time coming in during the coaching session on defending. Marlon's fear of a second white man degrading and undermining him was broken, as the outcome was that Marlon's marks improved considerably. His feelings of bewilderment reflected his having to function through uncertain rules, determined by the different moods and characteristics of two white men, who were privileged to act in highly unpredictable ways. As Marlon tried to examine the reason for this improvement his checking to see if the white tutors at the top table in the corner of the room were looking revealed a persistent fear of being caught out. Marlon's intermittently guarded and suspicious looks over his shoulder indicated the problems of relaxing in an environment where he could not predict how white men would respond in either their internal or their external worlds:

> I can't explain it. It just seemed easier and maybe it was because I knew this tutor as we both live in the same area of Islington. It's difficult to tell how these white men think. One is really miserable and gives me good marks; the other, the 'fat destroyer', gives me poor marks. The most difficult thing is getting used to the different approaches of the tutors. I don't know if it's racism or not, but I have been all over the country as a professional player and have seen different types of racism at different clubs, so I have developed a second sense to it and you kind of expect it at different levels. The worst kind of racism is not what they say. It's what they don't say in case they are accused of being racist.
>
> (Marlon Jenkins, July 1994)

What is pertinent from Marlon's analysis is that he measured inclusion through moments and exchanges, through the personal relationships that he had with the two white tutors. Racism was silent and inexplicable, taking place within an assessment process that reflected the unpredictable norm of whiteness. Whether Marlon received a good or a bad mark was not based on any objective appraisal, but on having to guess how white men would use their power to perceive him as fitting into a performance. This could fluctuate, depending on their feelings and perceptions. Whiteness retains its power through the way white men avoid being exposed as unreliable, vulnerable and fragile if they are not seen to be in control of their emotions. For the black participants the playing field represented a new threat to their dignity and self-esteem, and their ability to use the 'white mask' as a form of protection. Here they confronted more indirect and irrational acts by white men, without having any opportunity to speak out. Although they felt that, through the 'white mask', they had successfully copied the white tutor's coaching style, doubt emerged as to what 'meritocracy' meant in reality. Did it mean that white men could dominate the culture of the coaching qualification without having to reflect on their powers or the effects of their actions?

This privilege of white men led to feelings of victimisation and uncertainty in the black participants when they saw white students less competent than they were getting better marks because of their social links with the white tutors. The suspicion that white men were in a better position to pass the course, through their ability to operate within this mutual comfort zone, led the black participants to assess what it meant to 'play the white man' in their relationship with their white tutor. This example shows how the black participants had to reflect, using the 'white mask', on how they should deal with white tutors during the course:

> I just thought my tutor had very little real time for me. They said they were there to help, but during this period of time you were very lucky if you got two or three minutes with them. I feel their approach is rather teacher-like and they do seem to favour the teaching approach. Their approach is rather regimental. I like to have a laugh and joke. I don't feel there are any race problems with the tutors at the moment. The only politics I can see at the moment is the preferential treatment towards those who have some link with the Football Association.
>
> (black course member, 1994)

Implicit in this statement is the perception of white tutors as cold and distant. This form of alienation on the coaching stage was similar for the black participants to the classroom setting where white men swapped their suits for tracksuits. Consequently, both settings were experienced as regimented and controlling, as the black participants tried to sustain themselves while being uncertain as to whether they were being treated as candidates or as black men struggling in a white environment. In this environment they saw the power of white men to judge them as incompetent to operate inside their world.

The moments when racism became real as an experience depended on the ways in which the white norm influenced the lives of the black participants. Black footballers have to assess their ability to perform in an unsafe atmosphere where white men advocate equality and then act in highly preferential ways. This preference operates through the comfort of relating to other white men in a culture where men are not held accountable for acting white. Black footballers see that they do not have the luxury or the privilege of being ordinary, or of thinking that their race does not matter.

The tension when racism was taking place created an illusion that the privilege that white men hold was something in the black participants' imaginations, as the white tutors and candidates were reluctant to see whiteness as a series of actions. Instead they turned the mirror back onto the black players, claiming that they were the ones with a problem.

For example, one black player talked about a situation when the course tutor reprimanded him for wearing a baseball cap and sun glasses, and asked him not to swear in front of the other participants in the course. In this situation he used the 'white mask' as a mirror to reflect back the disrespect he felt from this white man, by parodying what the tutor said:

> You know that fat bastard, the 'fat destroyer'. How dare he come over to me and tell me to take my cap off because it didn't look appropriate for a coach. They want to get into the real world. When I'm down at my club there is no problem with me wearing a baseball cap. The funny thing about it [he begins to laugh] his fucking boss sitting in the corner with a fucking Umbro baseball cap and dark glasses. Who the fuck does he think he is? Not even my father talks to me like that. And you can't swear. Fucking hell, who does he think I am? A nun or something? The fucking prick.
>
> (black course member, 1994)

The comment showed the unintentional power of white men to put the black participants 'in their place' when they did not subscribe to the norms that they set and that only they could deviate from. They had the authority to dictate, interpret and reinvent the rules, despite the fact that at the start of each session each participant was told to wear a top and shorts, and to 'pull their socks up'. It was implied that one would automatically be guaranteed an A grade if one complied with these expectations.

For this black participant, while he tried to copy the white tutor's language, dress and actions, he faced the contradiction of the white assessor in the background wearing items of clothing associated with black culture, which he was being criticised for wearing, as contravening the dress code of the course. This showed how white men could normalise what was permissible in the internal culture of football, without any cognisance of the confusion that it could cause for the black participants. The white tutor could then control the environment in which the black participant was judged, particularly through having to wear a baseball cap, which had to be an Umbro cap to meet the conventions of the course.

The privilege that white men enjoyed to act without reflection was reinforced further in the freedom that the white participants had at the end of the course to shout 'hooray, hooray' and begin to mock the white tutors.

This typified the ease with which they could take risks that the black players would have had to think carefully about. This form of parody by white men of white men was made public and permissible, while the black participants had to assess more cautiously how they could parody white men, since their motives could be misunderstood.

It is symbolic of the lack of freedom that the black participants felt that they expressed their feelings in the absence of white players and became less inhibited, in their own private zone, by singing Gloria Gaynor's song 'I Will Survive'. The act of celebrating the sentiments of the song reflected their struggle in travelling through the contradictory ways in which white men influenced their chances to obtain the coaching qualification, as reflected in the following comment: 'I feel this course is just a mirror image of the personalities who run it. They are backward-thinking, racist and colonialist. You have a better chance of passing the course in America. Working-class and black people have no chance on this course' (black course member, 1994). This comment from the black player who had had the demoralising experience of being forced to take his glasses and cap off shows how he rationalised his experiences in this location as being linked to larger forms of racism outside the institutions of coaching. The temptation then was to see all the white men, without distinction, as being consistent in their dogma, and in the malicious manner that underpins the institutional world of football. This position, however, fails to recognise the complexity of these white men's individual capacity to exercise racism, especially in the private moments in which they performed in the absence of the black participants.

The black footballers on the course were excluded from the privileges that the white participants had to define themselves and their roles within the organisational culture of the coaching qualification, without any accountability for acting white. The black players then had to face white men who operated in what Goffman (1956) calls 'backstage'. In this case backstage was a space that was informal, closed and exclusive to white men.

The classroom setting and new forms of whiteness

The power of having a 'backstage' can be seen more clearly in the recent conversion from the FA full licence to the UEFA 'A' badge. The move from the coaching field to the classroom has enabled white men to operate on a more implicit level, through the subtle and unspoken ways in which they reaffirm their power. The conversion has moved the whole coaching and management structure of courses in English football towards the continental

European system. The major change involved is the shift away from the field, given the new requirement to complete 100 hours in the classroom studying the following components of the course:

- preparing for management;
- self-organisation;
- time management;
- managing people with the line of responsibility;
- counselling;
- communication;
- football food;
- football fitness.

The classroom setting has become the scene of new affiliations, where the additional hours are occupied in the presence of high-profile coaches and managers.

On the first day of the UEFA 'A' course in which I participated in 1996, a white male lecturer talked in great detail about the official route into the management role through the use of CVs. I sat next to another black player who was getting increasingly restless. I overheard him saying:

> What a load of shit. Do you think anybody in this room has ever got a job by filling out a CV? Do you really think any of these top white managers is going to respond to my CV, when they are more than likely going to give the job to their friends?
>
> (Darren Smith, 1996)

Darren's comment makes transparent the deceptiveness of a course where equality and citizenship are not connected to holding a coaching qualification. As he was aware, he would not be given the same powers as white men. He challenged the inherent contradiction between the way that white men preach the need for job descriptions and line-management responsibilities, and their simultaneous promotion of an informal route into coaching and management through networking with other white men. Networking was explicitly established as a working practice that took precedence over a coaching qualification in the following definition, taken from the section of the course materials on 'preparing for the management role':

> This refers to the activity of building up networks of contacts with individuals involved in the football profession who can potentially provide help and support for, and be involved in, the management role. If you list the people whom you know now or whom you have had contact with in the past, it is likely that you will discover you already

have a network of friends and acquaintances in the field. It is important to be proactive in networking, and think about whom you would like to meet, and who would potentially be an important source of support and advice. Knowing a network of people in the game is important in obtaining employment. They may be able to provide information about posts which are available or to act as referees, and comment on your personality and experience. Networking occurs naturally as your range of colleagues grows: however, there are ways of improving your networking skills, which are outlined as part of this module.

(Football Association 1996: 2)

This definition suggests that a directory of influential acquaintances is paramount in promoting one's career. It conveys the illusion that such a directory is open and equitable, and that all candidates can become a part of it. The implication that all candidates have the same rights and status disguises the performances necessary to enter and succeed in a network.

The necessity of having continually to perform, to sell one's self, is institutionalised in the following definition of 'impression management' and is closely linked to what Fanon (1967) calls 'becoming white or disappearing' in the struggles that black footballers face when trying to get jobs inside football:

The overall impression you create as an individual and as a professional is extremely important. The things you do and say help people to understand what you are about, they create an impression of you as a person. Learning to manage that impression is also an important part of preparing for, and building being successful in, the management role.

(Football Association 1996: 2)

This definition reinforces the need to develop personal relationships, to perform within social processes within which predominantly white men professionalise networks on an informal level. For black footballers these networks are formatted by the ways in which white men create rules of inclusion. Black footballers have little influence over reshaping and making explicit the sub-titles and textual messages that operationalise the power that white men hold.

The unwritten forms of white male power are embodied most prominently in the context of the classroom. This is where the performance needed effectively to become part of a network is revealed through the subtle powers of white men to define and approve how one is to act and how one is to talk. For example, on the UEFA 'A' course, during an afternoon discussion on networking, the white tutor asked what the important elements are in terms of communication. A black student enthusiastically put his hand up and said: 'I think it's important to try and work with people from different areas of the country, especially with more Asian people coming into the country. We need to find out how to work in the best way possible' (black participant, 1996). The tutor looked stunned and then responded apprehensively, with a vague look on his face. His smile dropped and his eyebrows rose as he said: 'Yeah, I am not sure what you mean, but let's move on.' A prominent ex-England coach put his hand up: the tutor responded with a very broad grin and warmly invited him to contribute, with a positive wave of his hand. The coach put his glasses at the end of his nose, and talked loudly and clearly, as if he hadn't left the coaching field: 'You see, at our club we have more and more players coming from the continent, more top players from the continent. There are many cultural and language barriers, and to get the best out of them we need to integrate them into our style of doing things' (Steve Bridges, 1996). The nods of approval from many of the white managers in the room indicated the almost telepathic manner in which they formalised a consensual response through the white male body.

Such moments are important indicators of how white men value each other, how they can talk and behave through pre-coded masculine modes that undermine the presence of black men, and their contributions to understanding the social and political worlds of coaching and management. In the first instance the voice of the black footballer, who talked about working with difference, was not heard or respected. This was in stark contrast to the acclaim given to the white manager, who talked about difference in the context of integration into his world. The ways in which participants in these courses conduct themselves in the classroom setting will affect whether they are seen as compatible with the cultural demands of the course and, more importantly, with the wider football culture, in which the institutional tensions between black and white are never challenged. Unlike on the football field, where white men demonstrate the norm of whiteness more publicly, in the classroom setting it features in these subtle processes of communication. This is where white men validate each other's experiences through unspoken moments of social approval, as the foundation of being included. This validation is based on mutual histories developed through social contexts that are enacted outside the classroom. The classroom represents these external locations where white men develop a sense of safety with each other and this is the basis upon which they reaffirm their co-dependency. It is these associations that permit an atmosphere of easiness for white footballers, which is at the centre of the problems that black players face, because these patterns of familiarity are not rooted in their histories.

Cheers: the bar of whiteness

In this section I want to consider the bar area as one of the most prominent examples of a 'backstage', where white men establish the institutional importance of white networking on an even more discreet but still significant level. The movement of white men from the field and the classroom into one of the symbolic spaces of white masculinity, the bar, reflects a football culture that has a special reference point in the power of white men. Through the rituals of drinking, particularly alcohol, the bar location, for white men, leads to the formation of networks.

Alcohol, as a means of inclusion, is illustrated in the following example taken from the UEFA 'A' conversion course in 1996, during which the white former England coach who had made the remark quoted above about foreign players integrating into the English game, retired to the bar. In the middle of the bar most of the white participants assembled around this white coach, drinking lager while listening intently to his amusing anecdotes about his coaching days. The laughter became louder and louder, as if they were at Speakers' Corner, as more white managers and coaches gravitated towards his performance. One or two of the black players situated themselves on the periphery of this process, in which the white coach was making a series of racist parodies of black players he had worked with. The white coach continued unaffected by the presence of the black players, while the other white members of the group were so intensely engaged that they were oblivious to the racialised content of the joke, an act that cannot be casually dismissed as just another case of 'unwitting prejudices':

> You know, I am standing in the coaching session trying to explain to this black geezer but nothing is going through. I say, fuck it, let's call it a day, so all the players get changed and shower. This thick black guy gets into the shower and comes out, and I tell you, he has the biggest dick I have ever seen in my life, and if he had tripped over he could have beaten the pole-vault record.
>
> (first team coach, 1996)

The punch line was accompanied by explosive laughter, a noise that reverberated throughout the room. The white tutors in the corner of the room colluded in the racist vernacular, unable to contain their enjoyment. The irony lay in the fact that these white men were caricaturing a black man's body while presenting a contrasting caricature of overweight white footballers resting against the bar.

The bar is an important feature of the coaching establishment and an intrinsic part of white male culture. It also represents an informal recruitment agency, with hierarchical forms of white male power, where the criteria for obtaining jobs are based on friendships, and thus on being secure within a relationship with another white man. On entry to the bar one noticed a group of white tutors lined up in order in one of the corners, separate from the students. The class divisions within whiteness were further reinforced by the separation between a group of players who had already got jobs but had been sent on the course to get the new UEFA qualification, and a group of white players who arrogantly stated that they didn't need the qualification.

For black footballers to break into these informal networks they needed to have been sponsored through a friendship with white players before, during and after the course. They had to adjust to the changing characteristics of the networks formed by white men, as illustrated by one incident. One of the black participants was sitting in the corner of the bar drinking an orange juice. Several white coaches and managers, drinking lager, surrounded him. One of the white men asked: 'Who is buying the second round?' The black footballer offered to do so and bought himself a pint of lager too, making his first attempt to force his way into this network. Speaking later about his experience of trying to assume a position alongside white men at that moment, he revealed the feelings hidden beneath his pretension:

> You know, I felt like a total outsider, although we laughed together and had a drink, it was hard being there. What was strange about it was these were the same people who were part of my group and when I had my session they did not want to work for me, and I even heard one of them say 'Let's make sure he gets a bad mark'.
>
> (black participant, 1996)

This comment shows the hidden barriers that black footballers have to grapple with and the false sense of inclusion that they can experience. Even when they share a drink with white men it is still unclear whether or not they are being accepted by their white colleagues. Although white men use their power in the environment of the bar in very crude ways, it is one of the three spheres that black footballers have to make sense of when adjusting to the norms of whiteness in the professional structures of English coaching and management.

Conclusion

In these different spheres – the field, the classroom and the bar – black footballers have to manage a series of relationships with white men in which they may have to 'play the white man' in comparatively different ways. This need to perform to the expectations of the white men who design the stages, and dictate the language and the social norms that define whiteness in the context of coaching qualifications, is executed by adopting the 'white mask'.

Black footballers face the unpredictability of the white norm through the individual capacity of white men who do not think about what it is to be white, or about the powers and privileges that they have in the systems that they produce. Whiteness is not fixed. It is a pattern of actions that has profound effects on black footballers, who cannot be certain that they are being integrated even when they comply with the norms of whiteness in their attempts to get a coaching qualification.

To change the outcomes of white men's behaviour in this regard, it is imperative that they begin to examine the processes and the actions that lead to forms of exclusion that are alienating black footballers and leading them to internalise their inferiority. If white men in the professional culture of football are to liberate themselves from their failure to see that what they do has implications, especially for those who cannot complain, they will have to review their privileged positions. They will have to see that racism in institutions is not simply a set of 'unwitting prejudices', based on ignorance and thoughtlessness, but is a behaviour that is practised. At present, there is no pressure to see and change the white norm as an intrinsic and unchallenged part of English football culture. To identify institutionalised racism is not simply a matter of whether black players pass a coaching course. It is also a matter of what they must do to 'play the white man' within the structures of English football.

10

Football and social responsibility in the 'new' Scotland: the case of Celtic FC

RAYMOND BOYLE

> Celtic have always been identified as a 'community club', representing the hopes and aspirations of a community, described generally – if somewhat mistakenly – as an Irish–Catholic enclave in Scotland.
>
> (Campbell 2001: 1)

This chapter examines the extent to which football clubs in Scotland in general, and Celtic in particular, influence social and political policy agendas that extend beyond football. To what degree does a multimillion-pound business such as Celtic plc address itself to wider social and community issues? Do concepts of community differ, for a club such as Celtic, from concepts applied elsewhere in Scotland or Britain? While the relationship between football and ethnic minorities has been viewed by some commentators as important within the English game, have concerns about sectarianism shaped a different agenda in Scotland? Before looking in detail at these issues it is worth making a number of initial observations about the specifically Scottish context.

The only game

Football simply overpowers all other sports in Scotland, whether measured by numbers of spectators, general public interest or media coverage (see Boyle 2000). Glasgow was recently recorded as third among European cities for average weekly football attendances, with only London and Rome ahead (*Sunday Herald*, 22 July 2001).[1] In addition, while commercialisation in general, and the selling of television rights in particular, have had significant influence on Scottish football since the early 1990s, this has not matched the effect of the television-driven financial boom experienced in English football. As a result, the dislocation felt by many football fans in

England as the game has been dramatically commercialised has not been felt so acutely in Scotland. While the cost of attending games has risen in Scotland as in England, and there has been a development of a 'corporate fan base' at some clubs, in many ways the pattern of support in Scotland remains more traditional than it does in England, where arguments about long-term fans being squeezed out of the game have recently been made. As I have argued elsewhere:

> In west central Scotland football has always been a part of a business and social network shot through with religious and cultural overtones. It is a network with its roots in a process of socialisation which involves family allegiances, the area you were brought up in, religion, schooling (with a strong Catholic state sector important) and work. While the new money and the new football supporters of the 1990s have moved into English football, the fan base in Scotland has remained largely unreconstructed. In many ways the people going to football in Scotland are remarkably similar to those who went 20 years ago. Yes, there are more corporate boxes and hospitality packages at Ibrox and Parkhead, but visit, say, Celtic Park and it isn't football's 'fat cats' dining there, rather the upwardly mobile Catholic working and business class, talking football and making deals.
>
> (Boyle 2000: 26)

Of course change has been marked in other aspects of the game, as the globalisation of the sport has had an impact in Scotland as it has elsewhere in the football world. The Scottish Premier League (SPL) is awash with foreign players. The former Scottish national football coach Craig Brown recently lamented the scarcity of opportunities for young domestic players at both Celtic and Rangers, where teams containing virtually no Scottish players are fielded increasingly often. Most of the leading clubs have become private companies in some form, with a range of shareholders (Morrow 2000). At the international level Scottish football is in crisis, as the national team failed either to qualify for Euro 2000 or to reach the World Cup finals in 2002. On the domestic front players' wages have continued to outstrip many clubs' income streams, resulting in most Scottish clubs, including Rangers, being in some form of financial difficulty. For example, Hearts, one of the bigger clubs outwith the 'Old Firm' (that is, Celtic and Rangers), reported a pre-tax loss of £3.8 million for the year ending 31 July 2001 (*Herald*, 12 October 2001), and later the same year Rangers admitted that it had an operating loss of £16.3 million. Indeed, one of the current concerns of Rangers and Celtic is that, despite their fan bases outwith Scotland and the strength of their 'brand identities' in markets such as North America, the revenues they receive from television, operating as they do in a relatively small domestic market, are paltry when compared with those of their English counterparts. On average the 'Old Firm' can expect between £3 million and £5 million a year in television revenues, while from 2002 onwards the average English Premiership club can expect at least £20 million. According to management at both Celtic and Rangers, this provides them with a structural funding problem that makes it difficult for them to compete at the elite European level.

The traditional rivalries in the Scottish game have also differed in some aspects from those south of the border. While both countries have rivalries between, and within, cities and regions, only Glasgow still has a football rivalry based in part on perceived religious, social and cultural differences. The sectarian overtones that inflect this rivalry can make issues of community liaison for the two 'Old Firm' clubs highly controversial and problematic.

Sport and politics in the 'new' Scotland

Before turning to focus on Celtic in particular, it is worth briefly examining the wider context of the developing interplay between politics, sport and public policy in Scotland since devolution began. With regard to sport and public policy the Scottish Executive, which to most intents and purposes is the Scottish government, has been active in two related areas of activity.

First, the Executive has backed a number of high-profile campaigns to attract major international sporting events to Scotland. The unsuccessful bid to secure the Ryder Cup golf tournament for 2010, led by the then First Minister Henry McLeish, also had as a key element a promise to make golf available to all under-9s who wished to try the sport. This formed part of a multi-agency approach that aimed both to boost Scotland as a destination for golfing holidays and to use golf, among other sports, to tackle aspects of social exclusion. It also signalled recognition by the Executive of the importance of major sporting events to the Scottish economy. As a result of the campaign the Ryder Cup tournament has been secured for Scotland for 2014, while a bid to attract the Euro 2008 international football tournament, partly on the grounds that it could be worth £450 million to the Scottish economy, was launched in 2001 (*Soccer Investor*, 16 October 2001). Second, the Executive's declared aim of pushing 'social justice' and the building of a more 'inclusive' Scottish society higher up the political agenda has not been insignificant for sport. A Poverty and Inclusion Ministerial Taskforce, under the Minister for Social Justice, has targeted health, education and housing as three key areas in which improvements must be made if the wider problem of social exclusion is to be tackled over the longer term. Across the country social inclusion partnerships (SIPs) have been working together, addressing the specific needs of various communities (Scottish Executive 2000). While sport may appear to some to be at the margins of this work, in 1999 the then Deputy Minister for Culture and Sport, Rhona Brankin, urged 'sports development officers to connect with social inclusion partnerships across Scotland to ensure that sport's contribution to this agenda is not overlooked. New partnerships need to be formed if we are to create a socially inclusive and cohesive Scotland. Sport is part of that solution' (Scottish Executive, news release, 3 November 1999). Since then sportscotland, the agency charged with developing Scottish sport, has stepped up its commitment to play a role in tackling social exclusion. Paul Kelly, the 'champion' of social inclusion at sportscotland, is clear about the role of that agency in relation to the Executive's policy agenda: 'sportscotland is convinced that sport can help achieve the aims of SIPs across Scotland by assisting them to engage with their client groups and, as a development tool in itself, assist with individual learning, reducing criminal activity within areas and promoting good citizenship amongst communities' (Kelly 2001: 19).

Research commissioned by the Scottish Executive and sportscotland, and published in 2000, indicated the difficulties and challenges to be faced in attempting to integrate sport into a wider social policy programme; in particular, programmes that seek to tackle urban poverty, crime and health issues, specifically in deprived parts of the country, require the targeting of resources (Coalter *et al.* 2000). However, little of this work has focused specifically on the role, if any, that professional and amateur sports clubs should play in such community-based policy. Initiatives that engage specifically with football and communities are, more often than not, driven by the clubs themselves, as in the case of Celtic (discussed below), or by clubs connecting with wider initiatives, such as anti-racism campaigns.

'Show racism the red card'

Perkins (2000) has argued that the 'Football in the Community' programme in England and Wales has helped encourage some clubs to enter into partnerships with local authorities (see also Chapter 3 of the present volume). This programme often encompasses issues relating to access to facilities, education and interaction with local groups. In some ways such developments in Scotland have been *ad hoc* and, it could be argued, have been patchier in their effects. Yet given the relatively small scale of most Scottish clubs, connecting with their communities should be of paramount importance and could be easily realised.

SPL clubs such as Kilmarnock and Livingston recognise the importance of multi-agency partnerships if they are to enjoy the support of their local communities. The former recognises the extent to which the cultural pull of Rangers and Celtic can easily eat into its potential fan base. This means that nurturing good relations with various actors in the local community makes good long-term business sense. Livingston FC, a relatively new club attempting to build a fan base, has worked closely with local government as it raises the profile of Livingston itself, which was built as a 'new town'. This can be viewed as part of what Perkins calls the 'place marketing' role that clubs can play in promoting a particular locality (Perkins 2000: 109). Both these clubs have community-based agendas similar to those of many clubs south of the border.

The growing anti-racism initiative in England has also found echoes in the Scottish context. In October 2001, for example, the Edinburgh and Lothians Racial Equality Council and Hibernian FC launched a partnership under which 'Hibs' became the first club in Scotland to launch an official policy on racism. This anti-racism programme followed on from an earlier initiative hosted by the Scottish Parliament in February 2001, at which the Show Racism the Red Card campaign launched a new video, with support from MSPs, both the Edinburgh SPL football clubs, Hearts and Hibs, and the Edinburgh and Lothians Racial Equality Council.

Hibernian's managing director said that he viewed the club's initiative as part of its wider community remit, and promised that it would seek to strengthen its links with ethnic minorities, which, it is estimated, make up about 8 per cent of the community living around the club's Easter Road stadium. He noted: 'We always strive to ensure that visitors to Easter Road are made welcome . . . This policy is a natural extension of that aim, and is very much in line with the modern, multicultural face of football' (quoted at . The club linked this initiative with other aspects of its strategy to attract new fans to the club, and thus deepen and extend its fan base. Arguably, then, it is the perilous financial situation of the Scottish game that has helped to focus the attention of at least some clubs on ways of attracting new spectators into their ground. This is not to imply that Hibernian was less than sincere about the anti-racism initiative; rather it is to point out that there are also financial benefits that might accrue from adopting a more progressive stance towards racism in the game. One might even ask why Scottish clubs have been so slow to recognise what many claim is a growing problem in Scottish society.

Celtic: markets, shareholders and stakeholders

While these aspects of the interaction between football clubs and their communities clearly resemble programmes and movements in the English game, on Scotland's west coast and in what might be regarded as the heartland of the Scottish game a very specific issue associated with football and its communities is on the agenda. With the exception of sport in Northern Ireland, the issue of sectarianism tends to be peculiar to the Scottish game and finds its most high-profile manifestation in and around the rivalry between the 'Old Firm' clubs, Celtic and Rangers (see Devine 2000).

The historical origins of Celtic have exercised a strong influence in the shaping of its character since the late nineteenth century. The club was founded by a Marist priest, Brother Walfrid (born Andrew Kerins in Ireland), to help the poor Irish Catholic immigrants in the East End of Glasgow. Celtic also attempted to help in facilitating the acceptance of the immigrant population into a predominantly hostile Protestant environment by playing the sport of the host community. This was an early example of football – the 'universal game' – being used as a vehicle to help to promote the social inclusion of a specific community marginalised by society at large. As has been noted: 'the Marist brother sought for the club to have both a Scottish and [an] Irish identity and hence the club's name "Celtic" came about, representing a bridge of cultures across the sea' (Carr *et al.* 2001: 71). The strong Irish Catholic dimension of the club, heightened as the rivalry with the Scottish Protestant club Rangers began to evolve, meant that Celtic became an important public expression of a particular form of cultural identity that remains part of the club's appeal to this day. The reasons for the longevity of this part of the club's identity have a great deal to do with the wider social, economic, political and cultural forces that have shaped Glasgow and the west of Scotland over the intervening years (see Boyle 1995).

In their economic analysis of the size and composition of football audiences, Dobson and Goddard suggest that cultural and political determinants have played little role in forming audiences, except in relation to Barcelona and Real Madrid in Spain, and the Glasgow teams Celtic and Rangers, their argument being that: 'in both cases it can be shown that social and cultural identities have played a crucial part in shaping the support the clubs attract' (Dobson and Goddard, 2001: 318; see also 335–42). In other words, the communities that these clubs come to represent have distinctive cultural and political identities that differentiate them from most other football clubs.

In Scotland Celtic has been accused of being an Irish club and, by implication, its supporters have been viewed by some as supporting organisations such as the Irish Republican Army (IRA). Both Rangers and Celtic have large numbers of supporters in Northern Ireland, and both have been accused of making money out of a football rivalry that has its origins in a wider ethnic and political conflict. The controversy in January 2002 over comments made in a radio interview by Dr John Reid MP, then Secretary of State for Northern Ireland, served to highlight the sensitivity surrounding the 'Old Firm' and its communities. Reid suggested that the Irish Catholic and Ulster Protestant diasporas had generated large fan bases for Celtic and Rangers in both North America and Australia. He also suggested that, from the point of view of marketing, Scottish football effectively amounted to Celtic and Rangers, as most other clubs were relatively unknown. One of the criticisms levelled at Reid afterwards was that, presmably inadvertently, he was reinforcing sectarian stereotypes about supporters of the 'Old Firm' teams. The proximity to Scotland of Northern Ireland, a society that has been in conflict for many years, has only added to the legacy in Scottish society of more than 100 years of migration and interaction involving Catholics and Protestants. Accordingly, any intervention by either of the clubs in this arena tends to be treated by sections of the media as highly controversial (see Devine 2000).

Celtic's Social Charter[2]

The protracted takeover of Celtic FC in 1994 by Fergus McCann, a Scottish multimillionaire based in Canada, has been well-documented (see Campbell and Woods 1996). McCann had emigrated to Canada in the 1960s, and had an extensive background in business and marketing, having created a very successful company specialising in golf tours in North America. More to the point, McCann was also a lifelong Celtic fan and had been the social convenor of his local Celtic supporters' club before he left Scotland. The board of directors that had previously controlled the club had been dominated by members of three families: it had been unresponsive to supporters' demands for change and had left the club in financial difficulties. McCann's takeover was widely welcomed by supporters at the time.

McCann set out to modernise and recapitalise the club, while attempting to retain and commercially develop aspects of the club's traditional links with the East End of Glasgow and its Irish origins, a task that most commentators thought would be impossible. The club extended its ownership base by being floated on the Alternative Investment Market at the beginning of 1995. The club raised £9.4 million through a share issue that was oversubscribed by almost £4.5 million and created 10,500 new shareholders. A subsequent share issue meant that by the time that McCann eventually left the club, in 1999, there were about 15,000 Celtic shareholders. The club invested more than £23 million in transforming Celtic Park into a modern all-seat stadium with a capacity of 60,000. A crucial element in making the redevelopment a success was the club's drive to increase sales of season tickets. In 1993/94 Celtic had 7,000 season-ticket holders, but within six years this number had risen to 53,388, the largest in Britain. The season-ticket holders help to ensure that Celtic's average home gate is almost up to the full capacity of 60,000, making the club the fifth best-supported in the world.

Peter McLean, a former director of public relations at Celtic who worked closely with McCann during his time there, was impressed by the clarity of McCann's vision. McLean claims that McCann recognised that: 'Celtic was firstly a football club and secondly a business, and thirdly a major social institution in Scottish life'; and that it therefore had 'wider responsibilities than just simply being a football club or a business' (interviewed by the present author, June 2000). However, it is also clear that McCann's main concern was to put the club on a sound financial footing and that the 'community' dimension of the club was not necessarily his first priority.

In April 1995 David Watt and Gerry Dunbar from the Celtic fanzine *Not The View* met McCann, and argued that his business vision for Celtic missed the important social and cultural dimensions of the club that were valued by supporters. David Watt, who has since become part-time Social Charter consultant at the club, drafted a social mission charter that, he felt, could reconnect Celtic to the founding principles that many supporters held to be part of the identity of the club. To his credit, McCann took these suggestions on board. He appreciated the importance that the club's Irish connections still had for many supporters:

> The traditional aspects are always something that is in people's hearts . . . That will never go away . . . It is up to us to make sure that it [Celtic Park] is an enjoyable place to be, it doesn't cost too much money, you can identify with it and maintain the contact with the community, schools and the punters themselves. All the initiatives we try to do is to ensure that we are a people's club rather than just an anonymous Marks and Spencers.
>
> (cited in Boyle and Haynes 1998)

One could argue, of course, that emphasising the traditional dimensions of the club helped to give Celtic a 'unique selling point' of the sort favoured by theorists of marketing. However, I suggest that the intense media environment surrounding both the 'Old Firm' clubs, as well as the wider politically charged debates relating to sectarianism in the west of Scotland, make some of these initiatives and interventions controversial and difficult to sustain.

In January 1996 the social charter drafted by those connected with *Not The View* was launched under the slightly misleading banner headline of the Bhoys Against Bigotry (BAB) campaign. The media focused not on reconnecting with the club's charitable origins but on McCann's attempt to stop the singing of Irish Republican songs at Celtic matches by announcing that fans who sang them could be ejected from the stadium. In addition, the launch focused on the message that the club was not a Catholic club, but rather one that, while remaining proud of its Irish connections, was open to all, regardless of ethnicity or religion. One feature of the campaign involved the club, in conjunction with Glasgow City Council, developing educational packs to be used in more than 300 schools in the city. The campaign attracted considerable attention, and in 1997 the European Commission made an award to the club in recognition of its attempts to stamp out bigotry and promote tolerance among supporters. In addition, the campaign promoted a positive reaction from Rangers, which had long appeared to be happy to play down the anti-Catholic culture associated with a section of its supporters.

Following the BAB campaign, the official club publication *The Celtic View* published the social charter and invited comments. More than 100 individuals and organisations responded, most of them welcoming this clear statement of the wider social and community responsibilities of the club. Some expressed concern that the Irish dimension of the club was being diluted, but that charge was rejected by the authors. Indeed, at least as of 2002 it could be argued that, with a number of major Irish shareholders, an Irish manager and some Irish players, these links have in fact been strengthened. Following the process of consultation several minor changes were made. What emerged was the Social Charter that now informs the club's community relations activities. It perhaps goes further than any equivalent document issued by any other football club in the United Kingdom in making the argument that football clubs are not simply businesses, but are also social institutions that bear a wider social responsibility. To this end it is worth quoting from it at some length.

The document begins with an introduction that attempts to address the question, 'why have a social charter?':

Celtic has always been more than a football club. Part of that extra quality of Celtic has been the social dimension linked to the reasons Brother Walfrid founded Celtic back in the 1880s.

Celtic Football Club has changed a great deal in recent years. The ownership of the Club has been transformed from few to many. The finances of the Club have been placed on a sound and solid basis. Celtic Park, while remaining on the site of past triumphs, has developed beyond recognition.

Celtic will continue to change in order to meet the aspirations of its fans and to live up to the principles behind Brother Walfrid's reasons for founding the Club. This will be carried out within a sound business plan ensuring development of the football set-up and continued improvement for Celtic Park.

Jock Stein always sought to impress upon the fans the importance of the founding principles of the Club and the need for the fans to live up to those principles.

High expectations of management, players and supporters continues [*sic*] to be the norm at Celtic Park, and the Social Charter aims to set out the best that Celtic stands for.

Celtic Football Club, from the supporters to the management and owners, welcome[s] the statement of intent in its Social Charter to set out the values and actions that are part of the best that Celtic stands for.

The best that Celtic stands for is supporting the charitable principles of its founder.

The best that Celtic stands for is promoting health and well-being, understanding, and positive social integration.

The best that Celtic stands for is as an inclusive organisation being open to all regardless of age, sex, race, religion or disability.

The best that Celtic stands for is upholding a shared set of positive values including success, fair play and appreciation of skills.

The best that Celtic stands for is building on the renowned qualities of our supporters.

(http://www.celticfc.co.uk/socialcharter/
introduction.htm)

As noted above, the charter explicitly draws on the historical origin of the club and focuses on its charitable responsibilities. It also clearly promotes the club as being an inclusive organisation open to all.

Until McCann's arrival and the transformation of the club into a public limited company with wide shareholding among supporters, there was a perception that the previous board had paid no more than lipservice to these principles. While the Celtic Charity Fund predates the changes of the 1990s, in recent times its aims and objectives have enjoyed both a higher profile and a clearer focus. In 1996, for instance, shortly after McCann began to introduce changes into the club, the company's annual report stated that:

> It is important for a club of Celtic's traditions to remember that, although the club must be a highly professional and international business to meet the aspirations of shareholders and supporters, there are several groups in our society to whom leisure activities such as professional football are very important but not readily available. Celtic will continue to recognise such circumstances and provide assistance where possible.
>
> (Celtic plc 1996: 21)

The Social Charter outlines the aims and objectives of the Charity Fund and related activities under the heading 'Charitable Principles':

> The best that Celtic stands for is supporting the charitable principles of its founder. Brother Walfrid set up Celtic as a way of raising money to support children in the East End of Glasgow by providing money for the Poor Children's Dinner Table.

Action to be taken

The Celtic Charity Fund has been set up by Celtic to put into practice Celtic's charitable principles. The Celtic Charity Fund is being used in three principal areas of support. These are:

- children's needs charities;
- community action on drugs;
- projects that develop and promote religious and ethnic harmony.

Other areas include:

- supporting the homeless;
- helping the unemployed;
- support and research for projects aiding the afflictions of illness, famine and innocent families within areas of war.
    (http://www.celticfc.co.uk/socialcharter/charitable_principles.htm)

Celtic plc noted that between June 2000 and June 2001 the Charity Fund had raised more than £100,000, bringing the figure raised in the three years between June 1998 and June 2001 to more than £700,000 (Celtic plc 2001). The club has also developed links with local charities in Glasgow, in particular those connected with drug rehabilitation, the unemployed and the homeless, such as Shelter and the Simon Community.

It is also significant that the particular cultural identity associated with the club, with its Irish Catholic connotations, is also recognised through the organisations supported by the Charity Fund. In addition to the homeless causes that chime with the historical origins of the club, there are more overt gestures that indicate that Celtic's community extends beyond the shores of Scotland. In 1999 the Charity Fund made a five-figure donation to support the building of a garden of remembrance in Newmarket, County Kilkenny, in the Irish Republic. The Gairdin an Ghorta (Famine Garden) commemorates those who died or fled the country during the Great Famine of the 1840s. Allan McDonald, then Chief Executive of Celtic plc, explained the donation on the club's website: 'Celtic's Irish connection is a factor we are very proud of and through this project the Club can mark and promote its joint Scottish/Irish identity' (at www.celticfc.co.uk). The club continues to focus attention on the communities from which it has traditionally drawn support, including both the Irish Republic and Northern Ireland. Among the activities supported in 2001, for example, were community-based projects committed to promoting closer links between the Catholic and Protestant communities in Northern Ireland.

In addition, there appears to be recognition that the notion of 'communities' is one that is continually evolving. The Charity Fund has developed the club's connections with other social groups and communities that may have been excluded from the mainstream football culture in the past. Since 1999 the club has hosted the National UK Asian Soccer Championships at Celtic Park, as well as making donations to the Scottish Asian Sports Association. Peter McLean, the former public relations director (already quoted above), was quite clear about the key symbolic role that an institution such as Celtic can play in Scottish society:

> The reason we are supporting so many minority groups – we recently had asylum seekers from Angola, Kosova and Iran, and so on – is that the people coming here, the different groups that these people represent, have faced a sort of similar challenge to that faced by the Irish in 1888.
> (interview by the present author, June 2000)

This explicit use of the origins of the club as a reference point for current policy is highly significant and, I suspect, rare in contemporary football culture in Britain.

Stakeholders, shareholders and communities

A criticism sometimes made of major football clubs is that, as they strive to become national and global businesses, they ignore the immediate or local communities that sustained them in the first place. Thus the issue of the location of any new stadium is always something that exercises supporters: being a fan of a club is tied in with issues of location, identity and territory. In Glasgow there is a perception that Rangers, based south of the Clyde in Govan, has developed better relations with its immediate environment than Celtic has with its community in the East End of the city. While both clubs enjoy global fan bases, through the various Scottish and Irish diasporas around the world, closer to home Rangers has been active for a number of years in cementing good relations with the Govan community, notably through its work with both denominational and non-denominational schools and community groups. The perception among sections of the East End Social Inclusion Partnership (SIP) is that Celtic have not always been so proactive in encouraging links with its immediate community. The East End of Glasgow contains some of the poorest areas in the United Kingdom. At the same time, the East End SIP admits that it has not been as proactive as it might have been in using Celtic. This is not to say that the club has not been involved with the local community, simply that it appears that the club views its various communities as extending well beyond the immediate environment.

It appears that Rangers has also begun to pay more attention, through its community programmes, to Scotland-wide issues such as combating bigotry and racism. However, Rangers also remains rooted in supporting its local community. One of Jack McConnell's last acts as Education Minister before assuming the office of First Minister of Scotland was to join Rangers' manager Dick Advocaat in opening an educational and learning centre, partly funded by the club, in the Govan area. This formed part of the wider social inclusion policies being pursued by the Scottish Executive through the Govan SIP.

The conversion of Celtic into a public limited company has given some of its fans a stake in the club, which fans had been systematically excluded from in the past. However, now that the club is evolving as a multimillion-pound business, it is not at all clear to what extent this can continue. Celtic plc now has about 420 full-time employees, of whom more than 200 work in its commercial divisions. This makes Celtic plc the second largest commercial football operation in Britain after Manchester United plc. When Fergus McCann decided to sell his interest in the company and leave Scotland, in 1999, he sold his shares to existing shareholders and season-ticket holders. As Cannon and Hamil have commented, this was in marked contrast to the decision by Martin Edwards of Manchester United, in the same month, to sell £41 million worth of shares to City of London investors (Cannon and Hamil 2000: 46). Ian McLeod, the current Chief Executive of

Celtic plc, presides over a company of which about 40 per cent of the shares are owned by individuals, mostly season-ticket holders, 40 per cent by directors of the company and about 20 per cent by institutions. This pattern of shareholdings is in stark contrast to that in most British football clubs that have been floated on the stock market and are now dominated, whatever their supporters may feel about it, by investors based in the City of London.

Stephen Morrow (1999 and 2000) has argued that for many clubs a 'stakeholder' model of mutuality may be a better form of ownership structure than a public limited company, which is required by law to put the interests of its shareholders first. Trading in the shares of Celtic plc runs at a very low level, probably because it has a large shareholder base among fans who view their shares as being as much an emotional investment as a financial one. This may not be the case at those clubs where large financial institutions own significant stakes. In addition, the fact that large numbers of Celtic fans are also shareholders – a situation promoted by McCann, who, in my opinion, deserves more credit than he has generally been given – may, arguably, help to guard Celtic plc against a takeover. As Steven Lloyd, a corporate financial adviser, has noted with regard to football club share flotations: 'One way is to enfranchise the supporter in the way that Celtic has done. Celtic issued preference shares, which have no voting rights, so supporters don't have control, they have a stake in the club' (quoted in Glendinning 2000).

However, it is also possible that the proportion of fans among the shareholders will be reduced following further share issues, as Celtic plc attempts to raise additional capital. Even at a club such as Celtic, with its acute awareness of the traditions of the institution and of its core supporters, many of whom are from working-class backgrounds, the shareholder model remains open to abuse and to shifts in the balance of power away from supporters, who are already in a relatively weak position since their holdings are outweighed by those of the directors and the institutions, and both the latter groups are much more likely to act in a concerted fashion. One reaction among fans has been the setting up of a Celtic Supporters Trust, which was formally registered in September 2000 (see Carr *et al.* 2001). The Trust aims to act as a mechanism to help ordinary shareholders and season-ticket holders to exert a greater influence over the running of the company. In addition, it seeks to buy additional shares and pool the existing shares currently scattered among small shareholders.

The 'stakeholder' model, as opposed to the shareholder model, also recognises and gives rights to supporters, rather than simply addressing them as consumers. Unlike Celtic, it appears that many clubs both in

England and in Scotland are only too happy to adopt the shareholder model, to treat fans simply as consumers, and to downplay or even deny the social and cultural dimensions of the game. However, the cultural and social position of a football club such as Celtic suggests that an undiluted application of this model, while it may be financially beneficial for a few 'super clubs' and their major shareholders, could be disastrous for the wider community of supporters, whose investment is not just financial but also emotional and cultural.

The Sense Over Sectarianism (SOS) campaign

While Celtic plc has been cool in its response to the Celtic Supporters Trust, on other fronts it continues to intervene in the wider public discussion about how sectarianism and bigotry should be tackled in the 'new' Scotland, where it often appears that old issues simply will not go away. While there has been an increasing recognition by the Scottish Executive of the need to tackle racism in Scottish society, moves to tackle sectarianism have been more muted.

Yet in other policy areas Scotland is adopting approaches that enhance its differences from England. October 2001 saw the launch of the Sense Over Sectarianism (SOS) campaign in Glasgow, with the support of both Celtic and Rangers, all the main churches in the city, Glasgow City Council, and the anti-sectarianism pressure group Nil by Mouth. The three-year campaign, funded by the Millennium Commission with contributions from the football clubs, aims to measure the scale of the problem of sectarianism in the west of Scotland, while encouraging projects that build understanding and tolerance between communities. Despite the media furore that erupted after Celtic's manager Martin O'Neill walked out at the end of the media briefing on the campaign, having failed to answer a question about the role that he could play in tackling sectarian chanting at matches, SOS marks a significant coming together of the two clubs in recognising that this issue requires joint action.

Over the years, as already mentioned above, both Glasgow clubs have been accused of allowing the rivalry between them to develop along sectarian lines, perhaps because it was good for business. The 'Old Firm' clubs, it can be argued, have had a mutually beneficial commercial interest in keeping old rivalries alive. The launch of the SOS campaign revived the Scottish media's interest in examining the role that the clubs have played and, many would argue, still play in fostering a culture of hate in Scottish society. The media's coverage of the launch of the SOS campaign sheds light on the very particular set of circumstances within which both Glasgow football clubs pursue community-related policies.

Ian McLeod, Chief Executive of Celtic plc, strongly defended the club's position in the biggest-selling newspaper in Scotland, the tabloid *Daily Record*. He claimed that the commercial interests of the club would be enhanced if sectarian overtones could be removed from the culture surrounding the club. He argued that there was no reason why the club would wish vestiges of older resentments to linger in the modern age. He continued: 'Martin O'Neill [the club's manager] and myself share the same objective of upholding what have been the club's aims since their formation in 1888. Celtic is about social integration of Irish and Scots, of Catholic and Protestant' (*Daily Record*, 15 October, 2001). McLeod also accused the Scottish Executive of dragging its feet on supporting both the 'Old Firm' clubs in their attempts to deal with bigoted supporters.

The following day a stinging attack on Celtic and Ian McLeod was to be found on the comment pages of the broadsheet newspaper the *Scotsman*, in a piece written by Michael Kelly, a former member of the board of Celtic plc. He accused the club of being less than serious about tackling the problem of sectarianism because ultimately it might result in ejecting a couple of thousand season-ticket holders from the ground. He claimed that: the club has been changed from a rather old-fashioned and paternalistic organisation that felt a duty to look after its fans to a modern money-making machine. Morality would not be allowed to interfere . . . The club now exists to serve its shareholders first, last and all the time. They cannot in law put the supporters first, and they should not pretend to do so (*Scotsman*, 16 October 2001).

There is more than a touch of unintended irony in this piece. The Celtic FC that Kelly laments the passing of was run solely in the interests of a few families, the Kellys among them, and was viewed by most Celtic fans as completely undemocratic and unaccountable. His claim that the club looked after its fans had a hollow ring for many Celtic supporters, who remember the decline of the club over the 20 years before McCann arrived. In addition, more than 10,000 supporters are now shareholders as well and there is no question that the singing of pro-IRA songs likely to give offence has substantially declined in recent years.

The wider point to be made is that in the goldfish bowl that is the Scottish media/political scene any profiling of the work being done by either of the 'Old Firm' clubs tends to be used for the settling of old scores and the creation of dramatic headlines, rather than for focused and rational debate. Thus, for example, the serious accusation raised by McLeod, that the Scottish Executive had been less than helpful in supporting antisectarian initiatives, was simply dismissed by Kelly and others. Yet the Executive's aparent slowness to respond was probably a reflection of the turmoil that surrounded changes in the personnel of the Executive in late 2001.

Conclusion

There can be little doubt that the opportunities to influence aspects of public policy debate relating to social inclusion are considerably greater for football clubs in Scotland than elsewhere in Britain. The devolved Scottish Parliament, the relatively small population of the country, and the well-established networks among the media, lobbyists, organised interests and the major public institutions provide ample scope for clubs such as Celtic and Rangers to exert influence (see Scheslinger, Miller and Dinan 2001).

The peculiarities of Scottish society and politics, and the extent to which the two main Glasgow clubs dominate Scottish football, have dominated the debate about football and social inclusion, to the extent that it has tended to focus, either explicitly or implicitly, on the role of sectarianism in Scottish society. As Dennis Canavan MSP, the convenor of the Parliament's cross-party group on sport, has stated:

> Sport can also have a divisive rather than [a] unifying effect. Sport did not invent racism or sectarianism, but sadly some sports, especially football, sometimes become a focus for bigots. At a recent meeting of the Parliament's cross-party sports group, attended by representatives from Rangers and Celtic, some constructive suggestions emerged on how to combat sectarianism in sport. Proposals are now being considered by ministers and hopefully the Scottish Executive will work in partnership with both members of the 'Old Firm' to kick racism and sectarianism out of sport and out of Scottish society.
>
> (Canavan 2001: 16)

No doubt both Celtic and Rangers, and indeed other Scottish football clubs, could do more to tackle the particular problems associated with the role played by football in the construction of specific aspects of wider social and cultural identities in Scottish society. However, it should be noted that football also allows the collective expression of many positive facets of these identities.

In 2001–02 the direct involvement of Ian McLeod of Celtic plc in the proposed relaunch of a Youth Against Bigotry campaign, targeted at schools across Glasgow and supported by the City Council, suggested that this positive side was being recognised. The clubs also need more support and recognition, notably from the media, for the positive work that they are already carrying out. Many in the Scottish media, and perhaps in the country's newspapers in particular, remain broadly cynical about such exercises and appear reluctant, despite their acknowledged influence over the forming of Scottish opinion, to tackle the issue.

It also should be noted that, while I have focused mainly on Celtic and, to a lesser extent, on Rangers in this chapter, a lot of community-based work is also being carried on at a range of smaller clubs throughout Scotland. Many examples of this work remain unreported beyond the confines of the local media. However, partly because of the smaller size of both the Scottish media market, as a financial underwriter of the sport, and of the Scottish football market itself, the level of social exclusion, of specific social groups and of supporters alike, appears to be less acute than in England. As a result, the blight of sectarianism in Scottish football has resulted in a differing agenda north of the border. Perhaps, as a colleague and I argued in another context:

> part of the problem lies in the usage of the word ['sectarian'] itself, carrying as it does many connotations associated with the Northern Ireland conflict. Despite the continued existence of religious labelling in some parts of Scottish society, Scotland is not Northern Ireland, and to simply transplant a framework for analysis which fails to take into account the specific economic, cultural and political development of Scotland is always likely to be of limited use.
>
> (Boyle and Lynch 1998: 197)

In place of the emotive term 'sectarianism', with all its historical baggage, the simpler terms 'prejudice', 'bigotry', 'dislike' and, at certain times, 'discrimination' would be perhaps a more useful lexicon for dealing with social differences, whether along the lines of ethnicity, race, geography or gender. While there is no longer systematic discrimination against Catholics in Scottish society, this does not mean that in certain social circumstances, particularly in the west of Scotland there are not situations in which Catholics can be made to feel uncomfortable, simply because their religion is viewed with suspicion or outright dislike. When similar attitudes are applied to ethnic minorities, we quite correctly label this racist. In other words, one of the issues that Scottish society has to face up to is tackling prejudice and discrimination at all levels and against any citizens. In British society over the past 100 years and more, concerns about social exclusion have tended to focus on issues of class and gender. More recently, ethnicity and race have moved onto the agenda too. In Scotland, however, one must still add concerns about religious and cultural identities to the list, and both have tended to become intertwined and also dominated by the Irish Catholic experience. The historical evolution of Celtic FC/Celtic plc has seen it become a vehicle through which an excluded community has helped gain a foothold in society, in part by playing the sport of the host community. As that community matures and a new Scottish political landscape slowly takes shape, both Celtic and Rangers, as major institutions in Scottish society, have a unique opportunity to continue to extend their role beyond the playing field and to exert influence in other social arenas. Their unique historical position and their continuing influence in Scottish life dictate that addressing and evolving their wider social responsibilities in a changing Scotland will continue to remain part of their remit for some time to come.

Acknowledgements

I would like to thank all the people whom I interviewed, on and off the record, while preparing this chapter. In particular, thanks are due to Will Dinan, Peter McLean, Helen Scammell and David Watt.

Notes

1   London was ranked first, with an average weekly attendance of 153,590 supporters; Glasgow came third, with 106,885 fans; Manchester came fifth, with 101,548 fans; and Liverpool came seventh, with 77,834 fans. Newcastle was ranked 12th and Sunderland 14th. Six cities in Britain were among the 15 cities that had the largest attendances in Europe.
2   This section substantially develops and expands on work that originally appeared in Boyle, R., and Haynes, R. (1998).

11

Football for children or children for football? A contemporary boys' league and the politics of childhood

PAUL DANIEL

Separately, children and football enjoy enormously high public profiles in the United Kingdom, reflected in extensive media and academic interest. Together, however, they appear to cancel each other out. Viewed from within, children's football is a thriving, vibrant subculture, with a committed and passionate membership. As Jim White, a sports journalist and himself a manager of a boys' football team, has put it: 'Boys' football is probably the most emotionally intense form of sport known to man; a pursuit peppered with tears, tantrums, even fisticuffs. And that's just among the parents' (White 2002). From the outside, however, children's football is rendered almost literally invisible, confined to pitches on the outskirts of towns, or plots of land adjoining semi-derelict playgrounds in the less salubrious urban areas, or perhaps located in those parts of a park that nobody else visits, such as a corner that slopes so badly that it cannot be used for much else, or a patch of ground that is permanently flooded from December to April. The result is that the closest that most people come to having any contact with organised children's football is catching sight of small huddles of boys standing on street corners with their boot bags in the early hours of a Sunday morning as they wait for their lift to the game.

If children's football is physically hidden from view, it is no more visible in media or academic coverage. Aside from the occasional flurry of interest when a Premiership club shows interest in a 6-year-old, or lays out several hundred thousand pounds for a boy not yet in his teens, children's football is almost totally ignored. Yet the Football Association (FA) has estimated that more than 2 million children aged 16 or under play football on a regular basis, 750,000 of whom belong to organised youth football clubs (according to data on the FA's website). Football plays a significant part in many children's lives. Indeed, many children, as we shall see below, regard football as the most important activity in which they are involved. Just as football matters to many children, so children's participation in the game is a major part of football. This is receiving increasing recognition from the FA, which recently set in motion a number of initiatives aimed at supporting and developing children's football.

It is clear, then, that the low profile of children's football should not be taken to indicate its insignificance. By the same token it should not be assumed that it evokes any less passion, controversy or conflict than the adult game does, whether professional or amateur. Most of this, it has to be said, is generated by adults and their concerns, rather than those of the children themselves. Indeed, in recent years children's football has become a prime site for many of the issues that are dealt with elsewhere in this book, and that raise fundamental questions about the identity and 'ownership' of the game. In the case of children's football this can be summed up in the question: is its purpose to provide football for children or to provide children for football?

Children's football, the FA and the youth academies

Traditionally, children's football has been organised and run by parents and other enthusiastic amateurs. It has been based upon an ethos of social inclusion and the widest possible participation, at least in relation to able-bodied boys. Organised leagues for girls or for children with disabilities have been thin on the ground, and on the whole references to 'children's football' should be read as references to boys' football. That aside, the emphasis has clearly been child-centred. This is well-illustrated by the following admonition, taken from 'The Spectators' Code' in one junior football league's handbook: 'Remember that children play organised sport for their own enjoyment. They are not there to entertain you and they are not miniature Peles' (Tandridge Junior Football League 2003).

This is not to deny that junior football is also highly competitive and has produced some of the best-known players in the professional game. The Wallsend club, for example, has among its old boys Alan Shearer, Peter Beardsley and Michael Carrick, and most junior leagues up and down the country number at least one 'success story' from their ranks. This does not alter the fact that turning out future stars has never been the purpose of children's football, nor the norm, and there have been no vested, particularly financial, interests pushing it in that direction.

However, in recent years, largely as a result of a much more active involvement by the FA in children's football, the picture has become less clear-cut. The result of the FA's initiatives has been to introduce conflicting and possibly incompatible aims and objectives into organised children's football. On the one hand, recent developments within the FA have led it to put a strong emphasis on a more socially inclusive approach to football in general and children's football in particular. Its newly created division, 'The National Game', which employs 40 people, has as its brief 'to increase the quantity, quality and enjoyment of participation in football' (FA 2001/02). In relation to children's football this translates into a commitment to ensure that 'a well-developed infrastructure will be in place so that boys and girls can take their first footballing steps at an early age and then develop over time. The infrastructure will be positive, socially inclusive, impactful [*sic*] and educational, with links between schools and clubs' (Ibid.). Leaving aside the obvious and ugly use of all-purpose 'mission statement speak' in this set of objectives, there does appear to be a genuine commitment to expanding and improving the quality of children's participation. This has been backed up by a number of initiatives, such as the introduction of Mini-Soccer, 'Charter Standards' for clubs and schools (discussed below), and a new child protection policy. Perhaps most important of all when it comes to social inclusion is the fact that the development of girls' football has been placed very high on the agenda and, in a joint initiative with the mobile phone company One to One, provision for children with disabilities has been expanded.

On the other hand, working with a very different agenda and set of values, the FA has also been responsible for the development of youth academies and centres of excellence. These have the explicit purpose of identifying 'players of outstanding ability, and placing them in a technical and educational programme designed to produce football excellence' (FA 1997). The background to this development lay in the failure of the England team to qualify for the World Cup in the United States in 1994. This led to a frenzy of media 'soul searching' about the relative lack of technical ability in the English game compared to other European nations, notably the Netherlands and France. It provoked the FA to appoint Howard Wilkinson, in 1997, to the role of technical director, with the task of producing a blueprint for the future development of young talent. After extensive research in continental Europe and beyond, Wilkinson came up with a model that was heavily influenced by Gerrard Houllier's work at the French national academy at Clairefontaine.

Wilkinson outlined his ideas in the 'Charter for Quality', published in 1997. The central principle in Wilkinson's scheme was to take talented children from a younger age than would have been previously the norm and give them an extensive programme of coaching by qualified, specialist experts. Although he recognised that there were pockets of good practice in the English game, notably at the national academy at Lilleshall and at one or two Premiership clubs, such as Manchester United and Liverpool, Wilkinson felt that too many children were reliant on well-meaning parents and unqualified coaches for their football development. In the 'Charter for Quality' he proposed that academies should be established by the leading professional clubs. In the case of Premiership clubs this was to be made mandatory, but other Nationwide clubs would also be encouraged to follow suit. The academies would be expected to take children from below the age of 9. They would not only provide high-quality coaching and facilities, but would also be required to cater for children's educational and social welfare – the 'buzz concept' in the 'Charter for Quality' was that youth development should take an 'holistic' approach. The academies' standards would be subject to regulation and licensing by the FA, and they would be expected to meet rigorous criteria on the amount of time children spent travelling to and from the academy, the number of matches they played, the qualifications of staff, and so on. While it is true that there was a heavy emphasis on the welfare needs of children selected for the academies, given the development of new child protection policies, for example, Wilkinson's primary motive was nonetheless clearly and forthrightly expressed: 'I'm looking for England to produce players capable of winning the World Cup and playing for their club teams, and dominating Europe in the European club competitions' (Bent *et al.* 2000: 129) .

Despite the fact that Wilkinson's proposals were, by and large, well-received within the game and received positive endorsement from the FA, they were certainly not unopposed within children's football circles. Reservations were mostly voiced by the 'well-meaning amateurs' whose involvement in youth coaching was so deprecated by Wilkinson. The National Council for School Sports, an umbrella organisation that covers 31 different sports, expressed concern about the possible impact of the new academies on children's opportunities to participate in the widest possible range of sports. If talented children were to be selected to join academies and specialise in football before they had left primary school this would restrict their choices at a later stage. This point was echoed by a number of academic sports scientists, such as Peter Warburton, Director of Sports Education at Durham University, who claimed that:

> This is a massive area of concern. I would definitely say [that] the balance of the programme we have now, which is games, gymnastics, dance, outdoor pursuits, swimming and athletics, is the ideal for any child. We really need to be giving them a clear balance throughout their time in school, from 4 to 11, with opportunities in all those areas. I'm not a great believer in saying that children can't

cope with a lot of physical activity. My concern is that it isn't going to be that balanced. Their whole life is going to be soccer.

(cited in Bent *et al*. 2000: 132)

The English Schools Football Association (ESFA) was also lukewarm about the proposals, fearing the impact that the new academies might have on football in schools. Malcolm Berry, the Chief Executive of the ESFA, put the point forcefully when he suggested that 'the selfishness of some clubs searching for the so-called elite youngster is removing the spirit from the schoolboy game and is bordering on exploitation' (Ibid.).

The issue of the academies thus brought out into the open the acrimony that had been simmering for many years between the FA and the ESFA. This centred on which organisation was best suited to the task of developing schoolboy talent. On the one hand, the ESFA believes that, with its members' expertise in education, it should be the body responsible for the schoolboy game. Thus, when the FA took control of the England under-15 team for the first time, in 1999, John Read, who had succeeded Malcolm Berry as Chief Executive of the ESFA, argued that: 'They should be under us. They are all schoolboys. We would be willing to work with FA coaches. They may say that we are not the best coaches but we may be the most appropriate, (quoted in Ridley 2001). On the other hand, the FA, taking Howard Wilkinson's line, is sceptical about the level of coaching expertise within schools and believes that it should have overall control of children's football, particularly when it comes to the development of the most promising young players. At the heart of the conflict between the FA and the ESFA lies a philosophical disagreement over the nature of children's football. At least most 'well-meaning amateurs' would accept that Howard Wilkinson was motivated by a disinterested concern for the future of English football. The problems really begin, it may be argued, once responsibility for taking Wilkinson's ideas forward is placed primarily in the hands of the leading professional clubs. This, in turn, means that a commercial imperative has entered the equation. The philosophical gap becomes a yawning chasm.

Premiership clubs increasingly view youth academies in cost–benefit terms. With the cost of players in the transfer market spiralling out of control, and faced with their own increasingly precarious financial conditions, clubs are looking to their youth development programmes to supply first-team players and/or future income. Manchester United, with its generation of Ryan Giggs, Paul Scholes, David Beckham and the Neville brothers, provides the template. Lower down the scale, Crewe Alexandra has provided itself with a steady income stream from developing and selling on the products of its youth scheme, including Danny Murphy and Seth

Johnson. The pressures on the directors of youth academies are considerable and therefore their priorities are clear. Again and again coaches working in academies have made the point expressed here by Alan Hill, the youth team director at Wilkinson's former club, Leeds United: 'I have a budget of £2 million a year and if I don't turn out kids who can play in the first team I am going to get the sack' (quoted at www.seniority.co.uk).

Hill made this remark in the context of explaining why he and other directors of academies are frequently driven to look overseas for recruits. He bemoaned the rule, introduced following the 'Charter for Quality', that restricts recruitment to boys living within 90 minutes travelling time of an academy, claiming that: 'The whole idea behind Howard's Charter was to sort out English football. But this one-and-a-half hour rule is forcing clubs to go abroad. I might soon need a centre-half and if I can't find one locally I will have no choice but to look overseas' (Ibid.). In this way a rule that was introduced in the interests of children's welfare but is a hindrance to the club's primary objective of turning out first-team material is leading to a completely perverse outcome. When it comes to a choice between the welfare of children, developing the skills of players for the national team in the future and producing merchantable assets for their clubs, there is no doubting where the academies' priorities lie. As Brian Eastick, the director of Birmingham's academy, has put it: 'my directors will say to me that it's my job to get the best young players and they won't care if they're English, Irish, Scottish, French or Mongolian' (quoted at www.givemefootball.com). Arsenal, despite having Liam Brady, one of the most highly respected coaches in the game, as the director of its academy, has built up a particular reputation for its aggressive overseas recruitment policy. When it won the FA Youth Cup in 2001 it was with a team containing an Italian centre-half, a German full-back and, in keeping with recent Arsenal tradition, a French striker.

Growing evidence of the exploitation by European clubs of young players, particularly from Africa, has led to concern being expressed within both the United Nations and the European Union. In 1999, for example, in her annual report to the United Nations Committee on Human Rights, Ofelia Calcetas-Santos, one of the committee's rapporteurs for children's rights, criticised the football world for what she saw as trafficking in young people (quoted in Education and Employment Select Committee 2000).

What all this indicates is that the academies are not hermetically sealed from the commercial values that determine so much that takes place in the contemporary professional game. Recruitment of young footballers is every bit as much an aggressive and competitive business as the transfer market in senior players. This point has been acknowledged by Howard Wilkinson himself: 'Finding the talented performers is not a problem these days, the clubs are extremely well-organised and very aware. These days the problem would be that many are aware of who and where the talented boy is, as a result of which, competition for his signature is very keen' (interview, 20 February 2002, at www.bbc.co.uk/education/getyourkiton).

One result of this competition is that clubs have begun to search out talented players at younger ages than would previously have been the case. For example, it was widely reported in 1999 that West Ham had targeted John Megicks, who was just 6 years old at the time. A second response has been to use a very fine-meshed net in trawling for youth talent. In order not to miss out on the next David Beckham or Rio Ferdinand, the academies' scouts tend to scoop up far too many boys who have only very remote potential to make the grade. As one disillusioned former inmate of Manchester United's academy put it: 'They do get too big a batch in, in the hope that one will make it . . . The academies are just a trawl so they don't miss out on a single young player. They are meat markets' (quoted at www.play_the_game, 21 February 2002).

The youth academies have clearly had a seismic effect on children's football. Although they are relatively few in number – there are currently only 40 academies operating in England, with about 5,000 registered players – the impact that they have had on the whole of children's football is profound and widespread, posing a challenge to the ethos of social inclusion. It is this issue – the relationship between the academies and junior league football – that forms the focus of the following case study. My hope is that it is as revealing about the contemporary politics of childhood as it is about the state of English football.

The case study: background

The approach adopted for the study was ethnographic. The material was gathered in the course of direct involvement as a manager of a boys' team over four years, during which the team progressed from the under-10s division to the under-13s division of one of the largest leagues in the country. Covering an area stretching over south London, Surrey, Kent and Sussex, it has a membership of more than 8,000 children, mainly boys, aged between 8 and 17. The data were gathered from documentary sources, such as league magazines, as well as from discussions with managers, parents, officials and, most importantly, the boys themselves. In the case of the adults, material was gathered from numerous informal conversations over the course of the four years in question. The boys' views were collected in a series of more structured group discussions with the members of three clubs, one in the under-12 age group and two in the under-13 age group. Between 50 and 60 boys were involved in these sessions.

The first point to note about the league at the centre of this case study is that, like other junior football leagues throughout England, it caters for clubs with very diverse organisational structures and resources. Among the 500 or so teams that make up the league there are some that are linked to a semi-professional adult club with a history going back more than 100 years and a pedigree that includes knocking a Premiership team out of the FA Cup tournament. At the other end of the scale there are clubs that run single youth teams on shoestring budgets. Some clubs are affiliated to broader youth, sports or church organisations. Others are freestanding and have no purpose other than football.

Indeed, one of the great strengths of youth football leagues such as this one is that they are open to such diverse teams. Their flexibility and the ease of access to them can be illustrated by the example of my own club's entry into the league, which happened, quite literally, overnight. As the father of a 9-year-old boy who had been one of a group of children that had met every Saturday morning for four years to play football in a local park, I made a tentative inquiry about joining the league. After being told that the league committee was meeting that evening, I attended with another father. At that stage we were not officially constituted as a club. We had no name, no ground, nor even any kit, just a nucleus of a dozen or so keen boys. We bluffed our way through the meeting and six days later had our first fixture in borrowed school rugby kit.

Of course, the fact that there are minimal bureaucratic and financial barriers to entering organised children's football has both positive and negative consequences. Perhaps the greatest benefit is the social inclusion that openness promotes. Entry is not limited to those with substantial organisational or financial resources. Children do not need to prove themselves through trials at one of the larger established clubs in order to play competitive league football. All it requires is 14 or 15 keen youngsters and a couple of supportive adults. On the other hand, ease of access also means that teams enter the league and then find that they cannot sustain their commitment. This leads to a degree of instability, causing the league problems in organising divisions and fixtures. This 'let a thousand flowers bloom' approach also means that some teams enter when a more rigorous vetting process might lead to their being rejected, on the grounds that the adults running the clubs are unsuitable. Several managers in the league have, for example, been suspended for over-aggressive behaviour on the touchline.

A recent response from the FA has been to introduce 'Charter Standards' in an attempt to raise the quality of the organisation of children's football. Encompassing both schools and youth football league clubs, the 'Charter' sets out a series of standards that clubs must achieve, in club administration, child protection and so on, in order to be awarded 'Charter' status. At present this is not mandatory and only a handful of clubs had successfully gone through the process by the end of 2002. While the aims behind the 'Charter Standards' may be considered laudable, efforts to achieve 'quality assurance' through the kind of bureaucratic processes that it requires have largely failed in other spheres, such as education and health. It would be a great shame if the effort to raise standards made the process of establishing children's football teams and joining youth leagues prohibitively bureaucratic. If it forced out the smaller, less established clubs and made it more difficult for Wilkinson's 'enthusiastic amateurs' to enter the field, then it would represent a serious blow to the diversity and inclusiveness of children's football.

All this is some way off, however. At present the league under discussion still comprises a wide variety of clubs. Equally, just as there is no template for the structure and organisation of the clubs, so there is no 'identikit' manager. The adults involved in running teams in the league come from a wide range of backgrounds, and have very different motivations and aims. Perhaps the single most common factor is having sons who play for the team. Having a football-mad child is what brings most managers into the league and, although some go on to outstay their children, for the majority the motivation to manage a youth football team is expressed by the sentiment that 'someone has to do it'. That is not to say that it is taken lightly, or seen as an unpleasant chore. In my conversations with dozens of managers over the four years under review here it became apparent that for many it had become a major part of their lives and a source of more satisfaction than they derive from their paid employment.

Many managers have played and enjoyed amateur football themselves. A commonly expressed view is that they want to instil in their young players an enthusiasm to continue a lifelong involvement with club football. It is easy to caricature adults involved in children's football as yearning to achieve vicariously the success that they would have loved to have in their own football careers. Certainly there is an element of this, but my conversations with managers in this league suggested that a genuine desire to foster a love of the game is much more widespread. Most managers do not see it as their role to produce professional players of the future. They sometimes talk of the 'one or two boys in the squad who, in the right circumstances, could go all the way to the top', but they also derive just as much satisfaction from 'the progress of the boy with two left feet who struggles to make the school team'.

The case study: the adults' views

It is not surprising, then, that most managers regard the academy system at best with suspicion and at worst with hostility. As a topic of conversation, the 'predatory academy scout' outstripped all others by some considerable distance, particularly among the adults involved with clubs in the under-10 and under-11 age groups. A graphic illustration of the impact that academies can have on clubs is provided by the following example. In the year in which my own team entered the league at the under-10 level one team won the division, the league cup and the Surrey county cup with a perfect winning record. Not only was it an outstanding football side, but its players were impeccably behaved and games against them were always enjoyable. As a result of its success, however, the team was deprived of the majority of its players by scouts from academies, including those at Arsenal, Wimbledon and Crystal Palace. The team never recovered. By the under-13 season it was at the bottom of the league and unable to fulfil its fixtures from Easter onwards because of a shortage of players. The team's manager, more in sorrow than in anger, expressed his concern that: 'Because the team was so successful as a team, average boys who appeared to be talented when playing alongside the very skilful were scouted as well as the best players. I wonder how long they will last.' This was an extreme case, but virtually every manager of an A or B division team could give examples of the adverse impact of academy scouts on their squads. Descriptive terms such as 'locusts', 'leeches', 'poachers' and 'parasites' peppered managers' conversation on this topic.

Of course, the responses were not all negative. Some managers took pride in the fact that they had been the first to spot and develop the promise of talented young players. One such manager expressed the view that 'it makes it all worthwhile if just one of our youngsters makes it to the Premiership'. One or two of the larger and longer-established clubs had served as unofficial feeder clubs, or 'quasi-academies', before the academy system was developed. One club, for example, prided itself on its role producing boys for Millwall. For these clubs and their managers there was a degree of ambivalence towards the academies. On the one hand, there was resentment of the academies for the slurs, both actual and implied, on their abilities as well-meaning amateurs to train and develop talent. To some extent their noses had been put out of joint. On the other hand, they shared the overall ethos of the academy system and in most cases developed good relations with local scouts.

A further positive reaction, even from those who were generally resentful of academies, was admiration of the facilities and the quality of the training on offer at the academies. A number of managers who had attended academy training sessions with their boys felt that they had been able to pick up useful ideas for new routines and exercises to take back to their own clubs. Others spoke approvingly of the improvement in the skills of boys who had attended an academy for short spells and then returned to their clubs. Few managers saw the transactions between the academies and their own clubs as purely one-way affairs. Nevertheless, the general view among this same group was that the academies ought to be doing much more in the way of sharing their skills and providing support to the 'grass roots'.

This came to a head at a meeting between the league's managers and staff at Crystal Palace's academy. The purpose of the meeting, at least as far as the academy's representatives were concerned, was to forge closer links with the league in order to enable Crystal Palace to have first pick of the talented boys. One of the academy's spokesmen began the session by describing how dismayed he had been at a recent game between one of the academy's sides and Arsenal by the discovery that a number of the best players in the north London side had been recruited from the junior league on Crystal Palace's own doorstep. Unfortunately for the academy's staff, however, they were met with a barrage of cynicism and anger from parents and managers who had experienced at first hand what they perceived to be exploitation by professional clubs. Most of the people in the audience had no wish to make it easier for Crystal Palace's, or indeed any other club's, academy to recruit boys from their teams. Instead, numerous suggestions were made from the floor about ways in which Crystal Palace might provide more support to league teams, whether through help with coaching or through provision of equipment and kit. It was widely felt that at the very least there should be some *quid pro quo* if professional teams did take a boy from a junior club side with limited resources. However, all the suggestions from the floor, at what turned out to be a stormy meeting, were met with a straight bat by the academy's staff and no offers of support were forthcoming.

What was most striking at the meeting was the number of complaints, particularly from parents, about boys being badly let down by broken promises or bad faith on the part of Crystal Palace. The club had recently been in financial chaos, leading to its being placed in administration, and a number of the satellite centres of the club's centre of excellence had been abruptly closed. Boys who had been recruited were suddenly dropped. The whole episode had been so badly handled that it left many boys distressed, and their parents feeling angry and vengeful.

This was not an isolated incident, or a problem peculiar to Crystal Palace. Again and again, when talking to other managers, I heard stories of professional clubs' insensitivity and lack of concern for young children's feelings. Managers complained about boys being selected at 9 and deselected at 10, other boys being kicked out unceremoniously without any explanation or softening of the blow, and still others being told in the week before Christmas that they would no longer be required. Employees of academies frequently make the point that even when boys are not retained they can console themselves with having had first-class training that will stand them in good stead in later life. This was felt by most managers to be scant compensation for the damage done to children's self-esteem and confidence. For all the formal emphasis on child welfare within the academies, there was a strong feeling that the professional clubs were neither sufficiently aware of the impact that rejection might have on a young child, nor adequately skilled in dealing with children's emotional needs. As one manager graphically put it: 'We are providing fodder to a huge machine that, make no mistake, will chew 'em up and spit 'em out.'

Particularly galling to many managers was the impression that academies were not subject to the same level of accountability that they themselves faced. As one manager put it: 'If we fail to comply with the rules which are there to protect our boys we face fines or disciplinary action. Quite rightly. If we as non-profit-making volunteers are held so accountable, then so should the vast money-making organisations which take our boys'. The general view was that the standards set out in 'Charter for Quality' were being widely flouted, with impunity. Neither the FA nor the junior leagues appeared to be able to do anything to check the abuses. In this respect it was notable that one of the main bargaining points that the Crystal Palace academy's staff used in trying to persuade league managers to enter into a partnership was that they would replace the current 'free for all' with a strict code of conduct for all scouts.

On the whole, then, managers were unequivocal in their condemnation of the way in which the academies are operating. Similar sentiments were expressed by parents of boys in the league, although it would be fair to say that there was a greater degree of ambivalence and polarisation among this group. Without the active support of parents the academies would find it difficult to operate. The business of ferrying children to and from training sessions on weekday evenings, and to and from matches at weekends, requires a major commitment on the part of parents. It was clear that for many parents having a son noticed by an academy's scout was a source of pride. Being told by an 'opposition' parent that 'our midfielder has been given a trial at Wimbledon' or the 'lad up front was once at the Charlton academy' was a fairly common experience at league matches. For some parents the possibility of their child being scouted by a professional club was the main reason why they had got involved with junior football in the first place. Indeed, it was not uncommon for parents to persuade their sons to change to a more successful and higher-profile club in order to improve their chances of being noticed by a scout. Widespread media allegations of payments made by league clubs to families in order to secure the services of promising youngsters clearly serve to stoke up these ambitions still further.

However, if parents' ambitions could be said to constitute one of the cornerstones of the academy system, when they are thwarted they can be transformed into the most vitriolic hostility. At the Crystal Palace meeting discussed above parents whose children had been rejected or let down by academies were among the most vocal and antagonistic participants. Having lived with their sons' disappointment and seen its effects at close quarters they voiced considerable scepticism as to whether the professional clubs were showing enough concern about children's welfare. This was summed up in the contribution of one mother, who angrily addressed the meeting with the following rhetorical question: 'Are they [the academies] aware of the detrimental effects on the psychological development of children as young as nine? Do they really care, or is it just a corporate exercise in pursuing their business interests?'

Case study: the boys' views

What is clear is that the adults involved in junior football, whether parents and/or managers on the one hand, or representatives of the professional clubs on the other, have their own agendas, and that these are not always mutually compatible. What of the boys' experiences and views? For all that the 'Charter for Quality' and the league's own statement of values both have a strong child-centred emphasis, there has been little or no attempt to discover children's perspectives on football. Children remain a muted group in British society – even in areas that are central to their lives, such as education – and football has certainly not provided a forum for children's voices to be heard. It is arguable, of course, that in this respect the position of children who play the game does not differ markedly from that of their adult counterparts. Football has never been run, at any level, on the basis of democratic decision-making or involvement of players in administration.

The boys involved in this study came from very diverse educational, class and ethnic backgrounds. They were in the age range 11 to 13 and were all playing in the A division of the league, for three separate clubs. Many had direct experience of academies, either during the four years under review or when they were younger. All had indirect experience, in that they knew boys who were, or had been, involved with professional clubs. What is missing, of course, from this sample are the views of the small proportion of boys who play exclusively for academy teams, so to that extent, at least, it does not give a complete picture. In all other respects, however, it is a reasonably good cross-section of boys involved in football in a large area in the southeast of England.

In my conversations with all three groups of boys one theme emerged particularly strongly and clearly: playing for their club was a central and important part of their lives. For many of them it was an all-consuming activity and there were echoes of Bill Shankly's famous dictum about football being 'more important than life or death'. For these boys football was not only their only sporting activity – even in summer, when regular five-a-side tournaments took the place of weekly league matches – but, aside from school, it occupied most of their waking lives.

At the other end of the spectrum, for boys at one club in particular football was only one of a wide range of activities. These boys played rugby and cricket as well as football at school. For a number of them football was not their best sport. Several competed nationally at swimming or athletics and others represented their county at cricket. Some also played golf, badminton and tennis. This group also included some talented musicians and academic high achievers. Yet even at this club, where boys were faced with a wealth of opportunities and choices, membership of their Sunday league team occupied a unique position in many of their lives, a fact confirmed, in separate discussions, by their parents.

Sunday morning football was not seen as just another activity in a crowded weekly schedule. Rather it was eagerly anticipated, generated a real 'buzz' of excitement and became a focus of discussion at school on Monday mornings. Again and again boys made comments such as the following:

Playing for [my team] is great . . . It is the best thing in my week.

I really look forward to Sunday mornings . . . I can't stand it if I have to miss a game, if we are away or something.

When I was injured and couldn't play for a few weeks it was terrible . . . just watching and not being able to join in.

When they were asked what they particularly liked about playing junior league football, most boys chose to focus less on the football itself and more on the context. The whole experience of being in a team with a shared history – many of the boys had played together since they were 5 or 6 years old – was seen by many as the key attraction. Great shared moments, such as cup final appearances, winning penalty shoot-outs and victories against old rivals, were mentioned frequently:

> What I really like about playing for [my team] is that we all know each other . . . Most of us go to the same school and have played together for years . . . There is a good spirit in the team.
>
> We have a really good squad of 17 or so players . . . Everyone wants to play . . . and when we won the cup it was down to the whole squad, not just one or two players.
>
> We have had some great times . . . like when we got to the cup finals . . . I even took my trophy on holiday with me that first year . . . Some boys have left but mostly the team is still the same as when we were in the under-10s.

The boys also stressed the competitiveness within the league. A number of them favourably contrasted playing for their Sunday league teams with their experience in school teams. The league was seen to be altogether more serious and competitive. Matches against certain clubs took on extra significance. Avenging past defeats or battling for league places gave the football an edge of excitement missing from the more sedate school games. Boys referred to checking results each week on the league's website, and to match reports, articles and photographs in its monthly magazine, as aspects of the league that enhanced their enjoyment and their sense of being participants in something important:

> We have had some really great games against [one opposing team] . . . I think we have won more than them but it is always a battle . . . I always look forward to playing them.
>
> One good thing about it is that I can check all the results on the website on Sunday night . . . It is interesting to see how we are doing in the league.
>
> Our club has appeared in the magazine loads of times . . . it is great seeing your picture on the front cover . . . and there was a brilliant action picture of [a team-mate] in it a few months ago.

What is most striking about the boys' responses is the fact that they enjoyed playing league football as an end in itself. It was clear that they were completely focused on their present enjoyment of the game, rather than being concerned about what it might lead to in the future. In contrast to the themes emphasised at the academies, none of the boys in this sample mentioned either the development of their skills or the possibility of going on to become professional players, let alone England internationals, as a reason for playing in the league. That is not to say that, when asked directly, they did not express any ambition to go all the way in the game. Indeed, for many of the boys this was their greatest wish. However, the ambition was generally tempered by a strong dose of realism about the uncertain and precarious nature of careers in professional football. This was particularly noticeable among boys who had spent some time in the academies before being let go.

Like their parents, the boys viewed the academies with a degree of ambivalence. On the positive side, 'being scouted' was a matter of some pride for most boys and even a badge of status among their peers. At one of the clubs that formed the basis of this study it was very much the norm and anyone overlooked by the scouts would have felt very second-rate. It was apparent that the presence, or suspected presence, of a scout at a league match caused a frisson of excitement. More than once, for example, when I attended a game as a neutral observer, I was asked by boys whether I was a scout from a professional club. Very few boys were negative about being invited to go for a trial with an academy team. It almost seemed that the fact of having been talent-spotted was more important than attending the academy.

When it came to talking about their views on the academies, a much less positive picture emerged. Many of their comments echoed the points made by parents and managers. Boys who had personal experience of the academy system generally commented favourably on the quality of the training and the facilities, although a number complained about the time spent travelling to and from training, which was often clearly well in excess of the 90 minutes permitted under the FA's regulations. A further cause of complaint was the fact that, although the training was enjoyable, there had been too few opportunities to play matches. Boys missed their regular weekly games in the league. Most were unhappy at what they perceived to be the lack of care and sensitivity in the way they had been released from the academies. Some felt that the experience had been very negative and had affected their confidence. Others were more phlegmatic, but nevertheless believed that their expectations had been falsely raised.

Leaving to one side though the negative comments of boys who had been disappointed and hurt by rejection, a number of more general points were made about the impact of the academies on children's football. Perhaps the one comment that was most frequently and vehemently voiced, both by boys who had been involved with an academy and by those who had not, was the divisive effect that academy recruitment had on junior clubs. Boys made comments such as the following:

> The worst thing about joining Chelsea was leaving my mates . . . I really missed playing for my old team . . . It was great to come back. In the end I left the Fulham academy because I couldn't stand not playing with my friends any more . . . In the end they persuaded me to leave.
>
> I wouldn't have minded if I could still have played for my old team . . . but most of the time I wasn't allowed and I hated not being part of it anymore.

One of the attractions of junior football, as discussed above, is the camaraderie that arises from belonging to a team. Losing contact with friends and not being able to play on a regular basis for their clubs or, in some cases, their school teams were major drawbacks for the boys who had attended academies. By the same token, those who were left behind when their friends went off to join an academy were concerned at the disruption that this caused to the team. In some cases, as in the example already cited, this could bring about the demise of a team. More frequently it might cost a championship or end a cup run. It also caused problems for team spirit when the 'academy boys' were available to play for their club sides on an occasional basis, returning to the team for vital games at the expense of other boys who had been playing regularly:

> One thing that wasn't fair was when [a team-mate] who was at the Wimbledon academy and not available to play for us most of the time kept being picked to play in the important games – like in the cup.
>
> It was a problem when three boys left to go for trials at academies in a short space of time . . . we weren't able to replace them and it messed up our season really.
>
> It caused bad feeling at the club when some boys couldn't decide if they were playing for us or not . . . In the end they came back, but team spirit was never the same again.

In summary, the boys expressed the view, although with less anger and passion than their parents and managers did, that the academies were unreliable and exerted a disruptive influence in their lives. Even at the age of 13 they looked cynically upon the motives and *modus operandi* of the professional clubs. There was a widespread recognition that the demands imposed upon boys at the academies were not compatible either with getting the most out of school or with keeping up their other sporting interests. In contrast, playing for their league teams was a relatively uncomplicated and relaxed affair.

Conclusion

In this final section I would like to draw out a few lessons from the case study. The first point relates to society's understanding of children and childhood. The dominant view of childhood in Britain, as in other industrialised countries, is based on locating it within a 'developmental framework', so that children are seen primarily as 'the future' or as 'human becomings' (see Quortrup 1994). In recent years this view has been challenged politically by the children's rights movement and from within academic circles by new thinking about the sociology of childhood (see, for example, James and Prout 1997). Briefly summarised, this new approach argues for seeing childhood experience as valid in its own right and for according children the status of full human beings rather than adults in waiting.

It is arguable, then, that what we have been discussing in this chapter reflects the conflict between these two ways of looking at childhood. The ethos of the academies is firmly posited within the developmental framework. Children's football is seen simply as a preparation, whether, in Howard Wilkinson's terms, for producing future England players, or, as the staff of the academies see it, for generating marketable assets for Premiership clubs. In contrast, it is clear that the boys in the sample wanted to play football for its own sake and were focused very much on the present. Although they had dreams of playing for Arsenal and England, it was enjoyment of the game rather than ambition that got them out of bed even on wet and windy Sunday mornings in November.

The second lesson that may be drawn from this case study relates to the contemporary state of football. In recent years the impact of commercial interests on professional football has come in for considerable scrutiny. This chapter has shown that children's football is by no means immune from these same pressures. On the contrary, it is increasingly being exposed to them. As transfer fees spiral upwards the eagerness to identify and sign 'the next David Beckham' becomes ever more acute. There is undoubtedly much to applaud in the 'Charter for Quality', but handing over the responsibility for its implementation to the clubs has effectively put King Herod in charge of the nursery. The professional clubs are not the only commercial organisations with a vested interest in children's football. The sporting goods manufacturers Nike and Umbro have launched separate and competing initiatives to support coaching for children's football; so too, somewhat more incongruously, has the fast food chain McDonalds. Young footballers are clearly seen as a profitable market that is well worth targeting.

Commercialism would be less of a cause for concern if there was an effective regulatory body for children's football. Unfortunately, however, this is an area rife with conflict and petty squabbles. As a result the interests of children are frequently lost in the acrimony between the FA, the County FAs and the ESFA (see Ridley 2001). The FA has palpably failed to rein in the excesses of the richest and most powerful Premiership clubs. Perhaps what is needed is a new regulatory authority, independent of the vested interests within the professional game. Certainly, without a much stronger commitment to enforcing the existing rules set out in the 'Charter for Quality', children's football will be increasingly open to exploitation. That would be a shame, for, while we should not romanticise or overplay the 'Corinthian' aspects of children's football as it currently operates, it does help us all to recognise that, although there may be 'only one David Beckham', there are several million children who enjoy participating in well-organised, competitive but non-elitist and inclusive football.

12

Pick the best, forget the rest? Training field dilemmas and children's football at the turn of the century

SIMON THORPE

Association Football – the 'people's game' (Walvin 1975) – which was first organised and codified in England in 1863 with the formation of the Football Association (FA) – was played originally by the amateur gentlemen of the public schools and universities. It rapidly spread among the working classes, its format ideally suited to the new industrial cities. Professional players soon emerged and appropriated the game from the amateur gentlemen. As clubs themselves grew increasingly professional, there developed specialised methods of training and a network of surveillance charged with the task of identifying potential physical capital in the shape of young new players. The football coach and the club scout were born.

League football, like most modern professional sports, was thus effectively a product of the industrial age, displaying the same characteristics and values such as the ethic of hard work and competitiveness. Although it dates from the latter half of the nineteenth century, it was not until the 1960s that critical studies of modern sport emerged. The emergence of such work can be viewed as the combination of two main factors. First, the nascent academic study of sport in the 1950s had viewed sport in functionalist terms, eulogising its ability to unite disparate peoples on the sports field and to provide a platform for individual success. And, second, the 1960s witnessed the evolution of the sport superstar and the potentially immense financial rewards available. The application of Marxist theory to the study of sport questioned such functionalist assumptions and drew attention to some of the consequences of the commercialisation of sport by capital. One such result, it was claimed, was alienation.

Marxist theory of alienation fundamentally concerns the estrangement and isolation of the individual within society. Naturally, writing in the mid-nineteenth century, Marx did not originally intend his work to be applied to the study of sport. The main pioneer of Marxist critiques of sport came from the French academy and the work of Jean-Marie Brohm, whose polemics against what he labelled 'capitalist sport' in the late 1960s and 1970s were published in an anthology entitled *Sport: A Prison of Measured Time* (1978).

Brohm's work was followed by other critics of sport, including those concerned with children's sport, mostly from the American academy in the 1970s. These papers were largely written by educationalists and those involved with youth and school sports, and promulgated a concern over the excessive infiltration of the values and imperatives of capitalism and the market into youth sports, which they claimed made them more competitive and thus alienating. Frequently only those most talented children would be chosen to play for a team, and the rest ignored. This concern also frequently found its legitimacy in the fact that professional sport naturally looked to youth and school sports for its supply of new physical capital. These writers thus warned against a system that only catered for the best, leaving the rest with few or poor sporting experiences.

Most of these American studies of children's sport, however, had a distinct social-psychological flavour to them. Although physical matters and the child's body were mentioned, these references were brief and usually secondary. Since the 1980s – and particularly the 1990s in the sub-discipline of sport, the sociological study of the body has emerged and redresses the balance. The sociology of the body has drawn on the work of post-structuralist theorists such as Michel Foucault and Pierre Bourdieu, who in turn have partly developed the work of Marx. The sociological study of the body is naturally a fertile ground for sport, where the use of the body is central to athletic endeavour. However, to date, there is still a clear dearth of such studies concerned with the child's body and children's sport, not to mention children's football.

A search of the literature concerned with children's football thus produces two main types of text: one is the physiological study or coaching manual; the second has a critical perspective. The former invariably is concerned with 'good practice' techniques and child protection, but naturally has no criticism of the sports or the system within which they operate. The latter, critical studies derived from a Marxist perspective, redress the balance, serving not only to draw attention to the potentially damaging social-psychological and physical effects on children of competitive sport but also to criticise the system within which they operate. The accuracy and legitimacy of such studies will be discussed, but they at least serve to provide an alternative perspective and some food for thought.

The present study is the culmination of two main factors particular to the author: first, a passion for the sport of football and, second, as a fledgling football coach, an interest in the development of the child in sport. Recent developments in children's football now render this subject particularly amenable to contemporary sociological analysis. These developments include the British government's re-direction in 1995 of the Sports Council's focus away from 'Sport For All' towards school sports and the development of excellence and, two years later, the re-structuring of the FA and its plans for children's football. These moves will be examined in further detail.

Why was the focus upon schoolchildren, when perhaps it may have been better to focus solely upon children who had been selected to train with professional clubs and thus stood the best chance of being alienated – if such a condition exists? There is a short answer to this question and it concerns access. This introductory section began with reference to James Walvin, who wrote a detailed social history of football, and it is symmetrical to end this introduction with a second reference to his work. He claims that he found two problems in his attempt to write his book: 'Professional clubs are generally suspicious of outside enquirers and in addition are singularly unhistorical in their attitude to their own past' (Walvin 1975: 5). Suffice to say that I have found they are equally suspicious with regard to their own future, and perhaps not a little sensitive, as that future hinges upon young physical capital – children, a sensitive subject in any context.

But this is not to say that this investigation into schoolchildren's football has been conducted solely because there was easy access to it. As stated, recent developments now make this area fertile ground for (thus far absent) sociological investigation. The present study is an ethnographic investigation of a children's after-school football club in a South London primary school, to examine the impact of these developments – if any, on the school and also the claims of critics that children's sports can be alienating.

Children's football

In 1995 the Union of European Football Associations (UEFA) published a policy document outlining a blueprint for the future of children's football and, apart from espousing a modified, smaller game, also claimed that: 'Children's football has suffered from adults' (UEFA 1995).

Subsequently, in November 1997, the English FA announced several structural changes to their organisation, which were the brainchild of the FA Technical Director Howard Wilkinson. From the 1998/9 season the responsibility for the development of excellence passed from the FA to individual professional clubs and thirty-four Football Academies were established. These Football Academies assumed responsibility for the development of promising young players from the age of eight onwards. The FA's National School of Excellence at Lilleshall, which since 1984 had previously played a major role in this process, stopped doing so in 1998.

As well as the establishment of Football Academies, and in line with the UEFA policy document, the FA's plans also addressed the type of football played by children. Since May 1993, with the publication of the *Mini-Soccer Handbook*, the FA had in fact promoted this format of football for children under eleven years of age (Russell 1993); but starting in September 1999 all football affiliated to the FA played by children must take the form of mini-soccer. The fundamental rationale of mini-soccer is that children will play a more simple game with fewer rules; it involves smaller pitches and goals and a reduced amount of players. In short, football in a format more conducive to the physical and cognitive abilities of children. The FA promote this format as being the 'real game' (FA 1999). Thus, in order to be recognised and insured by the FA, which is part of affiliation, all children in Little Leagues and schools must play mini-soccer. According to FA publicity material, resistance was only received by the English Schools' Football Association (ESFA), which requested it be allowed to continue with eleven-a-side football for children. This was rejected by the FA (FA 1999: 3).

Alongside this the FA has also promoted its 'Soccer Star Scheme' since 1988. The scheme, as with mini-soccer, is almost incongruously sponsored (there are, after all, healthier products) by Coca-Cola and requires that children perform six drills under test conditions: running with the ball; changing direction with and without the ball; dribbling; heading; shooting; passing and control (Russell 1988: 1). These tests can be conducted by children's club leaders or educators with no or very little training (FA, undated). But the FA also run the Junior Team Manager (JTM) coaching course for those involved in children's football, and this accompanies the scheme as it instructs coaches on how to conduct the tests.

The 'Soccer Star' publication explains, along with an accompanying video, how to conduct these tests. Organisers complete an official form for each child and a scoring system produces a grade; these sheets can then be sent to the FA for certificates to be produced, but a potentially greater prize awaits the most proficient bodies:

> If you reach the 6 star grade – the champion class – this will indicate you are in the top one per cent of all players for your age in the country, and on reaching this level we will recommend you for a trial at your local Football League club's Centre of Excellence.
>
> (Russell 1988: 2)

According to FA publicity material, since the launch of the scheme test results have been processed for over 150,000 boys and 5,000 girls; while over 7,000 teachers, coaches and youth leaders have conducted the scheme with their charges (FA, undated).

In 1995 the then Conservative government published a policy document entitled *Sport: Raising the Game*, within which Prime Minister John Major announced: 'My ambition is simply stated. It is to put sport back at the heart of weekly life in every school' (DNH 1995: 2). This document promulgated a major overhaul of the teaching of sport in the National Curriculum. From August 1995 a revised PE curriculum came into force, including an enhanced role for team games, and a requirement for all schools to compulsorily offer two hours per week of PE and sport within formal lesson time (DNH 1995: 3).

The government also announced that the Sports Council would now be directed away from its long-standing commitment to 'Sport For All' to concentrate on promoting sport in schools and the nurturing of excellence.

The Sports Council, in conjunction with the charity organisation the Youth Sport Trust, subsequently devised the TOP Sport Programmes, to provide a framework for the delivery of sport within schools, training for teachers and supply of some equipment. TOP Play introduces basic skills and fun sport to 4–9 year olds; while TOP Sport introduces specific sports to 7–11 year olds such as football (Youth Sport Trust 1998). According to the Youth Sport Trust's 1997/8 *Annual Report* these schemes had reached 6,975 schools (Youth Sport Trust 1998).

This brief review shows that it would not be an overstatement to claim that children's sport generally, let alone children's football, is currently quite a topical subject. This is possibly a by-product of the radical transformation of the structure of the FA and new government policy initiatives over the last few years. Naturally, some critics have expressed their concerns and questioned whether these changes – always couched in terms of proper child development and the ubiquitous catch-all phrase 'good practice' – are actually good for children. Celia Dodd, writing in the *Independent*'s Education Section, questioned the apparent concentration in schools on the naturally gifted children, leaving the less talented effectively disenfranchised in sport, as local clubs also mostly only want the best children (Dodd 1999: 2).

Also, while the promotion of mini-soccer appeared to be a good development, it was questioned why this had taken so long to be implemented, and why particularly was it being implemented now? To improve the bodily skills of all children, including those not good enough for the Football Academies, or to further reduce the likelihood of talented children 'slipping the net'? The Soccer Star Scheme also appeared potentially even more problematic, with its emphasis on drill-like movements and the proposed separation of those most proficient bodies for further testing.

There is, then, a need for critical studies to examine contemporary developments in children's football in England. The present study is an attempt to address this need.

An ethnographic study of a football club in a south London primary school

I spent six months, between January and July 1999 on Monday afternoons between 3.00 and 5.00, as an assistant to the football coach at Bigfield School, a south London state primary school consisting of approximately 320 children. In addition to the allocated time of the Monday afternoon for the children's training sessions, various school matches and events were also attended. The club consisted of twenty-nine children actually registered by the coach, out of which an approximate average of 18–23 regularly attended. All the children were aged between 9 and 11 years, that is, from academic years 5 and 6. The club was mixed sex and four girls were registered.

Access was obtained through two contacts: Colin, one of the teachers of a year 5 and 6 mixed class, and the coach Graham, the former giving permission for me to be present in the school and the latter his consent for me to work with him at the club itself. In the almost self-appointed role of assistant coach it was thus impossible in this study for the observer to have no effect on the observed. As I've argued, it is now generally agreed that it is impossible in research of this kind for the observer not to affect the observed in some way. In the context of the ethnographic research I actually instigated some events, such as training drills. This was mostly through necessity, as, for example, on one occasion when in the absence of the coach I led an entire session. But in the main I would follow the example of the coach.

According to Hammersley and Atkinson, many researchers embarking upon their first ethnographic study have to find their own way of producing field notes (Hammersley and Atkinson 1995: 176). The present study was no exception. Throughout the six-month period of ethnographic study a diary was kept in which field notes were recorded immediately upon return home after an event. After a month or so a Dictaphone was employed as an aid to memory for the recording of some thoughts on the journey home. Notes of the day's events were written immediately I got home and left to one side for the addition of any thought or event subsequently recalled. After an average twenty-four hours this rough data would be ready for word-processing, as no further recollections would normally occur beyond such a time period.

Interviews

Follow-up interviews were conducted with key individuals. According to Kidder the interview serves to reveal complex and emotionally laden information or probe the underlying sentiments of an individual's opinions (Kidder 1981: 153). However, as above this is once again dependent upon the skill of the investigator in eliciting this from the respondent. But interviews were conducted with the two key individuals: Colin the schoolteacher and Graham the coach, to discuss queries raised by my observations.

While I acknowledge the warnings of Waksler (1991) over the absence of children's voices in analyses such as this, it was felt that the subjects' actions would suffice for the purposes of this study, one of the main concerns after all being a focus on the child's body. With regard to the freedoms and/or constraints placed on the body, it was necessary to look to those who determined them, namely the teacher and the coach.

Ethnographic observations

The Bigfield after-school football club and the events it was involved in during the six-month period of ethnographic study were problematic on several levels. In order to analyse these problems it is useful to separate them into two categories: the methods of training employed for the children, which has the most implications for the child's body; and inter-school

matches and competitions/events the club were involved in, due to the introduction of 'real' competition.

Methods of training

From the moment the children arrived at the club they were told to get ready
quickly and then assemble in the centre circle area. They were not allowed to
play with any of the balls whilst awaiting their colleagues who were still
arriving and getting ready. Although they were anxious to kick a ball and
frequently did, this caused disruption to the coach's plans. On one occasion
I offered to amuse the children by engaging them in a simple game of
passing the ball around the centre-circle but was told not to by the coach
and to let the children wait. Once they were all assembled and ready the
coach, after waiting for silence, would then conduct some stretching exercises and a two lap jog of the pitch, this being the children's least favourite
part of the session and frequently eliciting complaints.

Often, immediately following the stretching and jogging, the coach would
employ extra drill-like activities, as a form of warm-up for the children, the
most common one being the children moving and performing certain
routines to his particular commands.

Following the warm-up exercises the coach would set up a drill for the
children, which I would replicate, in the opposite half of the pitch, with half
of them. This was always a simple routine involving the children in turn
weaving in and out of cones with a football and usually taking a strike at the
goal. But occasionally the goals were not used.

Apart from the occasional non-use of the goals which would bring
complaints, the main problem with the drills was the fact that only one child
could be occupied at a time, two if I replicated the drill in the other half of
the pitch. This left a large queue of children unoccupied and bored. The
unoccupied children would naturally be bickering and fooling around, especially the less mature ones.

Frequently the drills employed would be far too complex for the children.
Another problem that came to light with some of the drills was what I felt to
be the over-involvement of the adults present, that was mostly the coach and
myself, but frequently also the teacher Colin. As noted, the under-involve-
ment of the majority of the children as they waited their turn to perform a
drill was worrying enough, but this was exacerbated by an adult playing a
key role that I felt could have been performed by a child.

Clearly, drill demanded the most uniform and restrictive movements and
was thus the least liberating for the child's body. On one occasion in particular, whilst conducting one drill, I noted the problems encountered by most
children:

> We performed one drill, as the children stayed in their two lines and
> Graham and I threw a ball for each one to trap, control and pass back,

or head the ball back, basically to react to the way the ball was delivered. The main problems encountered by the children were manoeuvring their bodies to accommodate the type of ball they were actually receiving. ... Body shape and body position thus appeared important exercises to work on but I cannot see when there would ever be the time to work on such a skill as this would probably require lots of individual attention or at least a ball between two.

(Field Notes – Week 14 – 10 May)

But this perhaps went deeper than a lack of facilities. Naturally some children were more skilled than others were, but my overriding feeling was that no amount of drill would help the less skilled ones.

The training sessions ended with a competitive game and this was undoubtedly the children's favourite part of the day. Some often only turned up for this match, much to the chagrin of the coach who would usually not allow this unless the offender had a watertight excuse, to the displeasure of the offender's peers. The two main perpetrators of this 'offence' were Steve and Daniel, both of whom also trained with the professional club Fulham FC's Football Academy for children, making them appear, to me at least, like 'mini-stars' or special cases in some way.

The pitch used was very small, but adequate to accommodate a maximum of eight children a side, probably seven-a-side ideally. The problem was that the average turnout for the club was approximately twenty and sometimes as many as twenty-five. Thus, the match always averaged between ten and twelve-a-side. From the very outset, Week 1 itself, I reported a match scene that was to become typical viewing for me: 'I finally found the pitch but a wire fence still blocked my path. There was Graham refereeing a slightly overcrowded game, about twenty or so children on what for adults would be a six or seven-a-side pitch' (Field Notes – Week 1 – 11 January). This made the matches little more than chaos, in truth. Although positions were always allocated, apart from the fact that children have difficulty understanding these positions- let alone keeping them, the pitch was plainly too crowded. As I remarked on Week 2, my first proper training session at the club: 'If positions had been allocated they were ones I had not heard of, as the game resembled a rugby match more than a football game' (Field Notes – Week 2 – 18 January). By Week 17 I had clearly tired of the situation, simply reporting that: 'The only thing to report about the match was its unruliness and disorganisation' (Field Notes – Week 17 – 14 June).

On occasion the coach and I decided to relieve the congestion on the pitch by separating the children into three groups. I would take one of the groups to the side to do something else with them leaving the coach with a smaller-sided but more rational match, which was more manageable both for him to oversee and the children to play in. He would then rotate the groups every five minutes or so. With the separated group I would normally set up either a keep-ball game or a small pitch with cones for a mini-game. But sadly the very presence of other children enjoying a match on the 'proper' pitch was a major distraction for the separated group, who clearly wanted to be elsewhere:

> To say that the small game was a success would be a lie. ... At one poignant moment when the ball went out of play and I retrieved it I realised that I was returning to the backs of seven heads, all watching the 'real' game on the big pitch.
>
> (Field Notes – Week 11 – 29 March)

I concluded that: 'The second smaller game is obviously seen as an inferior relation to the 'main' one' (Field Notes – Week 11 – 29 March). This problem perhaps had as much to do with structural matters as methods of training as clearly better facilities would have alleviated this.

As had occurred with the drills, once again with the end of training matches the issue of the coach, myself or the teacher playing arose. In the early part of the research I would usually supervise one team from the side-line, shouting instructions – albeit largely in vain – and encouragement. But when occasionally the teacher Colin would turn up he would always play in the match. One week I was clearly annoyed by this: 'The game was not long underway when Colin turned up and Graham announced that he would be "playing" on my side. In truth I was not keen on this idea but naturally had little choice in the matter' (Field Notes – Week 14 – 10 May).

To be fair, further examination of the field notes proved that I actually found playing with the children more efficacious (Field Notes – Week 19 – 5 July). But this was mostly for training, in exercises such as 'Attackers and Defenders' where it was useful to be able to motivate the children by being amongst them (Field Notes – Week 16 – 24 May). But by the last few weeks I found myself playing in the matches every week, as the coach would be balancing the game by playing for the opposition. Perhaps this may have only been an issue for me, but it did raise the question as to who the training sessions were for? The apogee of the issue perhaps being on the very last day of the club, the Parents versus Children Fun Day, when the children were losing 3–4 with little of the match remaining:

> Within moments Leon had the ball and was shaping-up to shoot from quite a distance from his usual left side of midfield position. As usual the ball flew high and accurately towards goal as only Leon can make it. ... I thought this would be an excellent goal to finish on and end the afternoon in a draw. But as I was watching the ball sail into the roof of the net suddenly Graham threw himself under it and cleared it away with a header. The shot was quite powerful too and this was a good clearance. But I felt he should have let it go in.
>
> (Field Notes – Week 21 – 19 July – Parents versus Children Fun Day)

To be fair to the coach again, this was a fun day, but only one week previously little Darren had complained about Graham's numerous blocks and clearances off the line in the match that day:

> We equalised and Graham blew the whistle pretty soon afterwards, eliciting a particular complaint from little Darren who accused Graham of being too much of an obstacle to overcome. Graham was just laughing. In a way Darren was right and even I felt Graham perhaps made too many blocks.
>
> (Field Notes – Week 20 – 12 July)

Inter-school matches and competitions/events

At the very first event that I attended I was shocked to see that the children would be playing on a full-size eleven-a-side adult pitch which I remarked to a parent was bigger than the one my men's team played on (Field Notes – League Match – 19 February). This was because the junior pitch was apparently double-booked, but it begged the question as to why on such a large playing field only one junior pitch existed. This experience was repeated when Bigfield played in a play-off tournament, having to cope with a full-size pitch once again. In the first match Bigfield suffered a 0–5 rout and I commented at the time:

> Being a full-size pitch, obviously with full-size goals, one of the opposition's strikes that had been a rising shot had left Jason our goalkeeper hopelessly stranded, as he grasped at fresh air with no hope of ever reaching it.
>
> (Field Notes – League Leaders' Play-off Tournament – 25 March)

Apart from the seemingly perennial structural problems I also noted a potential point of philosophical interest at both matches I attended. I observed children not involved in the 'proper' match:

> What was interesting was that despite the fact that the half was only twenty minutes, within what seemed like two minutes this entire group had already broken off and started their own impromptu football game on an adjoining pitch, visible proof that children just want to play, if ever one needed it.
>
> (Field Notes – League Match: Bigfield v. Wandle – 19 February)

This was even more evident in the subsequent four-team tournament I attended, initially overhearing a conversation between a definite team member, Steve, and his father in which the boy was only really concerned about getting two games that day, his main fear being that defeat in the first game would mean elimination. And once again what was also observed amongst those not picked to play was:

As before, when I last observed a league match all the substitutes were far too busy messing around to watch the 'real' game in which their peers were involved. The existence of a long-jump sandpit at this school sport ground not helping matters in the least, as all concerned could not resist a jump. At one stage during the first game, Colin tried to restore order as 'non-match balls' spilled onto the playing field and bodies equally spilled and displaced the sand in the pit.

'You lot. Will you pack it in and come and support your class mates?'
It would be nice to say that they did.
(Field Notes – League Leaders' Play-off Tournament – 25 March)

The matter of player selection was also most salient and obviously only really an issue at competitive matches. At both the league match and the tournament I attended what would be considered the club's best players were always selected to play, with the others not being picked for the squad. At the first league match the two substitutes Richard and Horace were not even used by the coach. I questioned him about this on the telephone and he merely confirmed that they had not played, perhaps avoiding the issue? Ironically, the reason for this telephone call from the coach to me was to tell me that at that game one boy, Daniel, had been approached by a Millwall FC scout who was in attendance to invite him for trials at his club (Field Notes – Postscript: A Telephone Call from Graham that Night – 19 February).

At the tournament I attended the coach once again started the first match with his best players, only bringing on Rebecca, the first girl I had seen him use, near the very end, when the match was obviously lost. Similarly, in the second match when conversely it was obviously won, he finally fielded a few of the fringe players who I had not seen have a competitive game before. At the time I had questioned him about the substitutions:

'Bold decisions those substitutes, Graham?' I remarked as he shook my hand at the end of the game.
'Well it's only fair to give as many as I can a run out.'
But this was the second half of the third place-play off. And some substitutes were unused. Most notably Chris, the large boy who also always turns up to training.
(Field Notes – League Leader's Play-off Tournament – 25 March)

Ironically at this tournament Bigfield were effectively eliminated by one boy who had amazing pace and scored all five goals in their 0–5 first game demolition. I was to find out subsequently that this boy had not been to training for his school all season, turned up on the day and was picked by the coach, making the father of the boy he had displaced livid (Field Notes – Week 11 – 29 March).

At all the matches I attended, the league match and the play-off tourna-ment, there were scouts present from professional clubs. This fact particularly concerned little Steve to the point where it appeared to be his main concern at the league match, almost disrupting his concentration (Field Notes – League Match: Bigfield v. Wandle – 19 February). This issue is obviously related to player selection of a different kind, the separation of those most proficient children's bodies and thus those with the most potential physical capital. However, little meaning can be garnered from these observations at the events alone, and were thus one of the issues raised during the follow-up interviews.

Interview 1: the teacher

This interview was semi-structured and the questions were mostly based on the data that were produced during the ethnographic field research. With regard to player selection, I questioned him about the fact that at all the games I attended the school's best players always played, with the rest being unpicked or unused substitutes. He stated that it was important to win the matches and that was why this occurred. He even went as far as to admit that he had relaxed the school policy on good behaviour to enable Daniel to play:

> you know I hold my hands up. For the sake of the team, for the sake of the game I would do everything to get him in the team ... because I knew he would make a difference on the football field.

I questioned him further about this, enquiring whether the good players played whatever their behaviour and he reluctantly admitted that they did. He went on to reveal even more about this situation:

> I'm actually quite uneasy talking about it because ... you know it's ... I feel as though ... I do feel as though I've compromised myself really and I'm quite surprised that I've done that and talking about it I guess I have really for a couple of players during the season last year, particularly this one lad Daniel because you know ... and his younger brother actually ... it was pretty much the same.

Staying with the same subject, I went onto those children who did not get picked to play, this also elicited an interesting dialogue between myself and the teacher and is worth reproducing in full:

CT:	... you're always going to have these children around the edges and it's nice to give them a run out occasionally but you know what sort of manager in their right mind is going to ... it's kind of ... it's very much an interface with real world sort of dynamics I think in the terms of social structure ...
ST:	Socialisation?
CT:	Yeah I mean it's because there's a lot of harsh realities to face ...

ST: So this is what happens in the real world?

CT: Yeah.

ST: If you don't cut the grade you're not in?

CT: Yeah certainly ... I'd certainly say that ... it would be nice to give everyone a run out but at the end of the day you're not going to ... but we do at the end of the day try and recognise everyone's commitment and you know everyone who turns up for practices and turns up for games and stuff they always get a mention in the assemblies and things and they always get certificates at the end of the season ...

He went on to mention that he and the coach tried to get the children on the periphery a game in friendly matches. He subsequently betrayed perhaps the sad truth of the matter when he stated the importance of winning matches to himself, the coach and the children, in that order. I finally asked whether he felt these 'important' victories meant so much to the children who were not playing. He stated that:

> I mean I think that they were upset and so on and so forth but I think for the most part I think it meant more to the children who were actually playing and that had been in the team the whole way through.

This response perhaps missed the point somewhat.

Interview 2: the coach

With regard to the matches and events I had attended, whereas in my view what would be considered to be the school's best players had always been playing, with the rest given peripheral roles, the coach refuted this. Stating that he tried to get everyone a game, including the girls registered with the club. He added that I had probably not attended enough matches if this had been my observation. He also stated that the unused substitutes I had seen at the school match I attended (Field Notes – Friday 19 February – League Match) were almost all passed over for their own good. In such a tight match he did not want to put one of the lesser used players on the pitch in case they made a mistake and cost the school the match. This, apparently, was potentially worse than not playing at all for the child involved, due to the potential criticism they could receive from their peers. However, he still went on to admit that in all of the competitive matches that the school did play, the best players always played anyway.

Children's football and alienation

The concept of alienation may have slipped slightly out of vogue. However, as pointed out by Seeman (1983) it is certainly alive and well in one guise or another and in evidence in the present study, and it will be seen that Marx's notion of the alienation of the species, that is a person from their own body, serves to facilitate analysis even further.

The studies of children's sports conducted in the 1970s that condemned them as alienating experiences for children could be accused of being only partly accurate. It should be recognised that these studies were products of their time, written as they were in an era still in many respects feeling the effects of the so-called counter-cultural revolution which witnessed attacks on all of capitalist society's institutions. If their weakness was perhaps their over-impassioned condemnation of all products of capitalism, their main strength was perhaps their stressing that children's sport should above all other things be an educational experience. In this respect, particularly when it comes under the educational context, such as school football, it should be an all-inclusive, and thus what else but a non-alienating and empowering experience.

During the ethnographic field work with the Bigfield school football club some of the criticisms voiced in those 1970s studies were still valid nearly thirty years later. Although it was found that the club was effectively outside of the school, spatially and temporally, as an after-school club, this should not mean that the type of football played should also be placed outside of the educational context. Sadly this was largely the case.

Although the teacher and the coach provided an equal opportunity for any child wishing to be involved in the club, the same could not really be said on match days. At all of the events I attended the school's best players played the other schools with the rest being either unpicked for the final team or a substitute. This also appeared true for the matches I was not able to attend. This was further borne out by studying the end-of-year report produced by the coach himself (Bigfield FC Season 98/99 Report). Looking at the seven league matches he produced detailed information for, including a full list of names of the starting eleven, it can be seen that over these games a total of fifteen children were used. That is fifteen out of a club consisting of twenty-nine players listed on the first page of the report. This list is also missing one or two names that appear in the field notes, children who perhaps joined late. Out of those fifteen, ten started either every game or six of the seven. These admittedly basic statistics hardly, however, betoken a club that truly embraces all-comers or provides an opportunity for all children to get their chance to play in a 'real' game.

This was redolent of the type of situation warned against by Orlick (1974), when he claimed that children's sport appeared to be operating as a highly successful weeding-out process and only the best were ultimately required to play. However, Orlick identified children who were dropping out because of this. In fairness, despite the apparent monopoly of regular first team places by a minority of the children, not many – if any – actually dropped out of the Bigfield school football club despite this.

Hyland's (1978) view that competition can equally produce friendship and not solely alienation, and Mehl and Davis's (1978) view that competition can be good for children, have to be accepted. Competition is important and can be beneficial for children. What is at issue, as pointed out during the research process and also pointed out by Mehl and Davis, is that it is important to stipulate a certain type of competition for children and remember who children's sport is for. In this respect the involvement of the teacher and the coach in matches at the end of the training sessions was problematic. As pointed out during the field work on at least two occasions, the coach's involvement elicited complaints from the children. It may be that coaching children is easier in – or at least very near – the 'heart of the action', but this can surely be achieved without affecting the outcome of a game?

But perhaps more problematic is the continued existence of, and Bigfield's involvement in, a league system. This, coupled with knockout tournaments, is an element of competition criticised by educationalists. The existence of the league table, as was seen in the present study, promoted caution in team selection due to the necessity of winning, ensuring that, as ever, only the best children played in league matches. The removal of the league, contrary to popular belief, would not – or should not – spell the end of competitive football. What it should spell the end of is cautious team selections and questionable adult motives and behaviour. That is, vicariously playing the game through children and possibly criticising their mistakes. Ultimately what is not considered is the fact that given more opportunities to play, and play without unnecessary stress, more children may actually improve and become better players.

Children's football, alienation and the body

The method of drill favoured by the coach for the Bigfield school football club is one no longer promoted by the FA. The body discipline and rigidity of repeatedly manoeuvring around cones with a ball has now been proscribed in favour of what could be labelled a more expressive and playful method of allowing the children one ball each and nurturing ball skills this way. The drill-like movements practised could effectively be labelled a form of body-discipline, similar to Hargreaves' (1986) appropriation of the Foucauldian concept to facilitate analysis of school physical education. A lack of equipment may have left the coach no option but to adopt this discipline, but upon being asked whether he would abandon drill if he had more footballs he stated he would not, believing drills to be more beneficial for 'tactics'.

While the FA's blueprint for children's football may be admirable and for some qualify as 'good practice', other aspects of their plans require more analysis, and the work of Foucault again helps facilitate this. The JTM scheme to train people as football coaches of children and the concomitant Soccer Star Scheme, outlined at the outset, could be viewed as potential forms of panopticism. When Hargreaves applied the work of Foucault to school PE he also claimed that competitive sport did not expose the individual child adequately to the teacher's surveillance, to what he called the 'gaze of authority' (Hargreaves 1986: 165). Traditional PE in the form of drill, or routinised movements with or without apparatus offered more scope for discipline and surveillance. Progress could be monitored more effectively and the body scrutinised for efficiency.

The FA have attempted to make competitive sport more amenable to scrutiny and surveillance, by breaking down the constituent elements of the game of football and calling for them to be performed individually. The disciplined child's body can be placed under greater surveillance with the JTM and the Soccer Star Scheme: it can be measured and its performance recorded; performances collated and the most efficient bodies separated from those below the required standard. Once separated, efficient bodies can undergo further scrutiny at a professional football club's centre of excellence. The Soccer Star Scheme could be viewed as a form of panopticism, removing the necessity for the scout to ever leave their club as the JTM trained coach performs the role of spreading the network of surveillance. Self-disciplined children's bodies work towards the required standard and await the call for further scrutiny and testing. When the call arrives the most proficient and disciplined bodies will answer it. The ultimate prize being the opportunity to convert their physical capital into economic capital as a professional footballer.

Those most disciplined child's bodies thus stand even less chance of 'slipping the net', as it were, with the existence of the JTM, the Soccer Star Scheme and the professional football club centres of excellence. Bourdieu's notion of physical capital can be seen to be most salient here. While there can be little doubting that the FA's plans for children's football are commendable, a note of caution has to be raised when further analysing the motives of these three schemes. It is possible to see an implicit link between them, whereby it could be asked whether the real objective of the FA is to improve the opportunities for all children to play and simultaneously improve their bodily skills, or whether it is to ensure that no stone is left unturned in the incessant search for new potential physical capital?

In this respect the Bigfield School football club could be viewed as the first point of separation of those most efficient children's bodies from the rest, albeit covertly. Two children were found to have already been separated, although this had been by means other than the JTM or Soccer Star Scheme.

A new discourse

It is often argued by people who would be condemned as philistines by academics that much social research conducted within the academy is a waste of time, fruitless investigations of the obvious, or simply pointless. The present study could be a fine candidate for such condemnation, and the author felt this throughout. As stated at the outset, it could well be asked what is there to investigate in children's football? The best will always be the best, in the same fashion as cream will always rise to the top, and there is very little that can be done about it. But this is only partly true. The best will always exist, whether their talent is God-given or otherwise. But what can be done about it, especially in the educational context, is guarding against their separation from the rest at such a very young age. This separation is, to all intents and purposes, elitist and, as it always does, ultimately merely serves to impoverish all concerned.

The less talented are impoverished through their limited opportunity to compete with more talented children, which would produce more skill-sharing and could help to nurture latent ability. The more talented are frequently the target of outside agencies such as professional clubs' centres of excellence, and thus their separation from the rest potentially goes deeper than simply on school match days. The ultimate impoverishment could await them when they fail to make the grade at professional level, as the majority of potential physical capital does.

It is thus argued that a form of alienation exists and faces both sets of children. Believing with Seeman (1983) that alienation is very much still in existence and is most likely a situation-relevant variable (Seeman 1997) it can be seen that the less talented children face exclusion, or alienation from full participation due to their lack of ability. While the more talented children face a form of alienation that is less explicit but equally real; and it is at this point that a focus on the body utilising the work of Foucault and Bourdieu facilitates further analysis. Thus, while the FA's plans for children's football ostensibly appear to foster 'good practice' and a form of football for the non-alienation of all children who want to play, Foucault's concept of the panopticon renders it slightly more problematic, as does Bourdieu's delineation of the notion of physical capital.

The early studies of children's sport and alienation could thus effectively be viewed as progenitors for the present study, while the modern focus on the body serves to develop that work further. This was attempted in the present study. While Foucault has been labelled *the* theorist of the body, it can be seen that the work of Bourdieu requires further development. According to Frank, Bourdieu's theorising 'waxes' (as opposed to waning) and he suggested that Foucault's work has perhaps been 'mined enough' (Frank 1990: 154–5). According to Hall, the work of other post-structuralist theorists like Saussure and Barthes has also still not been exploited to its fullest potential in sociology, and thus the sub-discipline of sport sociology could benefit too from any development in the application of these theorists' work (Hall 1997: 62). Future studies examining children's football may thus benefit from the development of these theorists' work.

The limits of a micro-sociological ethnographic study such as the present one have been stated from the outset. Its generalisability to the thousands of school football clubs countrywide is virtually impossible. However, it is hoped that if nothing else, in true sociological tradition, it could serve to provoke further studies and stimulate debate around an ostensibly non-problematic social practice – a social practice around which the FA have created a new discourse – children's football.

Select bibliography

1. Fat City? British Football and the Politics of Social Exclusion at the Turn of the Twenty-first Century

STEPHEN WAGG

Armstrong, Gary (1998) *Football Hooligans: Knowing the Score*, Oxford: Berg.

Assinder, Nick (1999) 'Blair's programme fails to surprise' *BBC News Online: UK Politics*, 17 November (http://newsbbc.co.uk/1/low/ uk_politics/525242.stm, accessed 29 October 2002).

Blair, Tony (1996) 'A stakeholder society', *Fabian Review*, 18/1, February.

Bower, Tom (2003) *Broken Dreams: Vanity, Greed and the Souring of British Football*, London: Simon and Schuster.

Bradshaw, Bill (2001) 'The rise and fall of Woodgate', *Observer*, sport section, 16 December, 6–7.

Brick, Carlton (2002) 'Fandmonium: the discourse of authenticity in the consumption of the FA Carling Premier League', Ph.D. thesis, School of Sport, Exercise and Leisure, University of Surrey, Roehampton.

Brimson, Doug and Eddie (1996) *Everywhere We Go*, London: Headline.

Burnham, Andy (2002) 'Give the people's game back', *Guardian*, 2 April, 16.

Campbell, Denis (2001) 'Playmaker's global pitch', *Observer*, sport section, 7 October, 8.

——(2003) 'Dad, lad, gay icon, player – why Beckham is Britain's model man', *Observer*, 2 February, 9.

Chaudhary, Vivek (2002a) 'Football's profile is white and wealthy', *Guardian*, 27 February, 11.

——(2002b) 'Soccer watchdog "has no bite" ', *Guardian*, 14 March, 7.

——(2002c) 'Football to groom boys for life at the top', 22 March, 13.

——(2003) *Digger* column, *Guardian* sport section, 22 February, 7.

Clark, David (2002) 'The beautiful game needs protection from the market', *Guardian*, 15 August, 16.

Collins, Roy (2003) 'Cash-starved Ipswich strike out', *Guardian*, 11 February, 28.

Commission for Social Justice (1994) *Social Justice*, London: Vintage.

Conn, David (1997) *The Football Business*, Edinburgh: Mainstream.

Cope, Jon (2002) 'Pass the cash', *Guardian*, society section, 23 October, 2–3.

Curtis, Adrian and Steve Stammers (2002) 'Football thrown into chaos', *Evening Standard*, 10 January, 79–80.

Cox, Gerry (2002) 'Division One clubs in crisis', *Observer*, sport section, 29 September, 11.

Critcher, Chas (1979) 'Football since the war', in John Clarke, Chas Critcher and Richard Johnson (eds) *Working Class Culture: Studies in History and Theory*, London: Hutchinson, 161–84.

Denny, Charlotte (2002) 'Future for football's spent forces lies in the home game', *Guardian*, 1 April, 25.

Driver, Stephen and Luke Martell (1998) *New Labour: Politics After Thatcherism*, Cambridge: Polity Press.

Dunning, Eric, Patrick Murphy and John Williams (1988) *The Roots of Football Hooliganism*, London: Routledge and Kegan Paul.

Fifield, Dominic (2002) 'As Beckham gets set for £92,000 a week, 600 fellow footballers prepare for the dole', *Guardian*, 7 May, 3.

Fynn, Alex and Lynton Guest (1994) *Out of Time*, London: Simon and Schuster.

Giulianotti, Richard (1994) 'Social identity and public order: political and academic discourses on football violence', in Richard Giulianotti, Norman Bonney and Mike Hepworth (eds) *Football Violence and Social Identity*, London: Routledge, 10–36.

——(1999) *Football: A Sociology of the Global Game*, Cambridge: Polity Press.

Goldberg, Adrian and Simon Lowe (2002) *Political Football*, video, Birmingham: Argy Bhaji Productions.

Golding, Peter (1990) 'Political communication and citizenship: The media and democracy in an inegalitarian social order', in Marjorie Ferguson (ed.) *Public Communication: The New Imperatives*, London: Sage, 84–100.

Golding, Peter (1994) 'Telling stories: Sociology, journalism and the informed citizen' *European Journal of Communication*, 9, 461–84.

Hamil, Sean (1999) 'A whole new ball game? Why football needs a regulator', in Sean Hamil, Jonathan Michie and Christine Oughton (eds) *A Game of Two Halves? The Business of Football*, Edinburgh: Mainstream, 23–37.

Hamil, Sean, Jonathan Michie and Christine Oughton (1999) (eds) *A Game of Two Halves? The Business of Football*, Edinburgh: Mainstream.

Hebdige, Dick (1974) 'The Kray twins: A study of a system of closure', Stencilled Occasional Paper: Centre for Contemporary Cultural Studies, University of Birmingham.

Horrie, Chris (1997) *Premiership*, London: Simon and Schuster.

Kelly, Graham (with Bob Harris) (1999) *Sweet F.A.*, London: HarperCollins.

Kelso, Paul (2002) 'Footballers caught in murky world of club scene', *Guardian*, 23 August, 5.

King, Anthony (1998) *The End of the Terraces*, London: Leicester University Press.

Lomax, Brian (1999) 'Supporter representation on the board: The case of Northampton Town FC', in Sean Hamil, Jonathan Michie and Christine Oughton (1999) (eds) *A Game of Two Halves? The Business of Football*, Edinburgh: Mainstream, 195–201.

Martin King Shaw Trust (2002) *Lambeth Football Forum: Report and Strategy*, London: MKST, 127 Sudbourne Road, London SW2.

Morris, Steven, with Helena Smith and David Alexander (2002) 'Gadafy's new plan: Bring Libya in from the cold – through football', *Guardian*, 16 August, 3.

Murphy, Patrick, John Williams and Eric Dunning (1990) *Football on Trial*, London: Routledge.

North, Stephen and Paul Hodson (1997) *Build a Bonfire: How Football Fans United to Save Brighton and Hove Albion*, Edinburgh: Mainstream.

Palmer, Henry (2001) 'United front', *Guardian*, society section, 8 August, 2–3.

Redhead, Steve (ed.) (1993) *The Passion and the Fashion: Football Fandom and the New Europe*, Aldershot: Avebury.

Showstack Sassoon, Anne (1996) 'Beyond pessimism of the intellect: Agendas for social justice and change', in Mark Perryman (ed.) *The Blair Agenda*, London: Lawrence and Wishart, 147–69.

Social Issues Research Centre webpage: http://www.sirc.org/publik/ fvtheory.html ('Football violence in Europe').

Stack, Pat (2002) 'Over the bottom line', *Socialist Review*, September, 36.

Steel, Mark (2001) *Reasons to be Cheerful*, London: Scribner.

Sugden, John and Alan Tomlinson (1999) *Great Balls of Fire: How Big Money Is Hijacking World Football*, Edinburgh: Mainstream.

Taylor, Ian (1971) 'Soccer consciousness and soccer hooliganism', in Stanley Cohen (ed.) *Images of Deviance*, Harmondsworth: Penguin, 134–64.

Taylor, Rogan (2000) 'Why football needs a regulator', in Sean Hamil, Jonathan Michie, Christine Oughton and Steven Warby (eds) *Football in the Digital Age: Whose Game is it Anyway?*, Edinburgh: Mainstream, 55–61.

Thompson, Laura (2002) 'Arrogant brain-dead game', *Observer*, sport section, 18 August, 15.

Wagg, Stephen (1984) *The Football World: A Contemporary Social History*, Brighton: Harvester Press.

——(1992) 'One I made earlier: Media, popular culture and the politics of childhood', in Dominic Strinati and Stephen Wagg (eds) *Come on Down? Popular Media Culture in Post-war Britain*, London: Routledge, 150–78.

——(1998) 'Sack the board, sack the board, sack the board: Accountancy and accountability in contemporary English football culture', in Udo Merkel, Gill Lines and Ian McDonald (eds) *The Production and Consumption of Sport Cultures*, Brighton: Leisure Studies Association, 37–53.

——(2002) 'All this aggro is bad for business', *Evening Standard*, 11 January, 13.

Ward, Colin (1989) *Steaming In: The Journal of a Football Fan*, London: Sports Pages/Simon and Schuster.

Watkins, Trevor (1999) *Cherries in the Red: From Terrace to Boardroom – One Fan's Fight to Save His Club*, London: Headline.

Williams, John (1991) 'Having an away day: English football spectators and the hooligan debate', in John Williams and Stephen Wagg (eds) *British Football and Social Change*, Leicester: Leicester University Press, 160–84.

——(1999) *Is It All Over? Can Football Survive the Premier League?*, Reading: South Street Press.

Williams, John, Eric Dunning and Patrick Murphy (1984) *Hooligans Abroad*, London: Routledge and Kegan Paul.

2. 'You're not Welcome Anymore': The Football Crowd, Class and Social Exclusion

TIM CRABBE and ADAM BROWN

AGARI (1995) *Press Release: Football Unites Against Racism and Intimidation Campaign Launch for 1995/96 Season*, 28 September 1995, London: AGARI.

Back, L., Crabbe, T. and Solomos, J. (2001) *The Changing Face of Football: Racism, Identity and Multiculture in the English Game*, Oxford: Berg.

Bourdieu, P. (1984) *Distinction: A Social Critique of Judgement and Taste*, London: Routledge.

Brown, A. (1997) *Report to UEFA into Manchester United v. Porto, March 1997*, Manchester: FSA.

——(1994) 'Football Fans and Civil Liberties', *Journal of Sport and the Law*, vol. 1, no. 2, July 1994.

Brown, A. (ed.) (1998) *Fanatics! Power, Identity and Fandom in Football*, London: Routledge.

Brown, A. and Walsh, A. (1999) *Not for Sale: Manchester United, Murdoch and the Defeat of BskyB*, Edinburgh: Mainstream.

Brown, A., Cohen, S. and O'Connor, J. (2000) 'Local Music Policies Within a Global Music Industry: Manchester and Sheffield', *Geoforum*, vol. 31.

Champion, S. (1991) *And God Created Manchester*, Manchester: Wordsmith.

Coalition of Football Supporters (COFS) press release, 25 February 1999.

Collins, M., with Kay, T. (2003) *Sport and Social Exclusion*, London: Routledge.

Conn, D. (1997) *The Football Business: Fair Game in the 90s?*, Edinburgh and London: Mainstream.

Crabbe, T. (2000) 'A Sporting Chance? Using Sport to Tackle Drug Use and Crime', *Drugs: Education, Prevention and Policy*, vol. 7, no. 4.

——(2004) 'England Fans. A New Club for a New England? Social Inclusion, "Authenticity" and the Performance of Englishness at "Home" and "Away"', *Leisure Studies* 23, 1, 63–78.

Davies, P. (1990) *All Played Out: The Full Story of Italia '90*, London: Mandarin.

European Commission Com. (1999) 644 *Helsinki Report on Sport*, Brussels: European Commission.

Fiske, J. (1989) *Understanding Popular Culture*, London: Unwin Hyman.

Football Association (1991) *Blueprint for the Future of Football*, London: Football Association.

Football Supporters Association (1998) *Submission to the Football Task Force*, Liverpol: FSA.

Football Task Force (1999) *Final Report: Commercial Issues, Report One*, London: DCMS.

Foucault, M. (1979) 'On Governmentality', *Ideology and Consciousness*, vol. 6, 5–23.

——(1975) *The Birth of the Clinic*, New York: Vintage.

Giulianotti, R. (2002) ' "Supporters, Followers, Fans and Flaneurs": A Taxonomy of Spectator Identities', *Journal of Sport and Social Issues*, vol. 26, no. 1, February 2002, 25–46, London: Sage.

——(1999) *Football: A Sociology of the Global Game*, Cambridge: Polity Press.

Guardian (2002) 'Clubs' Revenue to Tumble as Viewers Switch Away', by Vivek Chaudhary, 11 January.

Hall, S. and Jacques, M. (1990) *New Times: The Changing Face of Politics in the 1990s*, London: Lawrence and Wishart.

Hall, S. and Jefferson, T. (1976) *Resistance Through Rituals: Youth Subcultures in Post-war Britain*, London: Hutchinson.

Hamil, S., Michie, J. and Oughton, C. (eds) (1999) *A Game of Two Halves: The Business of Football*, Edinburgh: Mainstream.

Hamil, S., Michie, J., Oughton, C. and Warby, S. (eds) (2000) *Football in the Digital Age: Whose Game Is It Anyway?*, Edinburgh: Mainstream.

Hochschild, A. R. (1983) *The Managed Heart: The Commercialisation of Human Feeling*, California: University of California Press.

King, A. (1998) *The End of the Terraces: The Transformation of English Football in the 1990s*, London: Leicester University Press.

Lash, S. and Urry, J. (1994) *Economies of Signs and Space*, London: Sage.

Lee, S. (1998) 'Grey Shirts to Grey Suits: The Political Economy of English Football in the 1990s', in Brown, A. (ed.) *Fanatics! Power, Identity and Fandom in Football*, London: Routledge.

O'Connor, J. and Wynne, D. (eds) (1996) *From the Margins to the Centre: Cultural Production and Consumption in the Post-industrial City*, Aldershot: Avebury.

Polhemus, T. (1994) *Streetstyle*, London: Thames and Hudson.

Redhead, S. (1997) *Post-Fandom and the Millennial Blues*, London: Routledge.

——(1991) *Football With Attitude*, Manchester: Wordsmith.

——(1990) *The End-of-the-century Party: Youth and Pop towards 2000*, Manchester: Manchester University Press.

Redhead, S. (ed.) (1993) *The Passion and the Fashion: Football Fandom in the New Europe*, Aldershot: Avebury.

Robson, G. (2000) *'No One Likes Us, We Don't Care': The Myth and Reality of Millwall Fandom*, Oxford: Berg.

Rojek, C. (1995) *Decentering Leisure*, London: Sage.

Ronstein, J. (2001) 'The Commodification of Football or Football's Colonisation by Capital', working paper, University of Barcelona.

Rubython, T. (1998) 'How Manchester United Was Sold Out so Cheaply', *Business Age*, October 1998, 68–72.

Russell, D. (1997) *Football and the English: A Social History of Association Football in England, 1863–1995*, Preston: Carnegie.

Taylor, I. (1995) ' "It's a Whole New Ball Game": Sports Television, the Cultural Industries and the Condition of Football in England', *Salford Papers in Sociology no. 17*, Salford: University of Salford.

——(1992) 'English Football in the 1990s: Taking Hillsborough Seriously?', in Williams, J. and Wagg, S. (eds) *British Football and Social Change: Getting into Europe*, Leicester: Leicester University Press.

Taylor, I., Evans, K. and Fraser, P. (1998) *A Tale of Two Cities*, London: Routledge.

Wickham, G. (1992) 'Sport, Manners, Persons, Government: Sport, Elias, Mauss, Foucault', *Cultural Studies*, vol. 6, no. 2, 219–31.

Williams, J. (2000) 'The Changing Face of Football: A Case for National Regulation?', in S. Hamil, J. Michie, C. Oughton and S. Warby (eds) (2000) *Football in the Digital Age: Whose Game Is It Anyway?*, Edinburgh: Mainstream.

Williams, J. and Wagg, S. (eds) (1992) *British Football and Social Change: Getting into Europe*, Leicester: Leicester University Press.

3. 'Giving Something Back':
Can Football Clubs and Their Communities Co-exist?

NEIL TAYLOR

Bradbury, S. (2001), *The New Football Communities*, Leicester: Sir Norman Chester Centre for Football Research, University of Leicester.

Charity Commission, website at charity-commission.gov.uk.

Collins, M., Henry, I.P., Houlihan, B., and Butler, J. (1999) *Research Report: Sport and Social Exclusion: A Report for the Department for Culture, Media and Sport*, London: DCMS Policy Action Team 10.

Department for Culture, Media and Sport, website at www.dcms.gov.uk.

Department for Culture, Media and Sport (2000), *A Sporting Future for All*, London: DCMS.

Department for Culture, Media and Sport (2001a), *Building on PAT 10*, London: DCMS.

Department for Culture, Media and Sport (2001b), *A Sporting Future for All: The Government's Plan for Sport*, London: DCMS.

Department for Education and Employment, *Playing for Success*, at www.dfee.gov.uk/playingforsuccess.

Department for Education and Skills, promotional material.

Evening Standard (2001), 26 July: 61.

Football Insider (1999), May/June: 14.

Football Task Force (1999), *Investing in the Community*, London: Department for Culture, Media and Sport.

Football Unites Racism Divides (FURD), website at www.furd.org.uk.

Garland, J., and Chakraborti (2001), *Evaluation of the Charlton Athletic Race Equality (CARE) Partnership Final Report*, Leicester: Scarman Centre, University of Leicester.

Give Me Football, website at www.givemefootball.co.uk.

Guardian (2001), Society section, 24 October: 1.

Hamil, S., Michie, J., Oughton, C., and Shailer (2001), *The State of the Game*, Football Governance Research Centre.

Independent (2001a), 5 March: 32.

Independent (2001b), 30 November.

Inglis, Simon (1986), *Guide to Football Grounds*.

Leyton Orient Community Sports Programme (LOCSP), website at www.locsp.freeserve.co.uk.

On the Line (2002), radio programme, May, BBC Radio 5 Live.

Scottish Executive (2000), *The Role of Sport in Regenerating Deprived Urban Areas*, Edinburgh: Scottish Executive.

Social Exclusion Unit (1998), *Bringing Britain Together: A National Strategy for Neighbourhood Renewal*, London: Social Exclusion Unit.

Sunday Times (2001), Sports section, 28 January: 8.

Watson, N., 'Football in the Community', in *Soccer and Society*, Vol. 1, number 1, Spring: 114–25.

When Saturday Comes (2001), November: 25.

4. A Day Out with the 'Old Boys'

PAT SLAUGHTER

Armstrong, G., and Hobbs, D. (1994), 'Tackled from Behind', in Guilianotti, R., Bonney, N., and Hepworth, M. (eds), *Football Violence and Social Identity*, London: Routledge: 196–228.

Beck, U. (1992), *Risk Society*, London: Sage.

Giddens, A. (1992), *The Transformation of Intimacy*, Cambridge: Polity.

Hancock, L., and Matthews, R. (2001), 'Crime, Community Safety and Toleration', in

Matthews, R., and Pitts, J. (eds), *Crime, Disorder and Community Safety*, London: Routledge: 99–119.

Lea, J. (2002), *Crime and Modernity*, London: Sage.

Katz, J. (1988), *The Seductions of Crime*, New York: Basic Books.

Young, J. (1999), *The Exclusive Society*, London: Sage.

5. 'With his Money, *I* Could Afford to be Depressed': Markets, Masculinity and Mental Distress in the English Football Press

STEPHEN WAGG

Adams, Tony with Ian Ridley (1998) *Addicted*, London: CollinsWillow.

Arlidge, John (2000) 'Share cropper' [Profile of Piers Morgan, editor of the *Daily Mirror*], *Observer*, 14 May.

Beattie, Kevin (1998) *The Beat*, Essex: Skript Publishing.

Borger, Julian (2000) 'Mother executed for killing her children', *Guardian*, 4 May.

Brown, Adam and Walsh, Andy (1999) *Not For Sale*, Edinburgh: Mainstream.

Buckley, Will (2000) 'Paging all sports fans', *Observer*, 26 March.

Burn, Gordon (1984) *Somebody's Husband, Somebody's Son: The Story of Peter Sutcliffe*, London: Heinemann.

Cassy, John (2000) 'Man Utd set to become the world's first £1bn club', *Guardian*, 8 March.

Dicken, Peter (1986) *Global Shift*, London: Harper and Row.

Earle, Robbie (1999) 'Mollycoddle Collymore', *Observer*, 31 January.

Goldberg, Adrian and Wagg, Stephen (1991) 'It's not a knockout: English football and globalisation', in John Williams and Stephen Wagg (eds) *British Football and Social Change*, London: Leicester University Press, 239–53.

Hall, Stuart and Jacques, Martin (1989) *New Times*, London: Lawrence and Wishart.

Horton, Ed (1995) *The Best World Cup Money Can Buy*, Oxford: Ed Horton.

Lash, Scott and Urry, John (1987) *The End of Organised Capitalism*, Cambridge: Polity Press.

Merson, Paul, with Ian Ridley (1999) *Hero and Villain*, London: CollinsWillow.

Ridley, Ian (1999) 'In defence of Stan', *Observer*, 31 January.

Sedgwick, Peter (1982) *Psycho Politics*, London: Pluto Press.

Smith, Alan (2000) 'Mad or sad? Colly is an insecure threat to Leicester', *Observer*, 13 February.

Sugden, John and Tomlinson, Alan (1998) *FIFA and the Contest for World Football*, Cambridge: Polity Press.

——(1999) *Great Balls of Fire: How Big Money is Hijacking World Football*, Edinburgh: Mainstream.

Taylor, Matthew (1997) 'Proud Preston: A history of the Football League, 1900–1939', Ph.D. thesis, De Montfort University, Leicester.

Vamplew, Wray (1988) *Pay Up and Play the Game: Professional Sport in Britain, 1875–1914*, Cambridge: Cambridge University Press.

Ward Jouve, Nicole (1988) *'The Streetcleaner': The Yorkshire Ripper Case on Trial*, London: Marion Boyars.

Whannel, Garry (2003) 'From pig's bladders to Ferraris: Media discourses of masculinity and morality in obituaries of Stanley Matthews', in Alina Bernstein and Neil Blain (eds) *Sport, Media, Culture*, London: Frank Cass, 73–94.

White, Jim (2000) 'Closing ranks behind the spoiled brats for whom self-knowledge is a closed book', *Guardian*, 17 February.

Williams, John (1999) *Is It All Over? Can Football Survive the Premier League?*, Reading: South Street Press.

Yallop, David (1999) *How They Stole the Game*, London: Poetic Publishing.

6. Still a Man's Game? Women Footballers, Personal Experience and Tabloid Myth

JOHN HARRIS

Barthes, R. (1977) 'The photographic image', in R. Barthes, *Image-Music-Text*, ed. S. Heath, London: Fontana.

Berger, J. (1972) *Ways of Seeing*, Harmondsworth: Penguin.

Blinde, E. and Taub, D. (1992) 'Women athletes as falsely accused deviants: Managing the lesbian stigma', *The Sociological Quarterly*, 33, pp. 521–33.

Caudwell, J. (1999) 'Women's football in the United Kingdon: Theorizing gender and unpacking the butch lesbian image', *Journal of Sport and Social Issues*, 23, pp. 390–402.

Chafetz, J. (1978) *Masculine, Feminine or Human?*, Itasca: F.E. Peacock.

Choi, P. (2000) *Femininity and the Physically Active Woman*, London: Routledge.

Clayton, B. (2001) 'The print manhood formula', unpublished B.A.(Hons) Leisure Management dissertation, University of Wales.

Coddington, A. (1997) *One of the Lads: Women Who Follow Football*, London: HarperCollins.

Cole, C. (1993) 'Resisting the canon: Feminist cultural studies, sport and technologies of the body', *Journal of Sport and Social Issues*, 17, pp. 77–97.

Cox, B. and Thompson, S. (2000) 'Multiple bodies: Sportswomen, soccer and sexuality', *International Review for the Sociology of Sport*, 35, pp. 5–21.

Crosset, T. (1995) *Outsiders in the Clubhouse: The World of Women's Professional golf*, Albany NY: State University of New York Press.

Davies, P. (1996) *I Lost My Heart to the Belles*, London: Heinemann.

Davis, D. (1990) 'Portrayals of women in prime-network television: Some demographic characteristics', *Sex Roles*, 23, pp. 325–32.

Duncan, M. (1990) 'Sports photographs and sexual difference: Images of women and men in the 1984 and 1988 Olympic Games', *Sociology of Sport Journal*, 7, pp. 22–41.

Dunphy, E. (1976) *Only a Game*, London: Kestrel Books.

Fiske, J. (1992) *Understanding Popular Culture*, London: Routledge.

Griffin, P. (1992) 'Changing the game: Homophobia, sexism, and lesbians in sport', *Quest*, 44, pp. 251–65.

——(1998) *Strong Women, Deep Closets: Lesbians and Homophobia in Sport*, Champaign IL: Human Kinetics.

Grose, R. (1989) *The Sun Station: Behind the Scenes at Britain's Best-selling Daily Newspaper*, London: Angus and Robertson.

Halbert, C. (1997) 'Tough enough and woman enough: Stereotypes, discrimination and impression management among women professional boxers', *Journal of Sport and Social Issues*, 21, pp. 7–36.

Hall, A. (1996) *Feminism and Sporting Bodies: Essays in Theory and Practice*, Champaign IL: Human Kinetics.

Hargreaves, J. (1994) *Sporting Females: Critical Issues in the History and Sociology of Women's Sport*, London: Routledge.

Harris, J. (1998) 'Defending like women: An interpretive sociological study of female collegiate football players', unpublished Ph.D. thesis, Brunel University.

——(1999) 'Lie back and think of England: The women of Euro 96', *Journal of Sport and Social Issues*, 23, pp. 96–110.

——(2001) 'Playing the man's game: Sites of resistance and incorporation in women's football', *World Leisure*, 43, 4, pp. 22–9.

Harris, J. and Clayton, B. (2002) 'Femininity, masculinity, physicality and the English tabloid press: The case of Anna Kournikova', *International Review for the Sociology of Sport*, 37, 3/4, pp. 397–413.

Haynes, R. (1995) *The Football Imagination: The Rise of Football Fanzine Culture*, Aldershot: Arena.

Hilliard, D. (1984) 'Media images of male and female professional athletes: An interpretive analysis of magazine articles', *Sociology of Sport Journal*, 1, pp. 251–61.

Hopcraft, A. (1968) *The Football Man*, London: Collins.

Hornby, N. (1992) *Fever Pitch*, London: Victor Gollancz.

Horton, E. (1995) *The Best World Cup Money Can Buy*, Oxford: Author.

Kolnes, L. (1995) 'Heterosexuality as an organising principle in women's sport', *International Review for the Sociology of Sport*, 30, pp. 61–77.

Kuhn, A. (1985) *The Power of the Image: Essays on Representation and Sexuality*, London: Routledge and Kegan Paul.

Lenskyj, H. (1986) *Out of Bounds: Women, Sport and Sexuality*, Toronto: Women's Press.

Lopez, S. (1997) *Women on the Ball: A Guide to Women's Football*, London: Scarlet Press.

Luebke, B. (1989) 'Out of focus: Images of women and men in newspaper photographs', *Sex Roles*, 20, pp. 121–33.

Maguire, J. and Mansfield, L. (1998) 'No-body's perfect: Women, aerobics and the body beautiful', *Sociology of Sport Journal*, 15, pp. 109–37.

Markula, P. (1995) 'Firm but shapely, fit but sexy, strong but thin: The postmodern aerobicizing female bodies', *Sociology of Sport Journal*, 12, pp. 424–53.

Mason, T. (1980) *Association Football and English Society, 1863–1915*, Brighton: Harvester Press.

Messner, M. (1992) *Power at Play*, Boston MA: Beacon Press.

Messner, M. and Sabo, D. (eds) (1990) *Sport, Men and the Gender Order: Critical Feminist Perspectives*, Champaign IL: Human Kinetics.

Miller, L. and Penz, O. (1991) 'Talking bodies: Female body builders colonize a male preserve', *Quest*, 43, pp. 148–63.

Morris, D. (1981) *The Soccer Tribe*, London: Jonathan Cape.

Parker, A. (2001) 'Soccer, servitude and sub-cultural identity: Football traineeship and masculine construction', *Soccer and Society*, 2, pp. 59–80.

Rinalta, J. and Birrel, S. (1984) 'Fair treatment for the active female: A content analysis of *Young Athlete* magazine', *Sociology of Sport Journal*, 8, pp. 16–32.

Rowe, D. (1995) *Popular Cultures*, London: Sage.

Sabo, D. and Panepinto, J. (1990) 'Football ritual and the social reproduction of masculinity', in M. Messner and D. Sabo (eds) *Sport, Men and the Gender Order: Critical Feminist Perspectives*, Champaign IL: Human Kinetics.

Schacht, S. (1996) 'Misogyny on and off the pitch: The gendered world of male rugby players', *Gender and Society*, 10, no. 5, pp. 550–65.

Sparkes, A. (1992) 'The paradigms debate: An extended review and a celebration of difference', in A. Sparkes (ed.) *Research in Physical Education and Sport: Exploring Alternative Visions*, Lewes: Falmer Press.

Sports Council (1994) *Women and Sport*, London: Sports Council.

Sports Council for Wales (1995) *Why Girls and Boys Come Out to Play*, Cardiff: Sports Council for Wales.

Sugden, J. and Tomlinson, A. (1998) *FIFA and the Contest for World Football*, Cambridge: Polity Press.

Tomkins, J. (1993) 'The football discourse: The generation and control of the male and female body and its impact on the football world', in C. Brackenridge (ed.) *Body Matters: Leisure Images and Lifestyles*, Eastbourne: Leisure Studies Association.

Tomlinson, A. (1995) 'Ideologies of physicality, masculinity and femininity: Comments on *Roy of the Rovers* and the women's fitness boom', in A. Tomlinson (ed.) *Gender, Sport and Leisure*, Brighton: Chelsea School Research Centre.

Vande Berg, L. and Streckfuss, D. (1992) 'Profile: Prime-time television's portrayal of women and the world of work: A demographic profile', *Journal of Broadcasting and Electronic Media*, 36, pp. 195–208.

Wagg, S. (1991) 'Playing the past: The media and the England football team', in J. Williams and S. Wagg (eds) *British Football and Social Change: Getting into Europe*, Leicester: Leicester University Press.

Wagg, S. (ed.) (1995) *Giving the Game Away: Football, Politics and Culture on Five Continents*, Leicester: Leicester University Press.

Walvin, J. (1975) *The People's Game*, London: Allen Lane.

Williams, J. and Woodhouse, J. (1991) 'Can play, will play? Women and football in Britain', in J. Williams and S. Wagg (eds) *British Football and Social Change: Getting into Europe*, Leicester: Leicester University Press.

Willis, P. (1982) 'Women in sport in ideology', in J. Hargreaves (ed.) *Sport, Culture and Ideology*, London: Routledge and Kegan Paul.

Woodhouse, J. (1991) *A National Survey of Female Football Fans*, Leicester University: unpublished.

Young, K. (1997) 'Women, sport and physicality: Preliminary findings from a Canadian study', *International Review for the Sociology of Sport*, 32, pp. 297–305.

7. Out on the Field: Women's Experiences of Gender and Sexuality in Football

JAYNE CAUDWELL

Alcoff, L., and Potter, E. (eds) (1993), *Feminist Epistemologies*, London: Routledge.

Back, L. (2000), 'Between Home and Belonging: Racism, Sexuality, and the Embodied

Geographies of Safety and Danger', paper presented at the conference Dangerous Erotics: Violence, Sexuality and Space, Manchester Metropolitan University, 24 March.

Bell, D., and Valentine, G. (1995), *Mapping Desire: Geographies of Sexualities*, London: Routledge.

Bland, L. (1995), *Banishing the Beast: English Feminism and Sexual Morality, 1885–1914*, London: Penguin.

Blasius, M., and Phelan, S. (eds) (1997), *We are Everywhere: A Historical Sourcebook of Gay and Lesbian Politics*, London: Routledge.

Bordo, S. (1993), *Unbearable Weight: Feminism, Western Culture, and the Body*, Los Angeles and Berkeley, CA: University of California Press.

Braidotti, R. (1992), 'On the Female Feminist Subject, or: From "She-Self" to "She-Other"', in Bock, G., and James, S. (eds), *Beyond Equality and Difference: Citizenship, Feminist Politics and Female Subjectivity*, London: Routledge: 177–192.

Butler, J. (1990), *Gender Trouble: Feminism and the Subversion of Identity*, London: Routledge.

Butler, J. (1993), *Bodies that Matter: On the Discursive Limits of Sex*, London: Routledge.

Caudwell, J. (2001), *Women's Experiences of Gender and Sexuality in Football Contexts in England and Wales*, PhD thesis, University of North London.

Caudwell, J. (1999), 'Women's Football in the United Kingdom: Theorising Gender and Unpacking the Butch Lesbian Image', in *Journal of Sport and Social Issues*, Vol. 23, number 4: 390–402.

Chaudhary, V. (2001), 'Women Players Get Football Fever', in the *Guardian*, 28 July.

Conboy, K., Medina, N., and Stanbury, S. (eds) (1997), *Writing on the Body: Female Embodiment and Feminist Theory*, New York: Columbia University Press.

Cox, B., and Thompson, S. (2000), 'Multiple Bodies – Sportswomen, Soccer and Sexuality', in *International Review for the Sociology of Sport*, Vol. 35, number 1: 5–20.

Creed, B. (1995), 'Lesbian Bodies: Tribades, Tomboys and Tarts', in Grosz, E., and Probyn, E. (eds), *Sexy Bodies: The Strange Carnalities of Feminism*, London: Routledge, pp. 86–103.

Crinnion, J. (1998), 'A Game of Two Sexes', in the *Guardian*, 13 August: 15.

Davies, M. (1991), 'Innings and Outings', in the *Guardian*, 12 December: 34.

Duke, V., and Crolley, L. (1996), *Football, Nationality and the State*, Harlow: Longman.

Duncan, N. (ed.) (1996), *Body Space*, London: Routledge.

Dworkin, S., and Messner, M. (1999), 'Just Do . . . What? Sport, Bodies, Gender', in Ferree, M., Lorber, J., and Hess, B. (eds), *Revisioning Gender*, London: Sage.

Finn, G., and Giulianotti, R. (2000), *Football Culture: Local Contests, Global Visions*, London: Frank Cass.

Fishwick, N. (1989), *English Football and Society, 1910–1950*, Manchester: Manchester University Press.

Fletcher, S. (1993), *Women First: The Female Tradition in English Physical Education, 1880–1980*, London : Athlone Press.

Foucault, M. (1975), *'Discipline and Punish': The Birth of the Prison*, reprinted 1991,, London: Penguin.

Foucault, M. (1976), *The History of Sexuality*, Volume 1, *The Will to Knowledge*, , reprinted 1990, London: Penguin.

Foucault, M. (1984a), *The History of Sexuality*, Volume 2, *The Use of Pleasure*, reprinted 1992, London: Penguin.

Foucault, M. (1984b), *The History of Sexuality*, Volume 3: *The Care of the Self*, reprinted 1990, London: Penguin.

Gatens, M. (1992), 'Power, Bodies and Difference', in Barrett, M., and Phillips, A. (eds), *Destabilising Theory*, Cambridge: Polity Press: 120–37.

Gibbs, C. (1995), 'Women Play Too: A Hidden Story', in Commission for Racial Equality (ed.), *Kick It Again*, London: Commission for Racial Equality: 16–18.

Gibson, M. (1997), 'Clitoral Corruption: Body Metaphors and American Doctors' Constructions of Female Homosexuality, 1870–1900', in Rosario, V. (ed.), *Science and Homosexualities*, London: Routledge: 108–32.

Giulianotti, R., and Williams, J. (eds) (1994), *Game without Frontiers: Football, Identity and Modernity*, Aldershot: Arena.

Glanville, B. (1969), *Soccer: A Panorama*, London: Eyre and Spottiswoode.

Griffin, P. (1998), *Strong Women, Deep Closets*, Champaign, IL, and Leeds: Human Kinetics.

Grosz, E. (1993), 'Bodies and Knowledge: Feminism and Crisis of Reason', in Alcoff, L., and Potter, E. (eds), *Feminist Epistemologies*, London: Routledge: 187–215.

Halberstam, J. (1998), *Female Masculinity*, Durham, NC, and London: Duke University Press.

Hall, M.A. (1996), *Feminism and Sporting Bodies*, Champaign, IL, and Leeds : Human Kinetics.

Haraway, D. (1988), 'Situated Knowledges: The Science Question in Feminism and the Privilege of Partial Perspective', as reprinted in Conboy, D., Medina, N., and Stanbury, S., (eds) (1997), *Writing on the Body*: 283–95.

Hargreaves, Jennifer (1994), *Sporting Females: Critical Issues in the History and Sociology of Women's Sports*, London : Routledge.

Henry, J., and Comeaux, P. (1999), 'Gender Egalitarianism in Co-Ed Sport: A Case Study of American Soccer', in *International Review for the Sociology of Sport*, Vol. 34, number 3: 277–90.

Holliday, R. (1999), 'The Comfort of Identity', *Sexualities*, Vol. 2, number 4: 475–91.

Ingram, B.G., Bouthilette, A.-M., and Retter, Y. (eds) (1997), *Queers in Space: Communities/ Public Places/ Sites of Resistance*, Seattle: WA: Bay Press.

Johnston, L., and Valentine, G. (1995), 'Wherever I Lay My Girlfriend That's My Home: The Performance and Surveillance of Lesbian Identities in Domestic Environments', in Bell, D., and Valentine, G. (eds), *Mapping Desire*: 99–113.

Kenway, J., and Willis, S. (1998), *Answering Back: Girls, Boys and Feminism in Schools*, London : Routledge.

Laporte, R. (1971), 'The Butch/Femme Question', in blasius, M., and Phelan, S. (eds) (1997), *We are Everywhere*: 355–64.

Lee, D. (2001), 'All-Women Football Academies are Shooting Up Everywhere', in the *Times*, 29 November.

Lenskyj, H. (1990), 'Power and Play: Gender and Sexuality Issues in Sport and Physical Activity', in *International Review for the Sociology of Sport*, Vol. 25, number 3: 234–43.

Lopez, S. (1997), *Women on the Ball: A Guide to Women's Football*, London: Scarlet Press.

Mason, T. (1996), 'Football, Sport of the North?', in Hill, J., and Williams, J. (eds), *Sport and Identity in the North of England*, Keele: Keele University Press: 41–52.

Massey, D. (1994), *Space, Place and Gender*, Cambridge: Polity Press.

McCrone, K. (1988), *Sport and the Physical Emanicipation of English Women*,

1870–1914, London: Routledge.

McCrone, K. (1991), 'Class, Gender and English Women's Sport, c. 1890–1914', in *Journal of Sport History*, Vol. 18, number 1: 159 – 74.

McKay, J., Messner, M., and Sabo, D. (2000), *Masculinities, Gender Relations and Sport*, London: Sage.

McNay, Lois (1992), *Foucault and Feminism: Power, Gender and the Self*, Cambridge: Polity.

Messner, M., and Sabo, D. (eds) (1990), *Sport, Men and the Gender Order: Critical Feminist Perspectives*, Champaign, IL, and Leeds: Human Kinetics.

Moorhouse, H.F. (1996), 'One State, Several Countries: Soccer and Nationality in a "United" Kingdom', in Mangan, J.A. (ed.), *Tribal Identities: Nationalism, Europe, Sport*, London: Frank Cass: 55–74.

Moyer, C. (1997), 'Do You Love the Dyke in Your Face?', in Ingram, G.B., Bouthilette, A.-M., and Retter, Y. (eds), *Queers in Space*: 439–46.

Munt, S. (ed.) (1998), *Butch/Femme: Inside Lesbian Gender*, London: Cassell.

Munt, S. (1995), 'The Lesbian Flaneur', in Bell, D., and Valentine, G. (eds), *Mapping Desire*, London: Routledge: 114–25.

Nestle, J. (1997), 'Restriction and Reclamation: Lesbian Bars and Beaches of the 1950s', in Ingram, B.G., Bouthilette, A.-M., and Retter, Y. (eds), *Queers in Space*: 61–68.

Newsham, G. (1997), *In a League of Their Own*, London: Scarlet Press.

Newton, E. (1991), *The Mythic Mannish Lesbian: Radclyffe Hall and the New Woman*, London: Penguin.

Parratt, C. (1989), 'Athletic "Womanhood": Exploring Sources for Female Sport in Victorian and Edwardian England', in *Journal of Sport History*, Vol. 16, number 2: 140–57.

Rothenberg, T. (1995), '"And She Told Two Friends": Lesbians Creating Urban Social Space', in Bell, D., and Valentine, G. (eds), *Mapping Desire*, London: Routledge: 165–81.

Sawicki, J. (1991), *Disciplining Foucault: Feminism, Power and the Body*, London: Routledge.

'S.B.D.' (1895), 'Feminine Footballers', in the *Sketch*, 6 February: 60.

Scraton, S., Fastings, K., Pfister, G., and Bunuel, A. (1999), 'It's Still a Man's Game? The Experience of Top-Level European Women Footballers', in *International Review for the Sociology of Sport*, Vol. 34, number 2: 99–111.

Scraton, S., and Flintoff, A. (eds) (2001), *Gender and Sport: A Reader*, London: Routledge.

Sedgwick, E.K. (1990), *Epistemology of the Closet*, London: Penguin.

Seidman, S., Meeks, C., and Traschen, F. (1999), 'Beyond the Closet? The Changing Social Meaning of Homosexuality in the United States', in *Sexualities*, Vol. 2, number 1: 9–34.

Skeggs, B. (2000), 'Violence, Sexuality and Space: Progress to Date', paper presented at the conference Dangerous Erotics: Violence, Sexuality and Space, Manchester Metropolitan University, 24 March.

Sommerville, S. (1998), Scientific Racism and the Invention of the Homosexual Body', in Bland, L., and Doan, L. (eds), *Sexology in Culture: Labelling Bodies and Desires*, London: Polity: 60–76.

Sugden, J., and Tomlinson, A. (1994), *Hosts and Champions: Soccer Cultures, National Identity and the USA World Cup*, Aldershot: Arena.

Taylor, A. (1998), 'Lesbian Space: More than One Imagined Territory', in Ainley, R. (ed.),

New Frontiers of Space, Bodies and Gender, London: Routledge: 129–41.

Tomlinson, A. (ed.) (1983), *Explorations in Football Culture*, Eastbourne: University of Brighton.

Valentine, G. (1993), 'Desperately Seeking Susan: A Geography of Lesbian Friendship', in *Area*, Vol. 25, number 2: 106–19.

Walvin, J. (1975), *The People's Game: The Social History of British Football*, London: Allen Lane.

Walvin, J. (1994), *The People's Game*, Edinburgh and London: Mainstream..

Williams, J., and Woodhouse, J. (1991), 'Can Play, will Play? Women and Football in Britain', in Williams, J., and Wagg, S. (eds), *British Football and Social Change: Getting into Europe*, London: Leicester University Press: 85–108.

Williamson, D. J. (1991), *Belles of the Ball: The Early History of Women's Football*, Exeter: R & D Associates.

Young, P. (1968), *A History of British Football*, London: Stanley Paul.

8. Talking to Me? Televised Football and Masculine Style

EILEEN KENNEDY

Brick, C. (2001), *Fandemonium: The Discourse of Authenticity in the Consumption of the FA Carling Premier League*, PhD thesis, University of Surrey, Roehampton.

Buscombe, E. (1975), *Football on Television*, London: BFI.

Cooper-Chen, A. (1994), 'Global Games, Entertainment and Leisure: Women as TV Spectators', in Creedon, P. (ed.), *Women, Media and Sport*, London: Sage.

Critcher, C. (1991), 'Putting on the Style: Aspects of Recent English Football', in Williams, J., and Wagg, S. (eds), *British Football and Social Change: Getting into Europe*, London: Leicester University Press.

Easthope, A. (1990), *What a Man's Gotta Do: The Masculine Myth in Popular Culture*, London: Unwin Hyman.

Finlay, F., and Johnson, S. (1997), 'Do Men Gossip? An Analysis of Football Talk on Television', in Johnson, S., and Meinhof, U. (eds), *Language and Masculinity*, Oxford: Blackwell.

Gray, A. (1987), 'Behind Closed Doors: Video Recorders in the Home', in Baehr, H., and Dyer, G. (eds), *Boxed In: Women and Television*, London: Pandora.

Horrocks, R. (1995), *Male Myths and Icons: Masculinity in Popular Culture*, London: Macmillan.

Kennedy, E. (2000), '"You Talk a Good Game": Football and Masculine Style on British Television', in *Men and Masculinities*, Vol. 3, number 1: 57–84.

Lee, M. (2000), 'Introduction', in Lee, M. (ed.), *The Consumer Society Reader*, Oxford: Blackwell.

Modleski, T. (1984), *Loving with a Vengeance: Mass-Produced Fantasies for Women*, London: Methuen.

Morley, D. (1986), *Family Television: Cultural Power and Domestic Leisure*, London: Comedia.

Real, M. (1998), 'MediaSport: Technology and the Commodification of Postmodern Sport' in Wenner, L. (ed.), *MediaSport*, London: Routledge.

Stoessl, S. (1987), 'Women as TV Audiences: A Marketing Perspective', in Baehr, H., and Dyer, G. (eds), *Boxed In: Women and Television*, London: Pandora.

Whannel, G. (1992), *Fields in Vision: Television Sport and Cultural Transformation*, London: Routledge.

9. 'Play the White Man': Identifying Institutional Racism in Professional Football

COLIN KING

Fanon, F. (1967), *Black Skin, White Mask* [translation by Markmann, C.L., of *Peau noire, masques blancs* (1952)], New York: Grove Press.

Football Association (1996), *The FA Advanced Coaching Licence UEFA 'A' Coaching Award*, course materials, London: Football Association.

Goffman, E. (1956), *The Presentation of Self in Everyday Life*, Garden City, NY: Doubleday.

Kovell, J. (1988), *White Racism: A Psychohistory*, Exeter: Short Run Press.

Macpherson, Sir W. (1999), *The Stephen Lawrence Inquiry: Report of an Inquiry by Sir William Macpherson of Cluny, Advised by Tom Cook, the Right Reverend Dr John Sentamu, Dr Richard Stone*, London: The Stationery Office.

Roediger, D. (1991), *The Wages of Whiteness: Race and the Making of the American Working Class*, New York and London: Verso.

10. Football and Social Responsibility in the 'New' Scotland: The Case of Celtic FC

RAYMOND BOYLE

Boyle, R. (1995), *A Tale of Two Cities: Football and Cultural Identity in Glasgow and Liverpool*, PhD thesis, University of Stirling.

Boyle, R. (2000), 'Why Football Matters (or, What Fitba Tells You about Scotland)', in *Critical Quarterly*, Vol. 42, number 4, *The Scottish Issue*, Winter: 21–29.

Boyle, R., and Haynes, R. (1998), 'Modernising Tradition: The Changing Face of British Football', in Lines, G., McDonald, I., and Merkel, U. (eds), *The Production and Consumption of Sport Cultures*, Brighton: Leisure Studies Association.

Boyle, R., and Lynch, P. (eds) (1998), *Out of the Ghetto? The Catholic Community in Modern Scotland*, Edinburgh: John Donald.

Bradley, J.M. (2001), *Imagining Scotland: Nationality, Cultural Identities, Football and Discourses of Scottishness*, Stirling: University of Stirling.

Brown, A., and Walsh, A. (1999), *Not for Sale: Manchester United, Murdoch and the Defeat of BSkyB*, Edinburgh and London: Mainstream.

Campbell, T. (2001), *Celtic's Paranoia . . . All in the Mind?*, Ayr: Fort Publishing.

Campbell, T., and Woods, P. (1996), *Dreams and Songs to Sing: A New History of Celtic*, Edinburgh and London: Mainstream.

Canavan, D. (2001), speech in the Scottish Parliament, Holyrood, Edinburgh, 1 October.

Carr, P., Findlay, J., Hamil, S., Hill, J., and Morrow, S. (2001), *The Celtic Trust*, in Hamil, S., Michie, J., Oughton, C. and Warby, S. (eds), *The Changing Face of the Football Business: Supporters Direct*, London: Frank Cass.

Celtic plc (1996), *Annual Report, Year Ended 30 June 1996*, Glasgow: Celtic plc.

Celtic plc (2001), *Annual Report, Year Ended 30 June 2001*, Glasgow: Celtic plc.

Coalter, F., Allison, M., and Taylor, J. (2000), *The Role of Sport in Regenerating Deprived Urban Areas*, Edinburgh: Scottish Executive Central Research Unit.

Devine, T.M. (ed.) (2000), *Scotland's Shame: Bigotry and Sectarianism in Modern Scotland*, Edinburgh and London: Mainstream.

Dobson, S., and Goddard, J. (2001), *The Economics of Football*, Cambridge: Cambridge University Press.

Glendinning, M. (2000), 'Clubs Examining Creative Funding Options', in *SportBusiness*, number 43, March.

Kelly, M. (2001), 'Why Celtic are Failing the Test of Sectarianism', in the *Scotsman*, 16 October.

Morrow, S. (1999), *The New Business of Football: Accountability and Finance in Football*, Basingstoke: Macmillan.

Morrow, S. (2000), 'Football Clubs on the Stock Exchange: An Inappropriate Match? The Case of Celtic plc', in *Irish Accounting Review*, Vol. 7, number 2: 61–90.

Perkins, S. (2000), 'Exploring Future Relationships between Football Clubs and Local Government', in Garland, J., Malcolm, D., and Rowe, M. (eds), *The Future of Football: Challenges in the Twenty-First Century*, London: Frank Cass.

Schlesinger, P., Miller, D., and Dinan, W. (2001), *Open Scotland? Journalists, Spin Doctors and Lobbyists*, Edinburgh, Edinburgh University Press.

Scottish Executive (2000), *Social Justice: A Scotland where Everyone Matters – Annual Report 2000*, Edinburgh: Scottish Executive.

11. Football for Children or Children for Football?
A Contemporary Boys' League and the Politics of Childhood

PAUL DANIEL

Bent, I., McIlroy, R., Mouseley, K., and Walsh, P. (2000), *Football Confidential*, London: BBC Books.

Education and Employment Select Committee of the House of Commons (2000), *Minutes of Evidence*, 15 March.

Football Association (1997), *Charter for Quality*, London: Football Association.

Football Association (2001/2), *The National Game: Developing Football at Every Level*, London: Football Association.

James, A., and Prout, A. (1997), *Constructing and Reconstructing Childhood*, London: Falmer.

Quortrup, J. (1994), *Childhood Matters: Social Theory, Practice and Politics*, Aldershot. Avebury.

Ridley, I. (2002), 'Too Many Cooks . . .', in the *Observer*, 4 February.

Tandridge Junior Football League (2003), *Handbook*, London: Tandridge Junior Football League.

White, J. (2002), 'Eat your Heart Out, Sven', in the *Guardian*, 13 March.

12. Pick the Best, Forget the Rest? Training Field Dilemmas and Children's Football at the Turn of the Century

SIMON THORPE

Brohm, J. (1978) *Sport: A Prison of Measured Time*, London: Ink Links.

Department of National Heritage (1995) *Sport: Raising the Game*, London: HMSO.

Dodd, C. (1999) 'Sport for the Also-Rans', *Independent*, Education Section, 13 May.

Football Association (1999) *Mini Soccer 1999 Fact Sheets*, England: Football Association.

——(undated) *The Soccer Star Scheme*, publicity material, England: Football Association.

Frank, A. (1990) 'Bringing Bodies Back in: A Decade Review', *Theory, Culture and Society*, 7, no. 1, 131–62.

Hall, S. (1997) *The Work of Representation*, London: Sage.

Hammersley, M. and P. Atkinson (1995) *Ethnography: Principles in Practice*, 2nd edn, London: Routledge.

Hargreaves, J. (1986) *Sport, Power and Culture*, Cambridge: Polity Press.

Hyland, D. (1978) 'Competition and Friendship', *Journal of the Philosophy of Sport*, V, 27–37.

Kidder, L. (1981) *Research Methods in Social Relations*, New York: Holt Saunders International Editions.

Mehl, J. and W. Davis (1978) 'Youth Sports for Fun – and Whose Benefit?', *Journal of Physical Education and Recreation*, 49, 48–9.

Orlick, T. (1974) 'The Athletic Drop-out: A High Price for Inefficiency', *CAHPER Journal*, November, 21–7.

Russell, R. (1988) *Soccer Star: An Official Football Association publication*, England: Football Association.

——(1993) *Mini-Soccer: The Handbook*, England: Football Association.

Seeman, M. (1983) 'Alienation Motifs in Contemporary Theorising: The Hidden Continuity of the Classic Themes', *Social Psychology Quarterly*, 46, no. 3, 171–84.

——(1997) 'The Elusive Situation in Social Psychology', *Social Psychology Quarterly*, 60, no. 1, 4–13.

UEFA (1995) *Children's Football in Europe: A Discussion Paper*.

Waksler, F. (ed.) (1991) *Studying the Social Worlds of Children: Sociological Readings*, London: Falmer Press.

Walvin, J. (1975) *The People's Game: The Social History of British Football*, London: Allen Lane.

Youth Sport Trust (1998) *Annual Report 1997/98*.

Index

24 Hour Party People (film) 39

Abbeydale Asian Youth Project 62
ABeeC Party 21
AC Milan FC 74
Adams, Tony 94
Advisory Group Against Racism and
    Intimidation (AGARI) 33
Advocaat, Dick
Alexander, Jeremy (*Guardian* reporter)
    102
Alternative Investment Market 193
Arkwright Sportswear 40
Arndale Centre, Manchester 40
Arsenal FC 8, 11, 13, 49, 214
Asians into Football project 57
Aston Villa FC 98, 100–1
Atkinson, P. 229
authenticity (of football supporters) 35

Baddiel, David 156, 164
Baine, John 21
Banks, Tony MP 5–6
Barcelona FC 191
Barclaycard 17
Barnes, John 159
Barnet FC 10
Barnsley FC 10
Bartky, Sandra 142
Bayern Munich FC 71
Beardsley, Peter 206
Beattie, Kevin 90–1, 95–7,101, 108
Beckham, David 3–4, 10, 92, 209, 211,
    222–3
Bergkamp, Denis 8
Berry, Malcolm (ex-Chief Executive,
    English Schools Football
    Association) 209

Best, George 94
Bhoys Against Bigotry (BAB) campaign
    194
black footballers 167–85
Blackburn Rovers FC 11
Blair, Rt Hon Tony MP 2, 15, 19
Bloomfield, Jimmy 97
Bolton Wanderers FC 161–2
Bond, John 97
Bordo, Susan 142
Bourdieu, Pierre 38, 40, 225, 239–40
Bournemouth FC 10
Bowyer, Lee 79
Bradford City FC 10
Brady, Liam 210
Braidotti, Rose 133
Brankin, Rhona (Deputy Minister for
    Culture and Sport, Scotland) 189
Brentford FC 21–2
Brick, Carlton 7
Bright, Mark 105, 159
Brighton and Hove Albion FC 10, 21,
    153
Brimson, Doug 11
Brimson, Eddie 12
Broadcasting Act (1989) 3
Brodkin, John (*Guardian* reporter) 101
Brohm, Jean-Marie 224–5
Brother Walfrid (founder of Celtic FC)
    191, 196
Brown, Craig 187
BSkyB 30, 32, 41, 50, 52, 72
Burnham, Andy MP 23
Buscombe, Edward 150–2, 155
Bush, President George W. 3
Bushwackers (Millwall FC 'hooligans')
    71
Butler, Judith 129

Calcetas-Santos, Ofelia (of UN
    Committee on Human Rights) 210
Canavan, Denis, MSP 202
Cantona, Eric 161
Cardiff City FC 27, 78; supporters of
    68–85
Carragher, Jamie 13
Carrick, Michael 206
Celtic Charity Fund 195–7
Celtic FC 186–204
Celtic Park football ground 193, 197
Celtic plc 197–9, 204
Celtic Supporters Trust 199–200
Celtic View, The (club publication) 194
Champions League 67
Charity Commission 59, 61
Charlton Athletic FC 217
Charlton Athletic Racial Equality
    (CARE) programme 57
Charlton, Bobby 159
Chelsea FC 49, 161, 221
Chester City FC 10
Chesterfield FC 10
children's football 205–41
Clayton, B. 122, 124
Clough, Brian 99
Clough, Frank (*Daily Mirror* reporter)
    96
Coca-Cola 10, 17, 227
Colchester United FC 57
Collymore, Stan 90, 95, 97–108, and 'fire
    extinguisher' incident 102–5
Commission for Social Justice 15
Cox, B. 117, 120
Craven Cottage football ground 153
Creed, Barbara 144
Crewe Alexandra FC 209
Critcher, Chas 5, 163–4
Crooks, Garth 161
Crystal Palace FC 10, 26, 97, 99, 101,
    214–17
Curry, Steve (*Daily Express* reporter) 96
Customer Care Unit (of Premier
    League) 14

Dad's Army 161
Daily Telegraph 28
Davis, W. 237–8
Dean, James 4
Death of Football (radio programme) 5
Department for Culture, Media and
    Sport (DCMS) 52, 56

Department for Education and Skills
    (DfES) 51, 63
Derby County FC 10, 27, 42
Dick, Kerr's Ladies football team 129
Dobson, S. 191
Dodd, Celia 228
Dr Feelgood (R'n'B band) 154
Driscoll, Bob (*Sun* reporter) 95
Dublin, Dion 101
Dunbar, Gerry 193
'Dykescapes' 140–1, 145

Earle, Robbie 100
Easter Road football ground 190
Easthope, Anthony 157–8
Eastick, Brian (Director, Birmingham
    City academy) 210
Edgeley Park football ground 26
Edinburgh and Lothians Racial Equality
    Council 190
Education Action Zones 52
Edwards, Martin 198
Edwards, Patrick 21
Elias, Norbert 11
Elland Road football ground 74, 85–6
Ellis, Havelock 142
English Schools Football Association
    (ESFA) 209, 227
Eriksson, Sven Goran 159
Euro 2000 (Belgium/Netherlands) 33–4,
    187
European Commission 194

FA Charter for Quality (1997) 207–8,
    210, 213, 217, 222
FA Junior Team Manager coaching
    course 227, 238–9
FA Talent Development Plan
Fanon, Frantz 167, 170–1, 181
Fantasy Football 156
Fast Show, The 2
Federation Internationale de Football
    Association (FIFA) 145
Federation of Stadium Communities
    (FSC) 50
female masculinity 144–5
feminist poststructuralism 128–9
Ferdinand, Rio 211
Ferguson, Sir Alex 3, 159–60
Finlay, F. 147, 157–9
Fiske, John 42–3
Fletcher, Sheila 129

football academies 206–11, 214–17,
    220–1, 226, 231
Football Against Racism in Europe
    (FARE) 63
Football Association 18, 52, 54, 125,
    130, 156, 168, 170, 172, 177, 179, 181,
    205–9, 220, 224–8, 238–9
Football in the Community schemes 20,
    47–66, 189
Football in the Community schemes,
    registered as independent charities
    59–60
Football (Disorder) Act 2000 34
Football Focus (BBC TV) 148, 153–4,
    158–61, 164–5
Football Foundation 18, 55
football hooliganism 4, 12, 68–9
football and sectarianism 186–204
Football Supporters' Association 34
Football Task Force 14, 30, 34, 47, 50–1,
    55
football on television 147–166
Football Trust 55
Football Unites Racism Divides
    (FURD) 57, 62–3
Footballers Further Education and
    Vocational Society (FFE&VTS)
    55–6, 58
footballing body, the 142–3
Foucault, Michel 37, 128–9, 225, 238
Fox, Samantha 124
Frank, A. 240
Freedman, Dougie 26
French national football academy,
    Clairefontaine 207
Freud, Sigmund 142
Fulham FC 18, 49–50, 221, 231

Gadafy, Col. Muammar
Galatasaray FC 71
Game Plan (government policy
    document for sport) 16–18
Gascoigne, Paul 94, 106, 162–4
Gatens, Moira 142
Gaynor, Gloria 179
Giddens, Prof. Anthony 15
Giggs, Ryan 209
Giulianotti, Richard 29–30, 34, 40, 43
Glasgow City Council 194
Glasgow Rangers FC 187, 191, 198, 200,
    202–3
Global Issues 8
Goddard, J. 191

Goffman, Erving 93, 167–9, 179
Goldberg, Adrian 21
Golding, Peter 18
Greaves, Jimmy 94, 157
Greechan, John (*Daily Mail* reporter)
    104
Gregory, John 98–101
Griffin, P. 119
Grimsby Town FC 26
Grosz, Elizabeth 130

Halberstam, J. 144
Halbert, C. 117
Hall, Stuart 43
Hamil, Sean 23
Hamman, Sam 27, 78
Hammersley, Martin 229
Haraway, Donna 127
Hargreaves, Jennifer 119, 125
Hargreaves, John 238
Harkness, Steve 98
Havelange, Joao 145
Headhunters (Chelsea FC 'hooligans')
    71
Health Action Zones 52
Hearts FC 187
Hebdige, Dick 4
Hibernian FC 190
Highbury football ground 48
Hill, Alan 210
Hinckley United FC 154–5
Hoddle, Glenn 106
Hodge, Margaret MP 106
Hoey, Kate 23
Hopcraft, Arthur 111
Horrocks, R. 163–4
Houllier, Gerard 207
Hub African Caribbean Centre 62
Hughes, Charles (FA Technical
    Director) 170
Hull City FC 10
Huddersfield Town FC 26
Hyland, D. 237

Ince, Paul 122, 160
Independent Football Commission 23
Independent Manchester United
    Supporters' Association (IMUSA) 42
institutional racism in football 167–85
Ipswich Town FC 10, 95
Irish Republican Army (IRA) 192
Irish/Scottish diasporas 192, 198
ITV Digital 10

J League 156
Jameson, Fredric 165
Jefferson, Tony 43
Jenkins, Marlon 175–6
Johnson, S. 147, 157–9
Johnson, Seth 209–10
Jones, Kelly 7
Jones, Vinnie 154, 164
Jowell, Rt Hon Tessa MP 23

Kashiwa Reysol FC 156
Keane, Roy 36–7, 92
Kelly, Michael 201–2
Kelly, Paul 189
Kenyon, Peter 10
Kick It Out campaign 18, 33, 57
Kidd, Brian 153
Kilmarnock FC 190
King, Anthony 6, 29, 31, 43
King, Colin 18
Kirton, Luke 21–2
Kolnes, L. 117
Kournikova, Anna 124
Kovell, J. 173

Lacey, David 88
Ladyman, Ian (*Daily Mail* reporter) 104
Laing, R.D. 93
Laporte, Rita 144
Lawrenson, Mark 105
Leeds United FC 27, 90, 210
Leeds United FC, supporters of 68–89
Leeds United Supporters Club 73, 83
Leicester City FC 10, 49, 96, 101–5, 107
Leyton Orient Community Sports
    Programme (LOCSP) 60–1
Leyton Orient FC 49, 57
Lincoln City FC 10, 22
Liverpool FC 13, 74, 98, 106, 208
Livingston FC 190
Lloyd, Steven (corporate financial
    advisor) 199
Lofthouse, Nat 162
Logan, Gaby 153, 159
Lomax, Brian 22

Macpherson Report (1999, on the death
    of Stephen Lawrence) 167, 169
Madame Tussaud's 36
Maguire, Joseph 115
Major, Rt Hon John 2, 227
managed capitalism 93
Manchester City FC 27

Manchester United FC 6, 8, 11, 21, 27,
    30–2, 36–9, 41–4, 52, 74, 88, 90, 92,
    108, 159–60, 208–9, 211
Manchester United plc 198
Mandelson, Rt Hon Peter MP 15
Manpower Services Commission 55
Mansfield, L. 115
Mansfield Town FC 10
Mastermind 161
Matthews, Stanley 40, 91
McCann, Fergus 192–6, 199, 201
McConnell, Jack (Scottish First
    Minister) 198
McDonald, Allan (ex-Chief Executive,
    Celtic plc) 197
McDonald's 17, 19, 223
McLean, Peter (PR director, Celtic FC)
    193, 197
McLeish, Henry (Scottish First
    Minister) 188
McLeod, Ian (Chief Executive, Celtic
    plc) 198–9, 201–2
McMenemy, Lawrie 5
Megicks, John 211
Mehl, J. 237–8
mental distress 90–108
Merson, Paul 94
Middlesborough FC 38
Milburn, Jackie 2
Millennium Commission 200
Miller, Harry (*Daily Mirror* reporter) 96
Miller, L. 115
Miller, Sgt Nigel 90
Millwall FC 47, 72, 214
Mini-Soccer 207
Mini-Soccer Handbook 226
Modleski, T. 150, 160
Morris, Desmond 123
Morris, Jody 9
Morrow, S. 199
Murdoch, Rupert 32
Murphy, Danny 209

National Association for the Care and
    Rehabilitation of Offenders
    (NACRO) 57
National Council for School Sports 208
National Game, The (division of the
    FA) 207
National Lottery 133
National Sports Centre/School of
    Excellence, Lilleshall 170, 208, 226
Neighbourhood Renewal Fund 52

neo-liberalism 93
Nestle 17, 19
Neville, Gary 209
Neville, Phil 209
'New Labour' 6, 14–24, 63
New Opportunities Fund 52
Newcastle United 30, 68
News Corporation 51
Newsham, Gail 129
Nike 223
Nil by Mouth (pressure group) 200
Ninian Park football ground 79–80, 88–9
Nistelrooy, Ruud van 8, 160
Northampton Town FC 22
Norwich City FC 97
Not The View (Celtic fanzine) 193–4
Nottingham Forest FC 10, 67, 97–8, 159
Notts County FC 10

O'Neill, Martin 200–1
Old Fashioned Football Shirt Company, The 40
'Old Firm' (Celtic Rangers rivalry) 187–8, 191, 194, 201
'Old Labour' 16
Old Trafford football ground 36, 38, 42
On the Ball (ITV) 148, 155, 159–60, 164–6
Operation Wild Boar 68
O-Regen ((community regeneration agency) 61
Orlick, T. 237
Oxford United FC 10
Oxnoble 'gastro pub' 41

Paphitis, Theo 47
Parry, Rick 13
Pearce, Stuart 125
Penz, O. 115
Perkins, S. 189
Perryman, Steve 156
Peterborough United FC 67
Pierce, Mary 124
Playing for Success scheme, football clubs involved in 51, 56, 63–4
Polhemus, Ted 45
Port Vale FC 21
Portsmouth FC 10, 26
Positive Futures (funding body) 18, 52
Poverty and Inclusion Ministerial Taskforce (in Scotland) 188
Premier League/ Premiership 9, 10, 30, 32–3, 40, 50, 67, 69–7, 189, 91–2, 101, 133, 154, 164, 208, 212, 214, 222
Presley, Elvis 4

Pride Park football ground 27
Priory clinic 98, 101
Professional Footballers Association (PFA) 10, 55

Queens Park Rangers FC 49
Quinn, Niall 99

Read, John (Chief Executive, English Schools Football Association) 209
Real, M. 165
Real Madrid FC 191
Redhead, Steve 29
Reid, Rt Hon Dr John MP 192
Reith, Lord (John) 3
Revie, Don 95–6
Ricketts, Michael 161–2
Ridley, Ian 94, 99–100
Riverside Stadium, Middlesborough 38
Robson, Bobby 95, 122
Robson, Garry 35, 37, 44
Rochdale FC 99
Roediger, D. 168
Rosenborg FC 104
Rushden and Diamonds FC 153

Sadler, John (*Sun* reporter) 104
Saint and Greavsie 157
Scholes, Paul 8, 209
Scottish Asian Sports Association 197
Scottish Premier League (SPL) 187, 190
Seeman, M. 236, 240
Sense Over Sectarianism campaign 200
Service Crew (Leeds United FC 'hooligans') 71, 75, 80–1
Shankly, Bill 218
Shearer, Alan 162, 206
Sheepshanks, David 10
Sheffield Race Equality Council 62
Sheffield United FC 57, 62–3
Sheffield Youth Service 62
Shelter 196
Sheringham, Teddy 123
Show Racism the Red Card 189–90
Simon Community 196
Sir Norman Chester Centre for Football Research 5, 11, 13, 49, 54
Skinner, Frank, 7, 156, 164
Sky-ification of football 48, 50
Slaughter, Pat 27
Smith, Alan 101
Smith, Rt Hon Chris MP 23
Smith, Rt Hon John MP 15
Soccer Star Scheme 228, 238–9
Social Charter 194–5

social class 2
social exclusion 87–8, 145–6; football and 1–23, 45
Social Exclusion Unit 14
social inclusion 188–9, 207; football and 32–9
Social Inclusion Partnership 198
Socialist Workers' Party 22
Somali Blades FC 62
Soul Crew (Cardiff City FC 'hooligans') 72–3, 84–5
Southend United FC 10, 97, 99
Spencer, Peter (sports editor, *Manchester Evening News*) 159–60
Sport: A Prison of Measured Time 224
Sport England 16, 18, 52, 54–5, 57–8, 60
Sport: Raising the Game 227
Sports Club Orient (SCORE) 61
Sports Council 170, 225, 227
sportscotland 189
St John, Ian 157
Stack, Pat 22
Stafford Rangers FC 97
Stamford Bridge football ground 88, 153
Stein, Jock 195
Stereophonics, The 7
Stoke City FC 71
Stubbs, Ray 158–60
Sunderland FC 68
Supporters Direct 52, 22–3
Sutcliffe, Peter ('Yorkshire Ripper') 93
Swansea City FC 10
Swindon Town FC 10
Szasz, Thomas 93

Taggart, Gerry 103
Taylor, Daniel (*Guardian* reporter) 104
Taylor, Graham 122, 156, 159
Taylor, Ian 4–5, 8, 11, 29, 35
Taylor, Rogan 5–6
Teletubbies 161
Terry, John 9, 161
Thomas, David 28
Thompson, Laura 9
Thompson, S. 117, 120
Thorpe, Martin (*Guardian* reporter) 98
Title IX (of US Education Act) 1972 134
TOP Sport Programmes 228
Tottenham Hotspur FC 156

UK Sport 16
Umbro 223
Union of European Football Associations (UEFA) 169, 179–81, 183–4, 226
Upton Park football ground 153

Venables, Terry 162
Vodaphone 31
von Krafft-Ebbing 142

Wagg, Stephen 68, 122
Waksler, F. 229
Walker, Jack 11
Wallsend FC 206
Walsall FC 97
Waltham Forest Housing Action Trust (WFHAT) 61
Walvin, James 126, 226
Warburton, Peter (Director, Sports Education, Durham University) 208
Ward, Colin 12
Waterman, Dennis 27
Watford FC 102
Watt, David 193
Weaver, Paul (*Guardian* reporter) 98–9
Weller, Keith 96–7
West Ham United FC 49, 57
Whannel, Garry 147–8
When Saturday Comes 6, 47, 69
White, Jim (football columnist) 20, 105–7, 205
White, Peter (*Guardian* reporter) 101
Whose-game-is-it-anyway? paradigm 1–4
Wilkinson, Howard 207–10, 222, 226
Williams, John 5–6, 11, 13, 29
Williams, Richard 13
Wilson, Bob 97
Wimbledon AFC 20
Wimbledon FC 100, 214, 217
Wimbledon Independent Supporters Association 21–2
Wolverhampton Wanderers FC 55, 97
women footballers 110–46
women's football, images of 113–17; and the media 120–6; and sexuality 114–46
Woodgate, Jonathan 9
Woodhouse, Jackie 123
World Cup 1974 (Germany) 155
World Cup 1990 (Italy) 29
World Cup 1994 (USA) 207, 210
World Cup 2002 (Japan/ Korea) 28, 37, 41, 155
World Cup Finals 2002 (Japan/Korea) 187

York City FC 10, 21
Young, Scott 82
Youth Against Bigotry campaign 202